PRIVACY AND THE MEDIA

PRAISE FOR *PRIVACY AND THE MEDIA*

'*Privacy and the Media* is a thoughtful survey of the privacy landscape. McStay reviews the intricate tensions and seeming contradictions to offer an accessible book for anyone curious about the contemporary debates in privacy.'

danah boyd, founder of Data & Society

'The only book that addresses the full spectrum of the innovation-privacy dynamic, ranging from advertising to intelligence to wearables. It is timely and necessary; essential reading.'

Gus Hosein, Privacy International

'McStay's great achievement here is to confront many of the pertinent and complex questions about media and privacy in a style that is both authoritative and easy to read. He provides an excellent overview of the perennial debates and considers the implications on privacy of an increasingly data-driven media environment. His book will prove an excellent companion for all students of this fascinating and crucial topic.'

Mireille Hildebrandt, Vrije Universiteit Brussel

'This pleasingly accessible book tackles all the major questions that arise in a world whose lifeblood is our personal information: liberty, choice, transparency, control. McStay argues that privacy is "not about isolation, going off-grid or being a digital hermit". Rather, it is about managing our online lives and controlling how much others know about us. This book persuades me more than ever that privacy is a branch of ethics; it is concerned with the age-old relationship between the self and the other. It will serve as a great introduction to informational privacy, not just for media studies students and privacy lawyers, but for any information rights professional needing a deeper understanding of the subject.'

Iain Bourne, Information Commissioner's Office

'Clearly and accessibly written, this book is a great resource for anyone interested in the broad range of ways in which privacy and contemporary media are entangled and in the big picture of privacy-media relations today. It challenges us to take privacy seriously as a media – and mediation – issue. I will definitely be assigning it for my students.'

Helen Kennedy, University of Sheffield

PRIVACY AND THE MEDIA

ANDREW MCSTAY

Los Angeles | London | New Delhi
Singapore | Washington DC | Melbourne

Los Angeles | London | New Delhi
Singapore | Washington DC | Melbourne

SAGE Publications Ltd
1 Oliver's Yard
55 City Road
London EC1Y 1SP

SAGE Publications Inc.
2455 Teller Road
Thousand Oaks, California 91320

SAGE Publications India Pvt Ltd
B 1/I 1 Mohan Cooperative Industrial Area
Mathura Road
New Delhi 110 044

SAGE Publications Asia-Pacific Pte Ltd
3 Church Street
#10-04 Samsung Hub
Singapore 049483

Editor: Michael Ainsley
Editorial assistant: John Nightingale
Production editor: Imogen Roome
Copyeditor: Neil Dowden
Proofreader: Jill Birch
Indexer: Adam Pozner
Marketing manager: Lucia Sweet
Cover design: Jennifer Crisp
Typeset by: C&M Digitals (P) Ltd, Chennai, India
Printed and bound by CPI Group (UK) Ltd,
Croydon, CR0 4YY

Library of Congress Control Number: 2017932218

British Library Cataloguing in Publication data

A catalogue record for this book is available from
the British Library

This work was generously supported by the UK's Arts
and Humanities Research Council [grant number
AH/M006654/1]

ISBN 978-1-4739-2492-5
ISBN 978-1-4739-2493-2 (pbk)

At SAGE we take sustainability seriously. Most of our products are printed in the UK using FSC papers and boards.
When we print overseas we ensure sustainable papers are used as measured by the PREPS grading system.
We undertake an annual audit to monitor our sustainability.

CONTENTS

1 Introduction   **1**

Privacy perception: not about hiding or shielding   3
Chapters   4

**PART 1   JOURNALISM, SURVEILLANCE AND
POLITICS OF ENCRYPTION**   **11**

2 Nothing to hide, nothing to fear: myth and Western roots of privacy   **13**

Back to Greece: time, place and cultural context   14
Negative approaches: the shifty citizen   16
Positive approaches: liberalism   18
Liberty versus security   21
Conclusion   24

3 Journalism: a complex relationship with privacy   **27**

Balancing the right to privacy with a free press   28
Acting in the public interest   32
Protecting journalists, sources and whistle-blowers   35
Warren and Brandeis: decency and the newsroom today   36
Conclusion   38

4 The Snowden leaks: a call for better surveillance   **41**

Background context   42
The leaks   44
Know it all   47
Pro-privacy does not mean anti-surveillance   49
How do the leaks inform our understanding of privacy?   50
Conclusion   53

5   Encryption: simultaneously public and private   57

What is encryption?   58
UK political situation   61
Tech industry reactions   62
Libertarian privacy   64
Privacy-by-design and the social construction of technology   65
Conclusion   67

PART 2   COMMERCIAL DIMENSIONS OF PRIVACY
AND MEDIA   69

6   Platforms: disruption, connection and new social actors   71

On platforms   73
What is a social institution?   75
Platform cultures   76
What of privacy?   77
Conclusion   79

7   Behavioural and programmatic advertising: consent,
    data alienation and problems with Marx   83

Pre-chapter suggestion   85
Techniques: how behavioural advertising works   86
Personal data and consent   91
Audience-as-commodity criticisms   96
Squaring audience-as-commodity ideas with property-based
views of privacy   98
Conclusion   99

8   The right to be forgotten: memory, deletion and expression   103

Legal context   104
Implementation   106
Publisher perspectives: Google and 'imparting' information   107
Private interests   108
Forced openness   109
Conflicting rights: towards a pragmatic view of privacy   111
Implications for understanding privacy   112
Conclusion   113

9   Big data: machine learning and the politics of algorithms   115

Big data   116
Policy and big data   122

Anonymisation 122
Politics of algorithms 125
Conclusion 131

PART 3   THE ROLE OF THE BODY **133**

10   Empathic media: towards ubiquitous emotional intelligence **135**

Pre-chapter suggestion 136
Affective computing 136
Contemporary technologies: the case of facial coding 138
Intimate, but not personal? 142
Conclusion 143

11   Re-introducing the body to privacy: intimate and wearable media **145**

Wearable media and the Internet of Things 146
Background to wearables 147
Quantifying the self and personal sousveillance 149
Critical concerns 154
Conclusion 157

12   Being young and social: inter-personal privacy and debunking seclusion **159**

Public contexts 161
The fallacy that 'kids' don't care 163
Privacy: a fact of life 169
Conclusion 170

13   Sexting: exposure, protocol and collective privacy **173**

Who does it? 174
What about younger people? 176
Towards non-male gratification 181
Networked norms 184
Conclusion 185

14   Conclusion: what do media developments tell us about privacy? **187**

The big picture 193

References 195
Index 205

1

INTRODUCTION

In this book, *Privacy and the Media*, we will consider the nature of privacy and its relationships with modern media and networked communication. The aim is to use ideas about privacy to better understand the modern media environment, but also that through close assessment of media, organisations, technologies and people's uses of media, we will develop a better understanding of privacy. This is a purposefully varied book that examines journalism, the Snowden leaks, encryption, platforms such as Google, advertising, big data and machine learning, technologies sensitive to emotions, wearable body-trackers, and social media and sexting. The diversity of privacy matters in society today leads me to argue that, among a multitude of competing interests, privacy may very well be *the* critical topic of media and society today.

There are thousands of journal papers that address privacy, and many books that touch upon it, but there are far fewer books written in an accessible manner dedicated to privacy and media itself. Those on privacy and media come from the law subject area and, while important, miss many dimensions and theoretical perspectives of interest to the media studies subject area. This book will act as a corrective to this, providing readers with a solid understanding of the importance of privacy, how we can understand it and how it figures within contemporary media culture. My intention in writing this book has been to depict the assorted relationships between privacy and media and it is by this breadth it should be judged. Specialist scholars in any of the individual topics dealt may feel that I have not provided enough detail or sophistication. This is inevitable in a book such as this and to that reader I suggest a swim in unusual waters and immersion in the more unfamiliar topics within this book.

If we recollect that media studies is typically interested in the history and effects of media content and technology, the need for such a book becomes clear. Indeed, perhaps the most significant change in the last twenty-five years or so to media technologies is how corporations and other organisations now make extensive use of data about us. This invites all sorts of questions germane to media studies, not least about how content is formed, economics, history, influence, organisations, policies, power, technologies, and how people use media in specific situations and contexts. This latter point is important in that unlike other disciplines that examine technologies, media studies is very interested in how media facilitates and integrates into everyday life, and how emergent communications technologies *mediate* it. To this end, this book employs an expansive understanding of media based on the idea that while very much connected to devices and content, what is increasingly important to understand is how information about ourselves and the lives of others is collected, transmitted, processed and, indeed, mediated.

Although this book provides the reader with a rich (but not exhaustive) overview of the relationships between privacy and media, it is up to the reader to put this understanding to work. Readers will be encouraged throughout to test theories, take up challenges and understand how privacy functions in practice. My task is to provide the reader with a wide range of case studies and perspectives, to convince you of the centrality of privacy to critical questions about media today, and to suggest ways in which modern use of media technologies is forcing us to re-evaluate basic assumptions about what privacy is. Your task is the more significant one: to put ideas to work. To help with this, I will make suggestions at the end of each chapter about potential projects and areas for investigation.

We should recognise before we proceed that the narrative of privacy and media is not as simple as good versus bad, or freedom versus state/corporate control. This book: a) does not seek to preach about what the reader should or should not do; and b) recognises that many companies and organisations that make use of large amounts of data about us have a lot to add to society. On readers, I make two requests: that those with a pre-existing passion for privacy matters avoid knee-jerk reactions and assess the detail of technologies and practices; and that readers with less interest in privacy (perhaps you are begrudgingly reading this for a class you have to take?) think carefully about the development of new technologies and what they portend. As will be assessed in Chapter 2, you might have 'nothing to hide', but those who want our information will continue to push for more insights. How much is too much for you?

We will come to definitions of privacy, but let us open with the recognition that privacy is not about hiding or shielding information away from others. It is better seen in terms of awareness of what is happening to us, consent, respect and control. This should apply both online and offline but, in reality, it does not. If we saw that the couple on the next coffee table were listening to our conversation too intently we would be irritated and would secure our communication so they could not hear. Yet, online, the information we communicate to friends and the companies we choose to do business with is intercepted, collected, analysed and stored. Can you imagine if people started doing this in cafes? Weird!

Although privacy is certainly not 'dead' it has become more difficult to achieve. There are quite a few reasons for this that this book will explore in relation to contemporary media. On social media for example, we cannot always separate out different groups. This runs the risk of 'context collision' whereby a close friend may see the same Facebook content as a boss who has felt compelled to 'friend' their employees. We also see an increasing convergence between what is private and what is public. Communication via written letters and telephone used to be private. Today our Gmail is read so that advertising can be better targeted, and mobile-phone data is logged for government agencies to inspect. This includes length of call, where we called/texted from, where our phones are, journeys we take, where we live, how long we go away for, where we go, who our contacts are and details about internet usage (such as file type, or size of any attachments sent or received with emails). Another characteristic of life with modern media is that we do not know who or what invisible trackers are watching. As Chapter 7 explores, the reader may be surprised at the number of 'third parties' making use of what we visit, say and do online. Away from laptops, tablets and phones, whereas only a few years ago it seemed ridiculous that our televisions would watch us back, this is no longer as assured as it once was.[1] There is an asymmetrical irony here in that as our behaviour and habits are increasingly transparent for watchers to see, we have very little idea of who is watching us, what is collected and how and why this information is used.

In the past, privacy has been a fringe interest for the media studies subject area but today it is increasingly moving into centre-stage. This is because the contemporary media environment (and its panoply of screens and devices) is utterly predicated on watching, sharing, tracking and gathering data about interests, behaviour, location, communication, purchasing, our bodies and even emotions. Clearly screens and watching go together, but data and the mediation of behaviour has certainly become more pronounced since the inception of the World Wide Web in the early 1990s.

PRIVACY PERCEPTION: NOT ABOUT HIDING OR SHIELDING

A question that is often asked in relation to people's use of online media is whether they *really* care about their data practices. After all, who actually reads terms and conditions and, if things are really that bad, why do people use these services? No one is putting a gun to our heads and forcing us to use Google, Facebook and other data intensive services. Colleagues and I studied this by looking at UK and European reports about the public's feelings about privacy, security and surveillance across 2013–15. We found that reports from the online advertising industry, market-research companies, non-governmental organisations and academia all pointed to high levels of concern about *control* over personal information (Bakir et al., 2015). This was unambiguous as surveys from all stakeholders continuously pointed to high levels of concern (80 per cent and into the 90s). Surveys from the US echo these findings where people are clearly uneasy about the lack of control over information about them. For example, a Pew Internet Survey (2014b) about perceptions of privacy, security, the US government and advertising found that 91 per cent of adults in the survey 'agree' or 'strongly agree' that consumers have lost control over how personal information is collected and used by companies.

Similarly, of the social media users sampled by Pew, the survey found that 80 per cent of social networking site users say that they are at least somewhat concerned about third parties such as advertisers or businesses accessing some of the information they share on those sites without their knowledge. However, while sceptical about supposed benefits of personal data sharing, the majority are willing to make trade-offs in certain circumstances when their sharing of information provides access to free services. This is indicated by the finding that 55 per cent 'agree' or 'strongly agree' with the statement: 'I am willing to share some information about myself with companies in order to use online services for free.' This concern about control over data yet willingness to share information provides us with an early lesson: privacy is not about isolation, going off-grid or being a digital hermit. Instead it has more to do with awareness, ability to manage digital life, meaningful consent and different privacy requirements depending on the situation we are in. This is echoed in another study by Pew that addresses the use of office surveillance cameras, smart thermostats, health data, retail loyalty cards, automobile insurance and social media. They found that the phrase that best captures Americans' views on the choice between privacy versus disclosure of personal information is 'it depends' (Pew Research Center, 2016). Key factors include how trustworthy they believe the company or organisation to be and what happens to their data after collection, particularly if the information is to be shared with third parties, and how long the data are retained. Again, a sense of control is key.

CHAPTERS

This book is broken down into three parts. I begin by addressing privacy in terms of journalism, surveillance and the politics of encryption (Chapters 2–5), and then progress to consider the commercial dimensions of privacy and media (Chapters 6–9). However, too often discussion of privacy tends to focus on abstract ideas of data, information and unseen technological practices. To this end, the last part considers the role of the body (Chapters 10–13).

Despite the seeming simplicity of the word, privacy is a slippery idea. Our first reactions are 'being alone', 'being secluded' or 'isolated'. A closer examination of everyday privacy practices reveals that these simplistic definitions fail to take into account a basic observation: privacy does not just involve being alone, but how we connect and interact with others, and how we control and manage access to ourselves and those we are close to. After all, there is nothing intrinsically wrong with either sharing or collecting information about people. Health is a good example, particularly for countries that have centralised health authorities paid for out of the public purse. Information sharing can help detect preventable illnesses, save lives, reduce hospitalisation, improve treatment healthcare and grant better opportunity for front-line practitioner care. Our first job is thus to engage in some ground clearance for how best to understand privacy, to dispel those misgivings about 'if you haven't done anything wrong, then you have nothing to hide' and develop a working understanding of what privacy is. In Chapter 2 we will do this by going on a brief philosophical and theoretical journey. Seen another way, this chapter details the *history of privacy*. Examination of philosophy helps with this in a number of ways. First, important theorising of being private and public comes from ancient Greece, Plato and Aristotle; second, contemporary understanding of privacy is virtually synonymous with a philosophical school known as liberalism; and third, philosophical ideas and writing on autonomy, consent and rights directly feeds into laws on privacy. To generalise: this means law-abiding citizens and groups who do no harm to others should be able to go about their business without being bothered by others. This becomes a little more difficult when we consider how we should keep societies secure from internal and external threats. Again, this modern tension about security and liberty has roots in philosophy and the writing of Thomas Hobbes.

Journalism is one of the most important media fields concerned with privacy. As Chapter 3 outlines, in the US, for example, there have long been concerns about the prurient encroachment of journalism into everyday life. Journalism and privacy have a long, difficult and paradoxical relationship. This chapter complicates the premise that privacy is innately a good thing because much of what journalists investigate are cover-ups of information people would prefer others do not know, abuses of power, financial wrongdoings and secret deals. At the level of principle, journalism exists to make situations publicly known, visible and *transparent*. However, journalism is also dependent on privacy to protect sources so no authorities or courts should be able to require a journalist to reveal the identity of an anonymous source. This involves a paradox in that transparency cannot be encouraged without privacy guarantees. Journalism is also a special case because the earliest writing on privacy and media studies is on the rise of photojournalism in the 1880s. This writing is both prescient and applicable to modern interests such as social media, celebrity injunctions and new ways of seeing by means of drones.

Chapter 4 continues discussion about the journalistic imperative to both make information public yet keep sources private by assessing the Edward Snowden leaks of 2013. These revealed the mass surveillance of citizens' telecommunications usage by US and UK intelligence agencies. The scale of surveillant activities surprised everyone, including the world's leading security experts, privacy researchers and computer scientists. This chapter provides a brief history of this series of leaks and events, and progresses to consider the relationship between transparency and privacy. Transparency and openness of knowledge is generally held as a good thing, but what happens when this collides with democratic laws and rights to privacy? This chapter examines these matters by recourse to the work of Jeremy Bentham, an eighteenth-century philosopher, who believed that absolute transparency is positive for societal net benefit and general happiness. It progresses to highlight the work of more recent media scholars, such as Clare Birchall, who have examined secrecy, transparency and media culture in depth.

Chapter 5 continues an interest in governmental surveillance by addressing encryption. Today, this is the practice of encoding data with a set of digital keys and decoding it at the other end with another set of digital keys. Many of our favourite apps and devices now use encryption by default. Paying particular attention to Apple, this chapter is interested in the debates taking place around the world regarding companies that encrypt communications and governments who demand access to the content of online communication. Centrally, this chapter uses encryption to explore the principle of privacy-by-design, or how social values such as privacy can be embedded or baked into media technologies.

Chapter 6 considers the role and nature of 'platforms' in modern media culture. These are software foundations upon which services and applications can be constructed. The names of these are probably recognisable as they include Airbnb, Amazon, Apple, eBay, Etsy, Facebook, Google, PayPal, Uber and Wikipedia. What is notable about many of these organisations is that much of everyday life is carried out upon them. Often this applies to both people and businesses as platforms such as Amazon become stages upon which others' businesses are conducted. I argue that these are new forms of social institutions that are transforming the world. What conjoins each of these platforms is a deep reliance on personal data both to function, but also for its revenue. Platforms also show us that individualistic accounts of privacy are problematic because of power, scale and the one-sided relationship we have with data-intensive institutions.

Chapter 7 assesses behavioural advertising – a practice that is the principal revenue for many of our favourite services, apps and arguably the web itself. This comprises advertising that is aimed at us by means of things we look at online, what we buy, who we communicate with, what we say and, in general, how we behave. You might be surprised to find out that online advertising is, by some margin, more popular with advertisers than any other medium – including television, newspapers, magazines and billboards. Thus, when we think about what advertising is, the first thing that should come to mind is not images from television or content seen on street billboards, but sponsored Google links and advertisements on the sides of our favourite webpages. If we recollect that the contemporary media economy is based on tracking potential consumers and getting to know us better, this invites questions about privacy. This chapter unpacks the mechanics of behavioural advertising, but proceeds to examine its privacy dimensions in relation to the notion of consent. This is a pivotal point of digital ethics and law that guides the use of data about people. The legal premise is that before companies can use personal data, people should be informed so to make a reasoned decision about whether they agree to this. What is clear today is that consent is simply enforced agreement. In exploring privacy and consent through examples in laws and behavioural advertising, this chapter highlights the roots of consent in liberal philosophies. It progresses to consider these roots in relation to questions of power, critical political economy and the suggestion that the principal output of the media industry is not content and services, but data about people.

Chapter 8 considers search engines, focusing on Google. I am particularly interested in the notion of memory and what rights a search engine has to hold and host information about us. In Europe this is crystallised in the 2014 legal case *Google Spain v AEPD and Mario Costeja González,* which found that individuals have the right to ask search engines to remove certain results about them. This is known as the 'right to be forgotten' ruling. It is significant for us interested in privacy because, in principle, it allows the web to forget so personal information that might otherwise have stayed high on Google searches begin to fade. Underpinning this are questions about rights to privacy versus freedom of expression, but also corporate ownership, who decides what should be publicly known, and issues of memory and temporality.

Chapter 9 examines a hot topic of recent years – big data. This can be defined in terms of large volumes of information, coming from a variety of sources, used at extreme velocity – often in real time. As Mark Andrejevic (2013) phrases it, it is about mapping human responses and activities in ways that influence everything from advertising to national security to healthcare. In exploring this premise, this chapter unpacks big data in relation to machine learning, mission creep, the increased impossibility of anonymity, and the all-too-human and cultural factors that inform algorithms. As we will see in discussion of data, gender bias, race and policing, despite being seemingly objective, machines can discriminate against the most susceptible in society. This problem is amplified when we consider that how machines make judgements is only understandable to a very small number of technologists.

Chapter 10 begins a series of chapters that are interested in bodies – a dimension that is often ignored in discussions of privacy and media technologies. Here I argue that many of our technologies are displaying qualities of empathy in that they are employed to understand our emotions and intentions. In this chapter I focus on advertising and retail, and how technologies developed by companies such as Affectiva are used to scan facial expressions to gauge emotions. In the case of advertising, this is currently being done without use of personal data (namely, that which identifies a person or generates a code that is linked to that person so they can be treated differently). This raises questions that go to the conceptual, ethical and legal heart of privacy. If the data in question is about our emotions then clearly it is intimate, yet privacy rules do not apply. Do we need to think 'beyond privacy'?

Chapter 11 focuses explicitly on wearable media that are worn both on and in the body (these are sometimes referred to as ingestibles or implantables).

Here I focus on the compulsion to self-track and quantify the body's performance, condition, moods and location. I outline the context and history of wearables and self-tracking and assess notable recent examples. To theorise and understand this we will examine the technological and theoretical work of Steve Mann who uses the term sousveillance to describe when we are doing the watching (rather than being watched). However, multiple actors such as employers, health providers and the insurance industry are keen to watch us watching ourselves, so to speak! This raises questions about who has access to our bodies. To explore and answer these, I make use of feminist approaches to privacy that are well versed on matters of access to the body and its objectification.

So far we have primarily discussed privacy in terms of governmental and corporate interest in our datafied selves. We only need think about privacy in our day-to-day lives to recognise that we also spend a great deal of time watching each other, particularly through social media. Chapter 12 is less interested in institutions than peer-based privacy and the ways in which social media users watch each other, and how social media users deal with this. The problem is one of context and while in offline life we manage different contexts and relationship types with relative ease (such as friends, families and work colleagues), online this is not quite so easy. This gives rise to context collision and difficulties in managing social life online and who sees what (Nissenbaum, 2010). This reinforces an argument being made throughout this book: privacy is not about hermitage or seclusion, but it is in large part about having control over what, when and with whom we share information. On this basis the chapter progresses to debunk the idea that young people do not care about privacy. In fact this could not be further from the truth, as they have to contend with unwanted sharing of images, tagging and misjudged comments from friends. They also have to negotiate parents who want to be 'friends', bosses who want to 'follow' them, but also less innocent others. As a minimum, this creates significant scope for potential embarrassment. In response, young people have developed innovative techniques to manage privacy and navigate online social contexts that we will assess.

Chapter 13 explores 'sexting', or the activity where people send nude and explicit images of themselves, typically through social media. It is also referred to as cybersex, sending nudes, sexts, dodgy pix, fanpics or simply selfies. Sexting draws together many of the privacy strands developed in this book because it requires we consider the privacy protocols that guide sexting, personal control, intimacy, management and respect for the sovereignty of others. This chapter adds an additional dimension in the form of affective privacy and corporeal experiences of privacy. Too often privacy is thought of in abstract terms, whereas in reality human experience of privacy matters can quite literally be gut wrenching. Sexting tells us a number of things about privacy and media. As a practice engaged in by around 20 per cent of all smartphone users, privacy becomes a collective responsibility. This brings into sharper relief the principles of protocol and care introduced earlier. It also shows us how media are being used to enhance emotional intimacy in relationships. Although readers who do not send nudes or sexts may wonder why people would send images that potentially expose themselves to any interested party, when one considers sexting in the context of trust and desire for open and authentic relationships with others, it makes more sense. However, the focus of this chapter is the experience of school children, where sexting is increasingly part of normal life.

Chapter 14 concludes the book and asks: what do media developments tell us about privacy? The chapter draws together lessons learned from earlier content and points out that privacy is a very basic affective fact of living in groups and that it is best conceived in terms of protocol, control and management that transcend questions of media. Only when offline privacy is comprehended should we progress to examine media-based examples, and how the technology industry, politics and user behaviour affects the broader social nature of privacy today. Although reports of the death of privacy are greatly exaggerated, as a dynamic social norm it is subject to change. Of who is dictating social change in privacy matters, these are very much matters for critical media studies.

NOTE

1 Indeed, in 2013, the UK's Information Commissioner's Office, a data-protection watchdog, looked into claims that LG's Smart TVs collected viewing habits and other data without user consent.

PART 1
JOURNALISM, SURVEILLANCE AND POLITICS OF ENCRYPTION

2

NOTHING TO HIDE, NOTHING TO FEAR

MYTH AND WESTERN ROOTS OF PRIVACY

Key questions

- Is privacy primarily a technological matter?
- What are the roots of privacy in the West?
- What are negative and positive accounts of privacy?
- Is the relationship between liberty and security as simple as it seems?

Key concepts

- Being public and private
- The shifty citizen
- Liberalism
- Social contract

How we pin down privacy is debatable, but what is obvious is that a life without privacy is impossible. This fact is lost on those who excitedly and disturbingly claim that privacy is somehow 'dead', or is no longer a social norm as Facebook's Mark Zuckerberg once foolishly claimed. Had he modified his claim, he would have had a point because privacy *has* developed and changed over the years. This is irrefutable. In some ways privacy has actually increased (such as smaller family groups and the fact that more of us grew up with our own bedrooms than the generation before us), but digital technologies continue to alter things. To this end, much of this book is dedicated to understanding how modern forms of media have impacted on how much we know about each other, what we allow others to know, what the actions of others might unwantedly reveal about us, corporate tracking, state surveillance, and also the types of knowledge generated by digital technologies. However, despite the role of new technologies and the intense connection between digital life and privacy, it is best understood by closing our laptops and putting down mobile phones. This is because privacy is less about technology than rights and social conventions that guide our most basic daily interactions with others. After all, although technologies are important, so is clothing, what we do in bathrooms, sex, conversation, gossip, growing up, politeness, sharing secrets and confidences. Notably, many of these involve being open with others, as well as being reserved. This reflects a key argument of this chapter: a positive account of privacy is much more preferable than a negative one.

Like words such as freedom, liberty and rights, we know privacy to be an important ideal but often struggle to delineate 'it' because it is one of those words that do not lend well to precise definitions. Although well versed in various approaches to privacy, specialist scholars struggle with defining it too. Perhaps it is best considered by its absence. By this I mean that like freedom, we do not notice it until it is lost. Indeed, the connection between freedom and privacy may be best appreciated by spending time in a country where freedoms are fewer than those where you reside. As will be developed, I suggest that privacy is a respected norm of group behaviour, and a set of either written or unwritten expectations about how people, organisations and technologies interact. It is acutely noticed when we do not have it or when expectations are not met.

Focusing on Western conceptions, in this chapter we will consider the background to privacy. What we call privacy today did not emerge fully formed, but it is a premise that has developed over millennia. To this end we will consider some of the key philosophical schools that have impacted on what privacy is today. There are many ways this can be approached but here, perhaps initially strangely, I focus on Ancient Greek contributions to our understanding of what is private and public; and liberalism that directly informs most of our thinking, laws and moral musing on privacy. For consideration of more diverse philosophical traditions and schools, see *Privacy and Philosophy* (McStay, 2014)

BACK TO GREECE: TIME, PLACE AND CULTURAL CONTEXT

Ancient Greece is a good place to start for three reasons: first, because it had a keen separation between being private and public; second, because ancient Greek thought remains influential on contemporary Western thought and politics; and third, because it thought being private was a bad thing. This may seem odd today given that we are often seeking to defend privacy, but for the ancient Greeks great virtue came from acts of citizenship and engagement in public life. For them, the city-state (or *polis*) was more than a collection of individuals, buildings and properties that occupy the city, but a living unity where the whole was more than the sum of its parts (Aristotle, 1995 [350 BC]). Whereas people and property pass away, the public life of the city goes on. This meant that the Greek city-state came before either the family or the individual. What is good and valuable is being public, engaging in political life and promoting the interests of the city. In distinction to the civic value in being public, privacy was seen in deeply negative terms. On the large assumption that most readers are studying in Western countries with democratic societies that privilege rights to privacy, this might appear strange. This is because democracies (or governance for the people by their elected representatives) innately value privacy because it promotes free development of the self, nonconformity, diversity of views, new ideas and opportunities to enjoy intimacy without unwanted scrutiny. In distinction to the privacy that citizens should have, democratic ideals demand openness, publicity and transparency of their governments to keep power in check.

To return back to ancient Greece, for Aristotle, the drive to be a public citizen was not an intellectual choice or a preference because 'man is by nature a political animal' (ibid.: 10 §1253a2). To be a proper politically active citizen is to be connected to goodness and justice. In contrast to be private is to lack participation in civic life. This creates quite a few dualisms because only free and very visible men were able to participate. Women by contrast were reduced to the private sphere (or *oikos*). For Aristotle, this is the household and family life that defined the role of women, children and slaves. A woman's lowly existence is a given in Aristotle and there is no possibility of entry into the *polis*. To live privately is to be devoid of status and significance. It is notable too the etymological roots of the word 'privacy' are *privo*, *privare* and *privatum* – all implying deficiency. *Privo* means to bereave, deprive, rob or strip of something; *privare* means to be free, released or delivered of something; the latter, *privatum* and its adjective *privatus*, means apart from the state, peculiar to one's self or belonging to an individual (Engelhardt, 2000: 121).

Although we are focusing on the West, a negative account of privacy is also evident in non-Western conceptions of privacy. Discussing Japanese history and public/private ideas, Hayashi (2006) says that whereas privacy in the West is frequently linked with autonomy (that Westerners see as a good thing), this is certainly not a global understanding of privacy. Hayashi points out that the premise of 'public' is historically and etymologically connected to the 'great residence' and then took the meaning of 'the master' at a later date in pre-modern Japan. The expression 'public interest' then connects to the idea of the 'master's interest', and thereby what is official. This sees the public domain belonging to 'them' (the masters), and not in terms of common ownership as in the West. This is not simply about ownership because there are moral and ethical aspects to this understanding of being private and public. Broadly aligning with the Greeks, Hayashi quotes:

> 'Public' is synonymous with the principles of heaven, and 'private' with human desires ... Hence a 'private' matter is an evil that must be rejected. The Chu Hsi scholars of the early Tokugawa period faithfully followed this interpretation. Hayashi Razan, for example, argued that 'a benevolent man is a person who has eliminated selfish desires and has adhered to the public good based on the principles of Heaven. Public good based on the principles of Heaven means righteousness ... This is the path that is natural and does not involve private considerations.' (Maruyama, 1974, cited in Hayashi, 2006: 615)

What is private is linked with that which is human (as opposed to a divine notion of public that is associated with fairness and being above criticism). This dualism leaves what is private as possibly dishonourable, redundant and containing what is evil.

NEGATIVE APPROACHES: THE SHIFTY CITIZEN

An important root of the contemporary meme 'nothing to hide, nothing to fear' can be found in Plato's book *The Laws*. He also phrases privacy in negative terms but whereas Aristotle sees privacy as negative since it is not public (and thereby good), Plato believed privacy to be innately bad because it connects with 'having something to hide'. For Plato privacy was a threat to the social good. He held that people should be well known to each other and should not be kept in the dark about a person's character. The idea that privacy might have a positive dimension does not occur to Plato anywhere in *The Laws*.

For Plato, people who conceal themselves and are unknown to others will not enjoy respect 'or fill the office he deserves or obtain the legal verdict to which he is entitled. So every citizen of every state should make a particular effort to show that he is *straightforward and genuine, not shifty*' (2004 [360 BC]: 160–161§5.738e; my emphasis). The last word 'shifty' is not one we would expect to find in Plato. Again, we see a dualism at play in that what is unknown is bad (rather than good) and immediately worthy of suspicion (as opposed to trust). This is quite arguably a strong root of the 'nothing to hide, nothing to fear ...' phrase, which is a great example of what advertising agencies call 'campaign lines' and what the rest of us call slogans or memes. These are ideological, highly memorable and repeatable, and encapsulate a rich set of values into one punchy line. It has become a shorthand means of saying that 'Law-abiding citizens have nothing to hide and should not be concerned'[1] and that a person should feel guilty for wanting any privacy; that is, if a person cares about privacy they must be shifty and have done something wrong. It is an insidious proposition because it entails *forced transparency*, has a coercive character, and runs counter to democratic ideals and citizens' rights to a private life.

On 'nothing to hide, nothing to fear', why do people always seem to use these precise words, what are the origins of the sentiment, and why don't people have anything to hide? After all, even the most virtuous among us have things we would prefer others not to know. Misdemeanours are a fact of life and while some are very bad, the suggestion that every aspect of our lives should be open to public inspection is an even more unpalatable suggestion. There are plenty of things we do in private that are not wrong, but we prefer not to share (such as being naked, toilet behaviour, sex both alone and with others, or even a predilection for 1980s power ballads). There is nothing immoral with any this, but we still may not want others to know. To speak of nothing to hide/fear is idiotic and impractical. Indeed, we might ask those who urge us to live this way to first do so themselves. 'Nothing to hide, nothing to fear' condenses a set of values and assumptions. First, it makes *us* into the potential criminal: it requires that *we* interrogate ourselves; and it demands absolute transparency of our lives and those who we connect with (be this social media 'friends' or close family members). It implies that all life should be made transparent because we should leave 'no thing' unavailable for inspection. This has a quasi-religious feel in that we should be physically, mentally and spiritually naked before our overseers. Where we are asked by our governments and corporations to be transparent in this way, this is to agree to: perpetual watching; to be OK with self-censorship ('I'd best not search for this idea because I don't want to be flagged up on a dodgy list'); and to be careful what we read about (such as reading ISIS material to understand their propaganda techniques).

One might still respond and say, 'Well, I haven't done anything wrong so what's the problem?' My answer is two-fold. First, I suggest you are unwittingly lying. Consider all the fun things you have done that might be illegal or possibly distasteful to some. Furthermore, we all gossip and possibly say hurtful and outrageous things behind the backs of others. I cannot answer why people do this (although I'm sure few of us want to hurt the person we are speaking of), but we do it nonetheless. While forced transparency about what we say and do may have abstract appeal, in reality it would be a deeply unpleasant proposition to make transparent everything that was once private. Again, privacy may best appreciated by considering its absence.

Second, this is not how healthy societies are meant to work. When we feel that we cannot look, search, or read certain things, this is wrong. The capacity to explore deviant ideas (assuming no harm to others), to think differently and to disagree with governments without their spying on us is a hard-won human right. Remember, history is littered with examples of when the status quo is wrong (I have laws and attitudes to homosexuality in mind). By 'human right', I do not mean a divine right, but instead principles that people have agreed to be right and that we think to be the morally right thing. We have abided by these principles and, for the most part, they have served us well. Without doubt though, moral principles are tested from time to time.

The 'nothing to hide ...' mnemonic assumes that secrecy is bad. Despite the fact that transparency is seen as inherently 'good' (being clear, good, connected with light and, to push the exposition, potentially godly), secrecy plays an important social role. This is because, paradoxically, the capacity to retain secrecy may help hold power-holders to account and make *them* transparent. The alternative to a modicum of secrecy should make us shudder because it involves *forced* openness. The delicious irony of modern life is that while greater transparency is demanded of citizens and consumers, both governments and corporations are very difficult to penetrate. This is the wrong way around. Historically, democracies have been based on the idea that societies can scrutinise those in power and hold them to account, that people are clear on what the laws of the land are and that seats of power can be inspected. Indeed, arguably of greater concern than national and transnational surveillance is the creation of secret laws and interpretations of laws. Although there is an argument to be made for the necessity of surveillance, we should not have a gulf between what the public thinks a law says and what the government secretly thinks the law says.

POSITIVE APPROACHES: LIBERALISM

This brings us neatly onto a liberal account of privacy. We cannot develop an understanding of privacy that progresses past common sense without understanding something of liberal philosophy. This is an area of political philosophy that emerged out of Europe in the late seventeenth and eighteenth centuries. It demands for citizens a minimum area of *personal freedom* from political authorities that must not be violated. As will be developed in later chapters, today this impacts on debates over the right to be forgotten (such as with Google in Europe); the right to be left alone (and not be tracked by corporations and governments); principles of informational self-determination that informs laws on privacy; and how we treat information we have been entrusted with (as with sexting). Key words and ideas expressed by liberal philosophers are freedom, consent, autonomy and non-interference from unwanted others. Notable philosophers from the past include Thomas Hobbes, John Locke, Jean-Jacques Rousseau, John Stuart Mill and Immanuel Kant. More modern ones include Isaiah Berlin, Richard Rorty, John Rawls and Michael Sandel.

The Greek approach to privacy is a deeply negative one in that it focuses on suspicion and the belief that privacy equates to deficiency. Although liberal philosophy is diverse and spans hundreds of years, in general it maintains a positive approach to privacy. This is an important development because (indirectly) it counters Plato's shifty citizen and the fallacy that privacy equates to 'having something to hide'. Instead it articulates privacy in terms of control, dignity and respect for self-hood regarding what one wishes to share, reveal or allow access to. When we consider how we feel when we have privacy breached (be this a broken lock on a toilet door, revenge porn or someone we trust breaking a confidence), we can see the value in an approach to privacy that values the experience of both individuals and groups.

As a philosophy it should be seen against the context of religious and moral doctrine that prescribed that deities and morality should be obeyed. What liberalism promotes is self-determination, free will and capacity to choose. Morally speaking this was a huge turn and even today is a controversial proposition. The idea of rights as naturally attributable to people begins with Hugo Grotius (2001 [1625]). His is a subtle but important point that human rights should ground and organise community law, rather than laws determining rights. For those of us interested in privacy, this means that we have privacy rights first and then laws have to be arranged around these rights.

Today's liberals express concern about the power of the state over individuals, improper uses of mass surveillance, social conformity and political sameness (liberals prefer a plurality of opinion). They are also concerned about the fact that when large amounts of data are collected that many people have access to, the likelihood of leaks and human error goes up. They also express concern about false positives (where data suggests someone is guilty when they are not), unintended uses and consequences (how information may be collected for one reason but used for another), fear of future governments (today's may be benign, but what about tomorrow?), and that once surveillant resources and powers are granted, they are incredibly hard to roll back (even in politically stable periods). Although liberalism is a political philosophy in the sense of being about the relationship between state, individuals and the power of corporations, it is also a personal philosophy. By this I mean it has a great deal to say about the value of personal experimentation, different ways of living, self-development, exploration of individuality, and developing possibly unusual ideas and practices free from unwanted interference from the state and other actors. The bottom line is that anything goes, as long as the behaviour of an individual or group does not negatively impact on others and that a common political good is still advanced.

A liberal approach to privacy typically emphasises the notion of *control* and *management*. This is important because rather than seeing privacy as that which involves keeping secrets, instead we can see it as the capacity to have a degree of control over who we share information with and what they do with our information. Inbuilt in this premise is a number of principles, discussed below.

CONTROL

The liberal approach to privacy is famously expressed by Alan Westin (1984 [1967]).[2] He sees privacy as the ability to control how much about ourselves we reveal to others. This is a highly individualistic but attractively simple definition of privacy. It is useful in that it depicts a positive account of privacy and it emphasises the rights of individuals to self-determination about how open or reserved they wish to be. However, the emphasis on control may lead us to strange and what many might consider bizarre outcomes. For example, if privacy is seen solely in terms of access and control is it violated each time we are purposefully looked at by another person? As Nissenbaum (2010) highlights, if a motorist peers at a pedestrian crossing the street, has a privacy breach occurred? Taking the control thesis and the doctrine of perfect inaccessibility by the letter, it would seem so.

RESPECT FOR SELF-DETERMINATION AND AUTONOMY

A positive approach does not place the burden on people to explain *why* they should have privacy, why they do not want to share information, or why they do not want others prying into their lives. The roots of this are deeply Western and philosophically can be found, for example, in Locke (2005 [1689]) and Kant (1983 [1784]). For Locke, liberal democracies are predicated on developing civil rights that allow for autonomy. Similarly, for Kant, he believed that for human life and understanding to flourish, freedom is required. From the point of view of privacy we see a privileging of individuality, subjectivity, self-determination, free choice, voluntariness, privacy and accepting responsibility for our choices. Indeed, privacy serves to guarantee autonomy and the right to personal choice, assuming no harm or conflict with others. At the level of politics, this requires governments to treat people with respect and dignity. For Kant, autonomy, self-determination and the ability to choose is the basis of social and moral life, and it is vital to protect this, and provide circumstances for it to develop elsewhere. The importance of liberal philosophy becomes clearer when we recognise that it holds sway over comprehension of human rights and the ethics that drive Western law.

RESPECT FOR OTHERS

Fried sees privacy as *the* enabler for love, friendship, trust and respectful relationships with others. He phrases it as 'the necessary atmosphere for these attitudes and actions, as oxygen is for combustion' (1984 [1968]: 205). This is best understood by attempting to subtract privacy from relationships with friends and people whom we love: the result is always negative. In addition to being desirable, this makes privacy a moral proposition connected to entitlements and duties one performs in relation to others. As we will see in Chapters 12 and 13 on social media and sexting, the notion of respect is an important one. This relates to liberal ideals but in addition to privacy being about self-determination and personal choice, we also make decisions on behalf of others (such as tagging and sharing information about others). This means that privacy also has a collective as well as personal character. Privacy then involves recognising the full existence of others and is tantamount to respect and obligations to others. It also recognises that privacy is that which comes to be because of interaction. Thus, if hypothetically we think of someone marooned on a desert island and who is entirely alone with no one knowing of their existence, they are not living in privacy but are simply alone. Privacy comes to be because of interaction with each other. This may involve face-to-face interaction or be mediated through machines.

LIBERTY VERSUS SECURITY

So far in this chapter we have considered negative accounts of privacy based on seclusion and hiding, and positive accounts of privacy based on respect, autonomy, control, management and freedom. The rest of this chapter explores this positive account of privacy in relation to security. The Universal Declaration of Human Rights[3] considers privacy to be a human right. However, this is not absolute like other rights (such as not to be tortured), but rather it may be encroached upon if there are other competing interests and public goods – such as security. The suggestion that people should give up some liberty (which encompasses privacy) for security is best expressed in the work of another old philosopher: Thomas Hobbes.

Hobbes (1985 [1651]; 1998 [1668/1642]) said that to guarantee a functioning society and avoid a collapse back into a 'state of nature', we need a central power for which we put aside a right to all things in favour of common interest, governance and mutual contracts with fellow humans. Today this *contract* takes form with each of our governments (see Rawls, 1999 [1971] for a full account of modern contract theory). Liberty, for Hobbes, means giving up some rights to establish peace via an authority that works on our behalf for the common interest (such as with defence and policing). In exchange, people obtain protection, providing they obey the law. This involves giving up some natural rights for the benefit of social stability. In doing so we lay aside the right to act with only self-interest, and grant others authority and power over us. The state, or what Hobbes (1985 [1651]) calls the 'Leviathan', is able to punish those who transgress the contract. This argument grafts well onto contemporary discussion of privacy (rights) and surveillance by the state (or sovereign). The primary task of the sovereign then is to keep us safe and offer protection, although Hobbes recognises that governance requires more than this – it requires people be happy too, although this has to be balanced with security needs. Hobbes sees that this is a balancing act and in his book *De Cive* ('The Citizen') says that safety cannot come at any cost or be the sole concern of life in society, but a society should also 'furnish their subjects abundantly, not only with the good things belonging to life, but also with those which advance to delectation' (1998 [1668/1642]): 259). This particular point is a fundamental one as it underpins and explains continuing tensions between protection and safety, and privacy and liberty.

21

In 2015–16 I co-organised a series of seminars that took place in the UK. This examined life after the Edward Snowden leaks of 2013 that revealed the extent of surveillance of citizens' digital communications by national security agencies. This series included delegates from academia, defence, industry and those charged with enforcing and creating laws around data protection. Each was asked to provide written statements and thoughts on how they see the ethics of surveillance. Iain Bourne, Group Manager of Policy Delivery for the UK's Information Commissioner's Office,[4] presented a rich and generous statement that both discussed his views in relation to Hobbes and crystallised the pro-surveillance argument. Note that the following passages discussing Iain Bourne are his own and *do not* represent the ICO.[5] He says that:

> I think there's a very compelling Hobbesian argument that by surrendering a degree of our privacy to the state through toleration of its surveillance, we are in fact safeguarding our security and ultimately our freedom. Of course this depends on what kind of state you are dealing with and what sort of person you are – and of course on how much privacy you are expected, or required, to surrender.

On the 'nothing to hide, nothing to fear' argument I unpacked earlier, Bourne also comments:

> 'If you have done nothing wrong you have nothing to fear.' Generally this argument is harshly rejected in privacy circles. However, in the context of surveillance it is largely true, again depending on what sort of society you inhabit. If the [surveillance] system is working right, it is likely that CCTV or electronic surveillance will have a more significant effect on someone who has broken the rules than on someone who hasn't. (Whether the rules are the right ones is of course a crucial matter.)

He progresses to point out that despite the increase in surveillance, people publicly share more information about themselves than they ever have done. He also argues that despite increased surveillance, people living in societies typically considered as 'free' have not been curtailed in notable ways. He posits that the reason why people have not changed their behaviour is because of the lack of 'negative effect of the expansion of data collection and analytical activity on ordinary people's lives'. He also urges that we consider the nature of political contexts. After all, Moscow, London, New York, Singapore, Tehran, Canberra and Pyongyang are all quite different places. Bourne says, 'It's easy to see it as the state versus citizens and to ignore the different types of state and the different types of citizen'.

He also makes a more subtle argument saying that it is too simplistic to claim that more privacy necessarily equals more freedom. He says:

Actually, I think most people make a Hobbesian surveillance–freedom trade-off most of the time, but won't articulate it as such. I think people are aware of CCTV cameras and of GCHQ and Snowden and have seen detective shows where the police use telecoms data to catch the baddies. Maybe they believe that state surveillance is there to stop bad guys doing bad things, not regular people doing good things, and that the world would be more dangerous and traditional freedoms would be eroded faster without surveillance. A perfectly understandable view.

He ends on a very Hobbesian point by presenting a hypothetical situation:

It would be interesting to see what would happen if we had a surveillance moratorium of say two weeks where we turn off all the cameras and shut down all the data feeds. Maybe we'd all enjoy a golden era of unrepressed, uninhibited freedom. Maybe it would make no difference at all. Or maybe very bad things would happen. Personally I would book a holiday somewhere else. James Madison – the 4th US president – said that 'if men were angels no government would be necessary'. Maybe the same is true of surveillance.[6]

Bourne makes strong arguments. However, if we inspect them a little more closely what appear as obvious truths are not as convincing as they first appear. For example, most people who argue for greater privacy rights do not think that surveillance is innately bad, or that we should not have security. The question is one of proportionality, type of surveillance, the role of indiscriminate surveillance and whether surveillance should be used to track innocent people. Most will admit too that the so-called choice between liberty and security is not entirely without merit. However, the opposing of liberty with security hides a lot of important complexity (we could phrase this as the 'devil in the detail rebuttal'). Again, it comes down to form of surveillance, type and proportionality, but also controls on how data is used to combat lesser crimes, and the role of reactionary politics by our politicians. For example, following any large-scale attack there is always a strong push for more surveillance powers and calls for attacks on other countries. As will be accounted for in later chapters, there is very little available evidence to suggest that mass surveillance prevents attacks.

We should also scrutinise the value and accuracy of invoking Hobbes. For example, the Leviathan is based on the hypothetical idea that before the inception of centralised states and governments, we lived in 'state of nature' and life was 'solitary, poor, nasty, brutish and short'. This does not graft well onto questions of surveillance and the political situation today is quite different from that which Hobbes was trying to understand. Also, a (social) contract usually implies terms that are understandable to its citizens. This is not the case with mass surveillance and instead we are asked to take it on faith that: a) surveillance is necessary; b) powers will not be exceeded; c) surveillance will not be used for lesser reasons (mission creep); d) data will be cared for and not lost or leaked. Further, if we are going by the social contract approach (that implies trust and stated obligations), then the state broke the last contract through indiscriminate surveillance. Lastly, the idea of a social contract is based on a hypothesis rather than a meaningful agreement between two parties who have explored and debated the terms of the contract. How valid is it?

Bourne also says that, '"If you have done nothing wrong you have nothing to fear" … it is likely that CCTV or electronic surveillance will have a more significant effect on someone who has broken the rules than on someone who hasn't.' There are a range of answers to this including the need to respect the consent of citizenry in democracies, the need for some healthy distance between citizenry and governments, problems with what happens when the next government comes to power, and how incumbents will choose to share this information without asking citizens (the UK, for example, has data collection and sharing programmes with the US). There is also the question of whether states can be trusted with increasingly granular information about us. After all, what both Wikileaks and the Snowden leaks highlight is that information is easily stolen and leaked.

CONCLUSION

The aim of this chapter has been to address head-on the key criticism levelled against people who campaign for stronger privacy rights. This is the question: 'If you've nothing hide, then what have you got to fear?' The roots of this principle go as far back as ancient Greece and Plato, and the belief that being public is good while being private is bad. This sees those interested in privacy as somehow 'shifty'. Today privacy is also discussed in relation to the Hobbesian choice between security and liberty. We explored the implications of this dualism in relation to an online discussion between myself and Iain Bourne, policy delivery manager for the UK's Information Commissioner's Office (ICO). Although not speaking in an official capacity he has a long-standing interest in these matters and raises many points and arguments used by those in governmental positions (also see Omand, 2010). Although I suspect some of his contributions were of a devil's advocate nature, he delineates and argues the case for mass surveillance well. Lastly, although this chapter disagrees with the choice between liberty and security on the basis that its simplicity hides questions about the effectiveness and ethics of surveillance techniques, the call for students of privacy and media to consider ethics in real-world political contexts is a good one.

Research and challenges

1 Identify and discuss problems with 'nothing to hide, nothing to fear'.

2 How satisfying do you find the liberty for security trade-off?

3 By means of ten vox pops recorded with a mobile phone, ask people to define privacy, and what they think about the relationship between security and liberty. Discuss findings in groups in relation to the content of this chapter.

NOTES

1 This line is a response to a survey from Pew Internet Center (2015) who carried out a survey of people's perceptions of privacy after the Snowden leaks.
2 Perhaps only Warren and Brandeis's (1984 [1890]) 'right to be let alone' defines the privacy field more absolutely.
3 Full list of rights available from www.un.org/en/universal-declaration-human-rights/.
4 The Information Commissioner's Office is the UK's data protection regulator. It is the agency that people complain to if they feel their data rights have been breached. They are also responsible for investigating companies and organisations deemed to have broken the data protection laws in the UK.
5 His full and extended blog post can be found at http://data-psst.blogspot.co.uk/2015/02/iain-bourne-group-manager-policy.html.
6 Again, note Bourne's disclaimer: 'These are my personal observations, intended to further discussion of an increasingly important issue. They do not reflect the view of the ICO, although we are keen to support and contribute to debate in this area.'

3

JOURNALISM
A COMPLEX RELATIONSHIP WITH PRIVACY

Key questions

- How have the connections between journalism, privacy and new technology developed since the 1890s?
- Given scope for intrusiveness, should journalism be subject to greater regulation? If so, why? If not, why?
- Do celebrities waive their right to privacy?

Key concepts

- Balancing the right to privacy with the right to free press
- The public interest formula
- Necessary tension
- Distinguishing what is private and public

Journalism and privacy have a long, difficult and paradoxical relationship. This chapter complicates the premise that privacy is innately a good thing, because good journalism reveals governmental misdoings, abuses of power, financial wrong-doings, secret deals and affairs that people in positions of power would prefer that the public do not know. Seen this way, journalism exists to fulfil the promise of democracy and make powerful institutions publicly known, transparent and accountable to citizens. However, although journalists may appear to be anti-privacy because their profession involves making uncomfortable truths public, they are also reliant on privacy. This is because their sources of information often need to be protected from reprisal from those whose secrets journalists have leaked. In practical terms, this means no authorities or courts should be able to require a journalist to reveal the identity of an anonymous source. There is another connection between journalism and privacy that we are all familiar with: this is when tabloid journalism goes after sensationalist stories and breaches people's privacy. Before publishing a sensitive story with personal information, a good journalist will ask: 'Is it in the public interest?' The formula used to answer this is that the more private or intimate the information is, the justification for public interest needs to be equal or greater. Again, note that 'what is in the public interest' and 'what is of interest to the public' are quite different things. There is a world of difference between *need* to know and *want* to know. The former is about things that we should know (such as crime, protecting public health or corporate/governmental institutional behaviour), and the latter what we like to know for all sorts of voyeuristic reasons. Another key connection to privacy is that the earliest writing on privacy and the media addresses the rise of photojournalism and what in the 1880s were new media technologies.

This chapter explores these topics by first examining the right to privacy and the need for a free press if democracies are to function properly. This sees two valuable principles of the 1950 European Convention for the Protection of Human Rights and Fundamental Freedoms go head-to-head: Article 8 (the right to privacy) and Article 10 (freedom of expression). We then progress to consider what many consider to be the origins of privacy scholarship in Samuel Warren and Louis Brandeis's essay 'The Right to Privacy', written in 1890. What is more interesting than being first on the scene is that this essay feels remarkable fresh, even when discussing media technologies. The question of journalism and invasion into personal lives thus allows us to think about what privacy actually is. Although typically framed in terms of 'control' and 'self-determination', there are also the matters of effects and harms when privacy is violated. As we progress towards the end of the chapter we will briefly consider new privacy questions in the context of journalism. The first is super-injunctions and the difficulty of gagging the press in an age of social media; the second is the rise of drones that offer new ways of obtaining pictures and access to private lives.

BALANCING THE RIGHT TO PRIVACY WITH A FREE PRESS

The need for a free press was well established by the Enlightenment in the eighteenth century. This led journalism to be called the 'Fourth Estate' and integral to the functioning of democracy. To quote the Scottish philosopher Thomas Carlyle commenting on the role of reporting parliamentary debates:

Whoever can speak, speaking now to the whole nation, becomes a power, a branch of government, with inalienable weight in law-making, in all acts of authority. It matters not what rank he has, what revenues or garnitures: the requisite thing is, that he have a tongue which others will listen to; this and nothing more is requisite. (2007 [1840]: 392)

Carlyle goes on to remark upon the power of ideas and words, the ways in which these frame reality itself, 'and how the Press is to such a degree superseding the Pulpit, the Senate, the Senatus Academicus and much else' (ibid.: 393). The press conceived in terms of the Fourth Estate is one in which it is independent of governmental influence and control; representative of enlightened public opinion;[1] and gives its readers information and free comment necessary to form a considered judgement on political matters (Boyce, 1978). Seen this way, journalists are clearly influential, important and play a pivotal civic role. In addition to power and capacity to shape narratives, they also serve to convey information. This is because democracy requires informed citizens. The key principle is that the press reports on what governments do and, if people do not like this, they can vote them out at the next election. Further, at least in theory, journalism should be balanced in that reports provide multiple perspectives of a debate within a single report. This view of journalism connects with liberal ideas, particularly the sort espoused by philosophers such as John Stuart Mill who argued that the liberty of the press is 'one of the securities against corrupt or tyrannical government' (1962 [1859]: 141). This is to see the press in its finest moments, illuminating the secret machinations of power, informing citizens of wrongdoing, acting as watchdog for the public and converting what was once private into information that is public and visible. Our press today still does this and plays a critical role in democratic functioning. By 'critical' I mean both senses of the word in both 'holding to account' and 'vital part'.

Some journalism scholars take issue with the narrative of the 'Fourth Estate'. Boyce (1978), writing about the nineteenth-century press, points out a number of problems, not least that nineteenth-century governments did not really listen to what the press said and were more receptive to parliamentary pressure than to what journalists were saying. There is also the question of to what extent the metropolitan press represented overall public opinion, particularly given the upper-class backgrounds of journalists. Boyce also argues that journalists were bribed by ministers, under influence of politicians, and that the natural position of the nineteenth-century press was that of being part of the political machine. Also, as the mass circulation press rose to prominence (such as the UK's *Daily Mail*, *Daily Mirror* and *Daily Express*), this posed financial problems for the 'quality' press. Boyce goes on to show how they received funds from the political patrons. Boyce's final criticism is that not all Victorian newspapers were in the business of enlightening the public, but many newspapers gave people what they wanted: sport and murder cases.

Today we have a diversity of news types and few publishers are able to resist click bait, sensationalism and excessive simplification. The drivers for this are the need to attract readers, app/website clicks and audience attention for advertisers (also see Chapter 7). The upshot is that commercial interests may dictate editorial decisions about how news is presented and what is reported. Even the most high-minded of publishers will tweak headlines to attract eyeballs and clicks.[2] Although journalism is rightly connected with principles of making governments and power-holders accountable, it also panders to less worthy instincts in all of us. This entails interest in celebrity news, gratuitous pictures, alarmism and freaky stories. On occasion this can sink to depravity, especially regarding the techniques employed to get a scoop. This is exemplified by a 2011 UK journalistic privacy scandal that involved UK newspapers illegally accessing the mobile-phone data and messages of celebrities, murdered schoolgirl Milly Dowler, families of dead British soldiers and victims of the 7 July 2005 London suicide bombings. This resulted in the closure of the tabloid newspaper *News of the World*, the cancellation of News Corporation's bid to increase majority share ownership of the British telecommunications company BSkyB, the resignation of the assistant commissioner of the Metropolitan Police and the Leveson inquiry (2012) that recommended a new independent body with greater control over the UK press (although this recommendation was rejected by the government). The key question is this: to what extent should the right to privacy be balanced with the need for a free press, however ugly it may be?

RIGHTS AND FUNDAMENTAL FREEDOMS

Another example of this tension is celebrities and public spaces, especially given the rise of paparazzi photographers who stalk celebrities to satisfy our prurient wants. Celebrities are often deemed to have sought to be in the 'public eye', which means one might argue they have lost the right to privacy. Even if one were to go along with this, the loss is not total and, for example, it would not be acceptable to broadcast their bank details, to access the inside of their homes, or to appropriate their name and likeness. However, they typically undergo public access to their affairs that most people do not for three reasons: 1) they have sought publicity, *arguably* consented to it and have lost right of complaint; 2) their personalities and affairs have already become public; and 3) the press has a professional right to inform the public about matters of public interest (Prosser, 1984 [1960]). We might look at it differently though. After all, celebrities do not sign a contract or consent in any meaningful way to the loss of their privacy, even when they are in public spaces rather than at home.

Whereas US law tends not to recognise privacy rights in public places, in Europe the situation is different. In Europe, privacy rights are underpinned by Article 8 of the 1950 European Convention for the Protection of Human Rights and Fundamental Freedoms. This is one of the earliest agreements within Europe and it remains one that all new member states must agree to if they wish to join the European Union. It states:

1 Everyone has the right to respect for his private and family life, his home and his correspondence.
2 There shall be no interference by a public authority with the exercise of this right except such as is in accordance with the law and is necessary in a democratic society in the interests of national security, public safety or the economic well-being of the country, for the prevention of disorder or crime, for the protection of health or morals, or for the protection of the rights and freedoms of others. (Council of Europe, 2010 [1950])

Article 8 is particularly important because in Europe the emphasis on 'everyone' may act as a defence for celebrities and public figures against publications intruding on a person's privacy.[3] Although it often appears that celebrities pass over their right to privacy because they seek public exposure on other occasions, there is no basis for this in UK law. This was illustrated in the UK when J.K. Rowling, author of the Harry Potter series, brought a legal case against paparazzi photographers who in November 2004 took photos of Rowling and her partner walking along an Edinburgh street with their 19-month-old child in a buggy. Rowling was also six months pregnant. The photos were taken covertly with a long lens and published by the *Sunday Express* newspaper. Court judges ruled that the children of famous parents should be protected from intrusive media attention.[4]

For journalists, the important part is that the Convention asks courts to balance Article 8 and the right to respect for private and family life with Article 10 of the 1950 European Convention for the Protection of Human Rights and Fundamental Freedoms. The latter says that:

1 Everyone has the right to freedom of expression. This right shall include freedom to hold opinions and to receive and impart information and ideas without interference by public authority and regardless of frontiers. This Article shall not prevent States from requiring the licensing of broadcasting, television or cinema enterprises.
2 The exercise of these freedoms, since it carries with it duties and responsibilities, may be subject to such formalities, conditions, restrictions or penalties as are prescribed by law and are necessary in a democratic society, in the interests of national security, territorial integrity or public safety, for the prevention of disorder or crime, for the protection of health or morals, for the protection of the reputation or rights of others, for preventing the disclosure of information received in confidence, or for maintaining the authority and impartiality of the judiciary. (Council of Europe, 2010 [1950])

Clearly there is possibility of conflict between Article 8 (the right to privacy) and Article 10 (freedom of expression). As Rozenburg (2004) points out, how can journalists write about us if they have to respect privacy, and how can we insist that journalists show respect to our family life if they have the right to say what they like about us in public? We should also keep in mind that while on the face of things both Articles 8 and 10 are straightforward, the second parts of both Articles add important caveats to the principles.

In relation to privacy this is especially important and, as Hosein (2004) notes, the second part of Article 8 complicates what was a straightforward principle. The consequence is that while privacy is important, it is what is known as a *derogable* human right in that there may be competing interests and ethics. This contrasts with *non-derogable* rights, such as the right to be free from torture or slavery. These are absolute and cannot be trumped. In sum, neither Articles 8 nor 10 dom- inate, but instead they provide a field of privacy coverage characterised by what we might designate as *necessary tension*. This means that no one norm should dominate because its implications would be unfavourable to all (unfettered access versus total gagging of journalists to report important wrongdoing).

ACTING IN THE PUBLIC INTEREST

The public's right to know is expressed in terms of allowances granted to journal- ism to engage in public interest investigations, which at times warrant intrusion (Lloyd, 2012). The UK's Press Complaints Commission defines this in terms of detecting or exposing crime or serious impropriety; protecting public health and safety; preventing the public from being misled by an action or statement of an individual or organisation; or public interest in freedom of expression itself. The privilege originates in the premise discussed above that journalism plays a democratic role and that it should only be exercised when acting on behalf of the public. In the UK, another way for people to know what is taking place is by means of the Freedom of Information Act 2000. This creates a public 'right of access' to information held by public authorities. However, although intended for citizenry, the press arguably became more aggressive in its pursuit of public figures. In his autobiography *A Journey*, ex-UK Prime Minister Blair describes the Act (intro- duced under his government) as: 'a quite extraordinary effort by a government to open itself and Parliament to scrutiny. Its consequences would be revolutionary; the power it handed to the tender mercy of the media was gigantic. We did it with care, but without foresight. Politicians are people and scandals will happen' (Blair, 2010: 127). He goes on to lambast himself as an 'idiot' and 'naïve, foolish, irresponsible nincompoop' for 'doing such a thing so utterly undermining of sensible government' (ibid, 2010: 516).

Although designed with openness and transparency in mind for UK citizens, he continues by saying that the FOI Act is not used for the most part by 'the people' but by journalists as a weapon. From the point of view of privacy (which in this case tips into secrecy and a clandestine wish to hide from view), Blair makes an interesting point by saying that it is a dangerous Act because governments, like any other organisation, needs to be able to debate, discuss and decide issues with a reasonable level of confidentiality. Without this cloak, people are inhibited and the consideration of options is limited in a way that is not conducive to good decision-making. In the jargon of privacy, this is what is known as the *chilling effect* (for more on this see Chapter 4) because actions and decisions are self-limited out of a vague fear of future publicity.

INVASION AND THE PUBLIC INTEREST

Alan Rusbridger (2012: 142), editor of the *Guardian* (1995–2015), suggests five practical points to justify privacy invasions by journalists: there must be sufficient cause along with prior assessment of harm to individuals and families; integrity of motive and justification that public good will follow; methods should be proportionate to the story and degree of public interest, and intrusion minimised; intrusion should be overseen by an authority; and there should be reasonable prospect of success and 'fishing expeditions are not justified'. Budding journalists should also know that UK editors and journalists are required to abide by the Press Complaints Commission (PCC) code of practice. Section 3 that addresses privacy states:

i.   Everyone is entitled to respect for his or her private and family life, home, health and correspondence, including digital communications.
ii. Editors will be expected to justify intrusions into any individual's private life without consent. Account will be taken of the complainant's own public disclosures of information.
iii. It is unacceptable to photograph individuals in private places without their consent.

The explanatory notes of the codes of journalistic practice are also useful as they reveal that, for journalists, a private place is a *'public or private property where there is a reasonable expectation of privacy'* (PCC, 2013; italics in original). The codes also address the role of new media technologies and use of surveillance equipment. Its Section 10 says:

i.   The press must not seek to obtain or publish material acquired by using hidden cameras or clandestine listening devices; or by intercepting private or mobile telephone calls, messages or emails; or by the unauthorised removal of documents or photographs; or by accessing digitally-held private information without consent.
ii. Engaging in misrepresentation or subterfuge, including by agents or intermediaries, can generally be justified only in the public interest and then only when the material cannot be obtained by other means.

Echoing the social value and responsibility placed on journalism discussed above, both of these sections are marked so to indicate there may be exceptions to the clauses when breaches can be demonstrated to be in the public interest. This includes detecting or exposing crime or serious impropriety; protecting public health and safety; and preventing the public from being misled by an action or statement of an individual or organisation. Beyond these specifics, there is also coverage for the public interest in freedom of expression itself and when the appeal to public interest is invoked, the PCC requires editors to demonstrate how journalistic activity is in the public interest.

Lessons for journalism can be also learned from Prosser, who suggests that privacy is comprised of four different kinds of invasion:

1 Intrusion upon the plaintiff's seclusion or solitude, or into his private affairs.
2 Public disclosure of embarrassing facts about the plaintiff.
3 Publicity which places the plaintiff in a false light in the public eye.
4 Appropriation, for the defendant's advantage, of the plaintiff's name or likeness. (1984 [1960]: 107)

These equate to freedom from mental distress (1 and 2), concern about reputation (3) and proprietary ownership (4). For Prosser, privacy has no unique qualities. Instead he thinks that the principle is an assemblage of other concerns. This means that as an ethical and legal principle, it is derivative. In other words, privacy has come about because of older pre-existing rights (such as freedom, property, trespass and defamation) and we can understand our modern concern in those original terms. This is one interpretation, but one could see it the other way around in that privacy can be read as the parent category of these other rights. So when we feel aggrieved that someone has intruded on an intimate moment, published an embarrassing photo in a magazine, misrepresented us in a story or has used our name in some way without our permission (for example using a photo of us in an advert without our permission), we will feel somewhere between being mildly irked, to extremely violated.

In regard to the nature of this container term, a variety of privacy law commentators have pointed to privacy as being a 'dignity tort', or that area of common law that deals in people's behaviour that has unfairly caused someone else to suffer loss or harm. For Bloustein (1984 [1964]) the equating of privacy with dignity sees privacy in terms of spiritual values rather than the impersonal discourse of property or reputation. Others, such as Cohen and Arato, refer to privacy as 'a domain of individual self-development and moral choice' (1992: 346), rather than simply as a realm of private economic interests. Journalists might also heed the advice of Ronald Dworkin (2011 [1977]), a legal philosopher, who says that in the case of privacy versus free speech, we might remember the key thrust behind privacy rights, which is to allow for the development of the self without unnecessary interference. Recognition of this allows us to distinguish between the protection of corrupt politicians and unwanted disclosure of information about a person.

PROTECTING JOURNALISTS, SOURCES AND WHISTLE-BLOWERS

Although journalists report and make information public, they often require privacy to be able to deliver knowledge that is potentially damaging. Following the Snowden leaks of 2013, in the UK (and elsewhere) journalists from the BBC, Reuters, the *Guardian*, the *New York Times*, *Le Monde*, the *Sun*, NBC and the *Washington Post* have been targeted by Government Communications Headquarters (GCHQ). An article from the *Guardian* says GCHQ captured 70,000 emails from journalists within ten minutes during a November 2008 test of their capacity to tap the internet's fibre-optic cables (Ball, 2015). The same article highlights that other documents leaked by Snowden revealed that a GCHQ information security assessment listed investigative journalists as a threat to security in a hierarchy alongside terrorists or hackers, particularly from journalists writing defence-related exposés. These activities sit against a wider context where a UK law, The Regulation of Investigatory Powers Act (RIPA), has been used to access journalists' records, for example the phone records of Tom Newton-Dunn, the *Sun*'s political editor (regarding the so-called 'Plebgate' investigation[5]), and *Mail on Sunday* reporters involved in coverage of the speeding case of Chris Huhne (a former UK Member of Parliament). RIPA is the law that stipulates how covert surveillance can be used by public bodies in the UK. This includes bugs, video surveillance and interceptions of private communications (for example phone calls and emails), and even undercover agents (or 'covert human intelligence sources'). There is a key point here because at the time of writing the law allows the police and security services to carry out surveillance without permission of a judge. Instead they only need permission from an assigned member of the same organisation who is not involved in the investigation. In 2014, Keith Vaz, then chair of the UK Home Affairs Select Committee that investigated how RIPA has been used, said: 'RIPA is not fit for purpose … Using RIPA to access telephone records of journalists is wrong and this practice must cease. The inevitable consequence is that this deters whistle-blowers from coming forward.' On BBC Radio 4's *Today* programme he said that journalists' records should be kept privileged, 'otherwise we get into a situation where legislation introduced for completely different purposes is being used in a mission creep to be able to control sections that were never intended to be controlled'.[6] This raises a number of critical and analytical points for consideration of privacy and governmental surveillance:

- Is oversight of surveillance practices adequate?
- Are the uses of these powers being properly recorded? (This is important because democratic governments should be accountable to its citizens and this means that there needs to be records of decisions and actions taken.)
- Is there evidence of mission creep, or to what extent is legislation introduced for one purpose being used for purposes that they were not intended?

WARREN AND BRANDEIS: DECENCY AND THE NEWSROOM TODAY

As we have seen, journalism makes for a good privacy debating point because it shows that privacy is not innately good and that which must always be defended. It also tallies neatly with the earliest writing on privacy and media, most notably the essay 'The Right to Privacy' by Samuel Warren and Louis Brandeis (1984 [1890]). Although written nearly 130 years ago when Kodak cameras using film rolls appeared, the essay is still fresh, frequently cited and discussed, and remains an essential read for any scholar of privacy. What is particularly interesting is that much of what it says about journalism and technology applies uncannily well to today's news environment. It raises alarm about the encroachment of yellow (sensationalist) journalism, the 'evil of the newsroom' and the overstepping of decency. The essay is an attack on when 'personal gossip attains the dignity of print, and crowds the space available for matters of real interest to the community' (ibid.: 196). For privacy scholars, Warren and Brandeis think of privacy as something more than physical interference with life and property. They also see it as different from slander and libel because in legal terms these are in 'nature material rather than spiritual'. This means that slander and libel are defined in relation to how a person's public reputation is lessened, rather than the personal damage inflicted on a person.

Echoing earlier discussion of paparazzi and telephoto lenses, Warren and Brandeis remark: 'Instantaneous photographs and newspaper enterprise have invaded the sacred precincts of private and domestic life; and numerous mechanical devices threaten to make good the prediction that "what is whispered in the closet shall be proclaimed from the house-tops"' (1984 [1890]: 76). This is all to establish the principle of the right to be a private individual and 'to prevent his public portraiture'. The argument continues to be of relevance as it is based on the observation that new media deeply affects the nature of journalism. This entails consideration of the affordances and properties of developing technologies, and the ways in which they contribute to new sensibilities, arrangements, communicating, image making and sensing. Critically for us it requires we think about the privacy implications of new technologies employed for gathering, processing, representing and distributing news. This is a view of journalism reminiscent of Marshall McLuhan. Certainly online media involves an increase in speed, scale, scope and the breaking down of space/time borders (communication is quicker than it has been and richer content can be shared).

It seems to be something of a truism today that new technologies and new societal arrangements (such as hyper-connectivity) mean fewer rights over information. However, Warren and Brandeis argued the opposite. Against the context of technological and industrial change, what they suggested is that 'Political, social, and economic changes entail the recognition of new rights … to meet the new demands of society' (ibid.: 193). This is a valuable contribution and reminder

36

for any discussion of privacy. In general, the essay argues that individuals in a new media environment still have the 'right to be let alone'. In addition to the 'right to be left alone', there are further points relevant to outcomes of press intrusion.

RYAN GIGGS AND THE PROBLEM OF SOCIAL MEDIA: INJUNCTIONS

A key question, possibly unique to the media milieu of today, is what is the role of privacy when everyone already knows what has happened? This occurs in the UK where media outlets have had gagging orders placed upon them, but stories have been reported in the international press and are the focus of discussion on social media. What is at stake here is a conflict between free speech and privacy. The resolution is clear because in most cases free speech should win. This is developed by Richards (2015) who argues that it is only in the most severe cases (he uses the example of sex tapes) that privacy should come before free expression. Today, a person can attempt to stop the press reporting an issue by means of injunctions and 'super-injunctions'. At a more general level, an injunction involves an urgent application to a court to compel a person or organisation to do or to refrain from doing something. In the case of journalism, this may be an injunction not to publish a story. This may be granted simultaneously with *another* injunction (the super-injunction) in order to prevent the fact of the injunction itself from being placed in the public domain. For example, a public figure might discover that a newspaper is about to run a negative story about them. They will arrange an immediate court hearing to obtain an injunction preventing the release of the story. In addition to halting the release of the story, the public figure will also want the fact that they have taken out an injunction hidden. This is because if the media can report on the injunction, they essentially get to report the story. This effectively gags the media. However, modern international media means super-injunctions can fail. One famous example of this is from 2010 when Ryan Giggs, the ex-Manchester United football player, secured an injunction blocking publication of details of his extra-marital affair with the model and *Big Brother* contestant Imogen Thomas. Giggs was married, a former BBC Sports Personality of the Year and generally considered to be a morally upstanding footballer with a reputation to protect (not least because his sponsorships worth £24 million were underpinned by his respectable family-man image). Although the press was gagged, the injunction could not stop discussion of Giggs's affair on social media as he was named on Twitter by the Scottish *Sunday Herald* newspaper and by John Hemming MP in the House of Commons. Other celebrities such as Fred Goodwin (banker), Andrew Marr (himself a journalist) and John Terry (another football player) have also taken out super-injunctions and seen them fail. The television presenter Jeremy Clarkson imposed an injunction regarding an affair, but lifted it saying to the *Telegraph* newspaper, 'If you take an injunction out it isn't an injunction because Twitter and Facebook mean that everybody knows anyway'.[7]

37

DRONES AND NOVEL WAYS OF SEEING

Unmanned aerial vehicles, or drones, are a modern-day manifestation of the concerns expressed by Warren and Brandeis. As aircraft controlled from afar by pilots on the ground that typically carry cameras, they grant new modes of visibility, seeing, image and data capture, and potential intrusion of people and their property. However, for public interest, drones also grant media access to places where it is too dangerous for journalists to enter, such as disaster areas. In the context of journalism, the effects of drones has precedent in the development of telephoto lenses because they allow photos to be taken across greater distances with higher levels of detail. Drones bring extra affordances in that they are able to overcome barriers and walls, and to obtain new perspectives and vantage points. With this comes scope for collateral intrusion by capturing more information than was intended.

In UK 2015, the civilian use of drones was assessed by a European Union Select Committee for the House of Lords. The function of this was to scrutinise EU documents in advance of decisions being taken on them in Brussels, in order for the House of Lords to influence the government's position and thereafter hold it to account. Part of the report[8] focuses explicitly on journalism and while the UK does not have an explicit privacy law, there is coverage in Section 32 of the current Data Protection Act,[9] which makes provision for the 'special importance of the public interest in freedom of expression'. David Smith, of the Information Commissioner's Office, who contributed insights and information for Committee members, said that drones are not just a data-protection (privacy) issue, but also one for media regulators on judging whether image and information gathered this way is suitable for publication or not. This part of the report concluded that although journalists should be able to act in the public interest and reveal a wrongdoing, it harbours concerns that journalists, particularly paparazzi, often overstep the privacy mark. It recommended consultation with the public about how to get the 'balance right between the need to reveal wrongdoing while at the same time ensuring that people have the right to privacy in their own gardens or houses'.[10] This is deeply reminiscent of the Warren and Brandeis quote above about mechanical devices that intrude upon 'what is whispered in the closet'.

CONCLUSION

Journalism has a complex relationship with privacy. In its finest hour it is a political practice that exposes facts that people in positions of power would prefer that the public do not know. This draws upon enlightenment principles of transparency and openness. Despite being a practice that intends to make information readily available, it requires privacy because journalists need to protect sources. Journalism's inbuilt tendency towards publicity means it sometimes has a difficult relationship with privacy. This is encapsulated in Article 8 and Article 10 of the European Convention on Human Rights that requires a balance to be struck between a person's right to a private and family life, and the media's right to freedom of expression. However, this tension is desirable in that each of the Articles helps keep the other in check. Journalism is also fertile ground for privacy scholars because the canonical essay by Samuel Warren and Louis Brandeis (1984 [1890]) 'The Right to Privacy' was squarely aimed at an intrusive press. What is remarkable about their essay is that although it is the oldest writing on privacy and media, it remains remarkably relevant, particularly on the prominence of new media in journalism. For Warren and Brandeis, their concern was with instant photographs, but we can read this more broadly to consider the privacy implications of new technologies (from social media to drones) employed for gathering, processing, reporting, representing and distributing news. However, although we should read their essay closely for historical value and its application to modern technology, we should reject the thesis that privacy equates to the 'right to be let alone' because it falls prey to the myth of seclusion. Although they are right to connect privacy with a sense of violation, the right to be alone is not encompassing enough as a concept. As we will see in later chapters, privacy is often better thought of as the terms by which we interact with others. In sum, it is social.

Research and challenges

1 Sensationalist journalists often breach people's privacy. Provide examples of stories where: readers can be said to *want* to know; when they *need* to know; and also find three stories where this distinction is unclear.

2 Do you agree that privacy is something spiritual rather than material, and different from slander and libel? If so, give reasons; if not, give reasons.

3 Divide a group into two and debate the following: do celebrities caught cheating on their partners have a right to privacy? If so, on what grounds; if not, on what grounds?

NOTES

1 Although we should remember that the vote was not extended to women or the working classes until the early twentieth century – so the House of Commons was not in any way a perfect representative of all classes, interests and opinions.

2 The *Guardian* newspaper has an active online readership via the web and its app. To measure readership they use an analytics tool they developed called Ophan. This helps them develop more popular headlines (for readers and search engines), trace how much time a person has given a story, understand readership city-by-city and understand how ads are performing. In general, data is informing how journalism is done.

3 There is no express right to privacy under English law, which means that there is no civil action available for a purported breach of such a right. There are, however, other areas of legislation that provide for privacy matters. These include: the Data Protection Act 1988, the Protection from Harassment Act 1997, the Criminal Justice and Police Act 2001 and The Sexual Offences Act 2003. The Human Rights Act 1998, however, is of particular importance as this has two Articles that have a direct bearing on journalism and privacy.

4 Case history available at www.5rb.com/case/murray-v-big-pictures-uk-ltd-ca/.

5 This case is based on the allegations that UK Conservative politician Andrew Mitchell called some police officers 'plebs' during a row in Downing Street. (Plebeian: a derisive term for 'the common people'.)

6 BBC News article at www.bbc.co.uk/news/uk-30351302.

7 *Telegraph* article: www.telegraph.co.uk/motoring/top-gear/8851987/Jeremy-Clarkson-injunction-pointless-after-Twitter-rumours.html.

8 Available from www.publications.parliament.uk/pa/ld201415/ldselect/ldeu com/122/122.pdf.

9 Available at www.legislation.gov.uk/ukpga/1998/29/section/32.

10 See sections 184–195 of report: www.publications.parliament.uk/pa/ld201415/ldselect/ldeucom/122/122.pdf.

4

THE SNOWDEN LEAKS
A CALL FOR BETTER SURVEILLANCE

In the end we can't be transparent about most of these issues and we have to, get comfortable, with the idea that we are delegating to somebody the ability to learn the secrets, to review what's being done and determine whether it's being done properly. We cannot simply bring everyone in off the street and tell them what is happening.[1] (Stewart Baker, Former National Security Agency (NSA) General Counsel)

I didn't want to change society. I wanted to give society a chance to determine if it should change itself. All I wanted was for the public to be able to have a say in how they are governed.[2] (Edward Snowden, former NSA employee)

Traditional, effective surveillance means targeting suspects. Not a population. Not a technology. Not a service. The suspect.[3] (Edward Snowden)

Key questions

- What is the current scope of digital data surveillance?
- What are the problems with mass surveillance?
- Is surveillance effective?
- How can security and intelligence agencies be made more accountable?

Key concepts

- Surveillance
- Chilling effect
- Accountability
- Absolute control (and its impossibility)

In June 2013, Edward Snowden, a US national security whistle-blower, revealed that intelligence agencies in so-called 'Five Eyes' nations (Australia, Canada, New Zealand, United Kingdom and the United States) are engaging in secret global surveillance. This comprises bulk data collection, storage and analysis of citizens' digital communications. Without Snowden it is quite possible that we might never have known about the existence of not just surveillance states, but a surveillance assemblage of states and corporate actors that spans the globe. Where only a few years ago such a sentence would have been cause for ridicule and accusations of tin-foil hat wearing, this is now recognised by critics and governments alike as fact. His actions represent a fundamental shift in what we know about surveillance. Critically it provided evidence of mass surveillance, which is paramount for anyone seeking to factually understand what is taking place. The reach and detail of the Snowden leaks surprised nearly everyone – including computer scientists, privacy scholars and privacy activists. The leaks reveal governments' indiscriminate data collection, or the 'grab everything and look through it later if it becomes relevant' approach. According to the leaks, this includes data from globally significant players such as Microsoft, Yahoo!, Google, Facebook, Pal-talk, YouTube, AOL, Skype and Apple. Revised approaches and legislation about surveillance and data interception began to appear in 2014 in the US and 2015 in the UK.

This chapter opens by outlining the background and consequences of the Snowden leaks and progresses to consider the implications for privacy, particularly in terms of the 'chilling effect' of mass surveillance. Although I will summarise the leaks, what data is collected and why this happened, I will not go into detail about the nature of the surveillance programmes. There are a number of sources that do this in a far more engaging manner than can be achieved here. The *Guardian* newspaper has a publicly available multimedia exposition of the Snowden revelations, interviews with key actors and rich explanations of surveillance programmes at a website titled 'NSA Files: Decoded'.[4] Please spend time looking through this resource. *The Intercept* also provides readable but in-depth ongoing coverage of the leaks. Also of interest is the Snowden Archives[5] that detail every published leak made by Snowden (note that only a tiny fraction have been published in the press). The filmmaker Laura Poitras also documented events in *Citizenfour* (2014). For further academic sources, see the journal *Surveillance & Society*, especially the 2015 special issue titled 'Surveillance and Security Intelligence after Snowden'.[6] You might also want to follow Edward Snowden himself on Twitter at @Snowden.

BACKGROUND CONTEXT

Why might the Snowden leaks matter to you? The reader is entirely forgiven for not being able to comprehend the scale of this situation, or possibly the connection with media. To bring this into focus pick up your phone and consider that it is *this* device, that is *your* device, that mediates *your* life, that is having its call, location, searches and internet communications tracked. Note too that surveillance is not applied on us from above, but it is something that works *through* our devices. Importantly too we participated, and continue to do so, in our own surveillance by posting on Facebook, Twitter and beyond, and using services such as Google Docs (Lyon, 2015).

What Snowden revealed is of profound historical importance. Although some of the technologies discussed in this book will undoubtedly not seem as important in five, ten or twenty years' time, Snowden's actions *will* stand the test of time and take their place in the line-up of key events in the early twenty-first century. The significance of what Snowden revealed is that for those of us living in the US, Australia, Canada, New Zealand and the United Kingdom, all forms of our net-worked communication are potentially being watched by our governments. This changes how we think about media and communication, and what we consider as private and public. In a pre-digital era, only totalitarian countries would trace our mail and record details about our telephone calls (Koehler, 1999). (For an excellent depiction of this, see the 2007 film *The Lives of Others*.) This is now routine in democratic countries. Time will tell whether this is the new normal. The Snowden leaks have forced society to answer some difficult questions because security and intelligence services *do* play a pivotal role in protecting national security and upholding the rule of law.[7] They do this by collecting, analysing and disseminating a wide range of information types, although here we will focus on signals intelligence (interception of data on digital networks).[8] The questions we need to address include: how should we react to governments that wilfully kept secret they were spying on their citizens' communications; what is the balance between rights and societal obligations; to what extent should we accept curbs on our rights in the name of protecting society; how do we decide limits on what should be surveilled; and how are we to have this discussion when the terms of the discussion are secret and/or technically difficult to understand?

I do not want either myself or readers of this chapter to lapse into lazy emotive arguments that depict American, Australian, Canadian, New Zealand and the United Kingdom governments as malevolent or evilly acting against their citizens, but I also urge that readers leave any mention of 'nothing to hide, nothing to fear' at the door for reasons dealt with in Chapter 2. We should also be clear that what is taking place *is* surveillance and that usage of this word is not hyperbole or excessive in any way. It is quite the opposite in that it is a more accurate diagnosis than any other word one might think of. David Lyon, for example, an expert in surveillance studies, says surveillance is 'any collection and processing of personal data, whether identifiable or not, for the purposes of influencing or managing those whose data have been garnered' (2001: 2). Another leader of surveillance studies, Gary Marx, defines it as 'the use of technical means to extract or create personal data' (2002: 12). These definitions may appear counterintuitive: after all, surely surveillance is about tracking suspicious individuals? This has changed and, as this chapter will discuss, *all* people are tracked today to provide a background against which unusual behaviour may be judged. In addition to the extent of surveillance that is taking place, what Snowden showed is that our mediated selves are increasingly visible and transparent, but conversely those who do the watching are very difficult to see, despite the scope of the infrastructure. As highlighted in Chapter 2, this is not the way that democracy was originally conceived. In the US alone, the surveillance assemblage is huge. For example the Utah facility of the National Security Agency (NSA) is a $1.5 billion centre. Employed to collect and analyse data from the internet, the building possesses its own water-treatment facility, uses over a million gallons of water a day, has an electric substation and 60 back-up diesel generators. *The Economist*[9] cites a source saying that its data-storage capacity would be enough to store a year of footage of round-the-clock video recording of over a million people. It achieves its data collection of communications from across the globe by tapping directly into the fibre-optic backbone of the internet.

My point is that the material structure of surveillance is very real, yet we are asked to take on trust that the secrecy (before Snowden) surrounding surveillance by the state is necessary. Historically, democracies have worked the other way around in that we grant the state licence to act on our behalf but we ensure it is accountable to citizenry; and that citizens are free from unwanted inspection as long as they behave in accordance with the law. Snowden revealed that both these principles were broken. Although transparency is a conceptual term, it is one that sits at the heart of what is often posited as the debate between security and liberty, or the question of how much secrecy we should allow the state and its intelligence agencies.

To understand the rise of US-led mass global surveillance, we have to understand something of what took place in September 2001 – the month that the US was attacked by al-Qaeda, the Islamist terrorist group. These were not just physical attacks, but symbolic attacks on globalisation, world trade and the pre-eminent global superpower. This was a co-ordinated spectacle that transfixed the world. The US government reacted quickly and by 13 September US senators had introduced the first version of the USA Patriot Act, which stands for Uniting and Strengthening America by Providing Appropriate Tools Required to Intercept and Obstruct Terrorism Act of 2001. State surveillance has a much older history and one that consistently entails agencies pushing for greater powers, but events post-2001 dramatically extended US surveillance powers and led to the creation of the global, pervasive surveillance programmes that Edward Snowden revealed in June 2013.

THE LEAKS

This section provides an overview of the leaks, but for a more detailed coverage see the *Guardian*,[10] *The Intercept*[11] and ACLU.[12] Although Snowden stole the documents, he did not leak them himself. Instead he worked with Laura

Poitras (a documentary maker) and Glenn Greenwald (a lawyer and journalist) to organise transmission of the documents to a range of news outlets. These include the *Guardian* (Britain), *Der Spiegel* (Germany), *The Washington Post* and *The New York Times* (US), *O Globo* (Brazil), *Le Monde* (France), and other outlets in Sweden, Canada, Italy, Netherlands, Norway, Spain and Australia. Each released edited extracts from the leaks and provided local reporting about their implications. The key revelation from the leaks is that intelligence agencies from the US, Australia, Canada, New Zealand and the United Kingdom routinely collect en masse, and analyse, the communications of their citizens. This includes email, instant messages, the search terms in Google searches, web browsing histories and file transfers. It also includes what is called 'communications data' (in the UK) and 'metadata' (in the USA) (or data about data). Such records of online and mobile activity includes: names, addresses, who is called, call records, length of service, types of service used, number used including temporarily assigned IP address, record of web domains visited, location data of senders and receivers, and means and source of payment. Today, in countries including the UK, the most important metadata may be obtained *without* the permission of a court[13] (Anderson, 2015). This data assists in identifying people of interest, building profiles and contributing to decisions about whether a person should be under targeted surveillance. The attraction of mass surveillance is that information can be collected at a fraction of the cost of tracking through traditional methods. The consequence is that to find suspicious individuals, entire societies are placed under surveillance.

THE PROGRAMMES

Intelligence agencies' mass surveillance relies on global internet and telecommunications companies. This is done by bulk collecting data from companies' servers, and by directly tapping fibre-optic cables carrying internet traffic. It also relies on citizens' own behaviour online as we unwittingly offer up plentiful data about ourselves through our everyday digital communications and digital footprints left across all forms of online activity. The global surveillance apparatus is achieved through several inter-related programmes. These are detailed below.

PRISM: With this programme internet and telecommunications companies were secretly compelled by intelligence agencies in the USA, UK and other liberal democracies to collect and hand over citizens' digital communications. It included tapping into the central servers of leading US internet companies, extracting audio and video chats, photographs, emails, documents and connection logs that enable analysts to track foreign targets (Gellman and Poitras, 2013). Companies that the NSA extracted data from include US service providers Microsoft, Yahoo!, Google, Facebook, PalTalk,[14] AOL, Skype, YouTube and Apple.

45

UPSTREAM: Whereas PRISM collected data from the servers of US service providers, UPSTREAM is the collection of data traffic as it flows through the fibre-optic cables that comprise the internet.

XKEYSCORE: Disclosed by Glenn Greenwald in an article for the *Guardian*,[15] this is an NSA programme allowing analysts to search databases covering nearly everything a typical user does on the internet, as well as engaging in real-time interception of an individual's internet activity. The leaks showed that the NSA harvests social media activity, browsing history, email, instant messaging contact lists and the location of cell phones. This creates a 'social graph' of individuals' lives in order to identify their associates and search for foreign terrorists, as well as to assemble a person's locations over time. It also piggybacks on cookie data used for advertising and, separately, also attempts to undermine efforts to encrypt communication.

TEMPORA: This is a covert operation by the British government (or what is referred to as 'black-ops'). The surveillance programme is conducted by GCHQ, on behalf of the UK government. It refers to the data interceptors on fibre-optic cables placed by GCHQ that carry internet data in and out of the UK. In operation since 2011, this was done with participation of BT, Vodafone Cable, Verizon Business, Global Crossing, Level 3, Viatel and Interoute. For sense of context, between 10 and 25 per cent of global internet traffic enters British territory making the UK an important internet traffic hub. TEMPORA stores this data flowing in and out of the UK, sharing it with the USA (Bakir, 2015).

LEGAL COMPLEXITY

One of the most notable features of the leaks is the care that governments have taken to interpret technical and legal frameworks that circumvent national constitutional or human rights protections governing interferences with the right to privacy of communications. Governments have assembled lawyers to provide workarounds and interpretations that are for the most part legal (although as indicated below, they have also overstepped the mark). This is extremely complex and even David Anderson (2015: 8), the independent Queens Counsel (QC) that led the review of the UK's anti-terrorism laws, said that interception laws such as RIPA are obscure and patched up so many times that they are incomprehensible to all but a tiny band of initiates.

In the UK, what is clear is that GCHQ admitted to what were once secret 'arrangements' to accessing bulk material collected by the NSA. This was made public as non-governmental organisations (NGOs) launched a legal challenge against GCHQ's extensive surveillance practices in 2014, arguing that the activities of the government intelligence services breached Articles 8 and 10 of the European Convention on Human Rights (also discussed in Chapter 3). In response to a legal challenge made by Privacy International, Liberty and Amnesty International about international surveillance techniques the government submitted evidence to the Investigatory Powers Tribunal in which it states that obtaining warrants for data isn't necessary in all circumstances. It argued that 'RIPA [Regulation of Investigatory Powers Act] interception warrant is not as a matter of law required in all cases in which unanalysed intercepted communications might be sought from a foreign government',[16] and that the practice doesn't involve 'deliberate circumvention' of RIPA. The consequence of this statement is that any call, internet search or website a person has visited can be stored in GCHQ's database and analysed at will. This can be done without a warrant to collect this information about UK citizens. The US and UK have a reciprocal deal whereby the US collects information about UK citizens, which is then handed back to the UK, so to get around the UK's interception laws.

In addition to penetrating communications networks and companies that run these, governments and their agencies have created complicated legal arrangements that are justified in private by arguments that stretch credulity and arguably break it. The legality is questionable, but the principal problem from a civic point of view is that because people did not know about these practices and legal arrangements, they were unable to challenge it. This is a fundamental point because governments and agencies created a global surveillance infrastructure to monitor citizens in democracies, without informing their citizens. Put otherwise, governments and defence agencies acted without external, public oversight, relying instead on secretive internal oversight mechanisms such as parliamentary or congressional intelligence oversight committees. This removes the public's capacity to challenge intelligence agency's actions: the public cannot hold their governments accountable when actions of key agencies are hidden through secret arrangements and covert legal frameworks.

KNOW IT ALL

Journalist Glenn Greenwald's (2014) book *No Place to Hide* summarises the intention and objective of the NSA surveillance apparatus through a leaked slide that says: 'Collect it All', 'Process it All', 'Exploit it All', 'Partner it All', 'Sniff it All' and 'Know it All'. What Snowden revealed is the wish to gain the fullest picture possible and the belief that harnessing all possible data might actually be useful. Defenders of surveillance argue that it is necessary to collect all available data to provide a background against which suspicious signals can be detected (signal to noise ratio). Mass surveillance and bulk collection of data is justified by saying that the aim is not to treat all citizens as suspects, but to provide a background of normalcy so unusual terrorist activity will stand out. This is a key factor of the story: data about networked behaviour is not collected because everyone is a suspect, but the logic instead is that normal behaviour is required to contextualise abnormal behaviour.

Next, the argument is that if armed with 'all' of the data, agencies are not just able to identify terrorist suspects after an event has happened, but they will be able to *pre-empt* terrorism by means of identifying unusual patterns in information. For what is unusual to be established, a 'usual' is required. This is why police and surveillance organisations feel justified in demanding warrantless access to information held by ISPs, and other large organisations that hold and process our information. What this means is that today surveillance is always on. Surveillance is not just applied on suspicion of wrongdoing as used to be the case, but instead it is a socio-technical perpetual condition that is potentially applied to everybody. As Andrejevic (2013) highlights, it is ubiquitous and the surveillance process itself generates the targets to be pursued. As fully explained in Chapter 9, this is done through machine learning and identification of trends, correlations and standout patterns. This information is both horizontal (everywhere and now) and vertical (chronological), and entails retaining records for as long as legally possible.

The argument made by security and intelligence agencies is that from a security/ surveillant point of view, analysts do not know when information may be relevant. What is utterly inconsequential now may provide insight a year down the line as new geo-political/policing events unfold. This is illustrated by a now famous article for the *Huffington Post* from 2013 where Gus Hunt, the ex-CIA Chief Technology Officer, boasted in a presentation given while still in post that, 'It is really very nearly within our grasp to be able to compute on all human generated information'. Moreover, 'The value of any piece of information is only known when you can connect it with something else that arrives at a future point in time' and 'Since you can't connect dots you don't have, it drives us into a mode of, we fundamentally try to collect everything and hang on to it forever' (Sledge, 2013). The situation is less about gross display of power, but that politicians and security technologists are impelled by panicked urgency to not miss *anything* and to defend against every eventuality. Further, this is justified at a policy level by the fact that it is machines rather than people doing the watching in the first instance. This is important: GCHQ and the UK government argue that mass electronic collection of personal data is not surveillance because human eyes only see the data when a potential threat is flagged by the system. Pro-privacy groups say that electronic collection and processing of personal data is still mass surveillance. The question is this: is it surveillance if human eyes do not see nearly all of the data? The answer becomes clearer if hypothetically we were to have cameras installed in bathrooms, bedrooms and living areas. It may only be machines examining most of the data, but presumably we would agree it is surveillance?

Quite arguably, the politico-ethical problem of our time is not state malevolence, but anxiety, over-reach, misunderstanding of what is technically possible, and a political desire to collect and interpret everything in the name of protecting citizens from terrorists and criminals. A less forgiving diagnosis says that the state wants the ability to readily identify, and hence target and control, its population, including dissenters. While the stated intention is to prevent risks from actualising, the consequence is a politics of absolute control that runs counter to all political persuasions other than those that seek total control. The problem with this is that even if we put privacy and the ethics of 'interfering' with our media technologies to one side, the idea that processing any and every piece of data will make any-body safer is deeply problematic. First it is impossible to collect and store data on all human behaviour and, second, it is highly inefficient to collecting irrelevant, outdated and incorrect information.

PRO-PRIVACY DOES NOT MEAN ANTI-SURVEILLANCE

Very few people interested in the surveillance debate suggest that there should be no surveillance. Instead pro-privacy campaigners argue there should be targeted surveillance rather than indiscriminate surveillance. As will be developed, in addi-tion to scepticism about the value of 'big data' techniques (explored in Chapter 9), the concern is that there is not enough oversight of how dragnet surveillance is used, and that these powers might be abused. To highlight the possibility that pow-ers developed and assumed to fight terrorism can be abused, in 2015 Big Brother Watch[17] reported that a total of 733,237 requests to access surveillance data were made by the UK police force between 1 January 2012 and 31 December 2014 ask-ing to see the 'who, where and when of any text, email, phone call or web search'. For a country as small as the UK, this is a rather large figure. The total number of 733,237 requests is equivalent to 670 requests a day, 28 requests an hour, or one every two minutes; 92.6 per cent of requests were accepted. What this points to is *mission creep*, where the use of powers granted for one purpose are used for another. While many citizens may be willing to grant access to their communica-tions believing this will help stop atrocities, a question remains whether this civic trust is being abused.

SOME PRACTICALITIES

The wish to collect all of the data all of the time is the mission goal, but it is unclear what is gained by this. This is somewhat exasperating for privacy and intelligence scholars. We are told that surveillance works, but few case studies have been presented. We also have little understanding of what is missed by sur-veillance (with exception of atrocities) or how many false positives are generated. William Binney for example carried out Signals Intelligence (SIGINT) operations and research for the NSA for 36 years.[18] He argues that while the technologies used for mass surveillance and bulk data collection are powerful and far-reaching, the resulting data swamps human analysts. Today arguing that mass surveillance does not work, he goes as far to say that 'It is 99 per cent useless' and even that it 'costs lives, and has cost lives in Britain because it inundates analysts with too much data'. On presenting his arguments to UK parliament in advance of the Investigatory Powers Bill in 2016, he also claims that security mistakes were made before 9/11 because the US had collected information from the terrorists involved in the attacks, but had not been able to check them because of resources. In a video interview posted by Open Rights Group[19] he argues that bulk collection actually gets in the way of stopping attacks in advance because analysts cannot discern intentions and capabilities. For Binney, excess irrelevant information causes inertia, dysfunction and incapacity to act.

As a privacy and media studies academic, I am not privy to sensitive information about the effectiveness of surveillance, but what Binney did is complicate the over-simplistic narratives of 'security versus liberty' and 'nothing to hide, nothing to fear' because, in addition to over-reach into citizens' lives, the fact that so much data is being collected makes the work of the intelligence agencies harder. Having officially managed thousands of analysts during his time at the NSA, he is well placed to judge. The practical problem is the noise to signal ratio, or the proportion of useful information to useless information in any given batch of data. Security agencies are not alone because this is a problem that faces the commercial data-mining industry too in that although they can collect a great deal of information about people, extracting meaningful insights is much harder. One wonders if reallocating resources to human policing, investigative work and building positive relationships within communities might raise effectiveness.

HOW DO THE LEAKS INFORM OUR UNDERSTANDING OF PRIVACY?

In 2013 Robert Hannigan took over the role of head of UK's GCHQ and used his opening speech to point out that privacy is not an absolute right. He will not find a serious privacy campaigner that disagrees with him, because no one believes that privacy trumps all other considerations. This is because, in a liberal democratic society, privacy is a *qualified* right. As explained in earlier chapters, in the hierarchy of rights, privacy is not an absolute right (unlike for example the right not to be tortured), but it is a right that can be encroached upon if there are other more important interests. The real question is whether GCHQ has a good enough reason for initiating a programme of global surveillance with questionable legality and effectiveness, and whether it should have been able to do so without external oversight. In the modern online era, some access to communications data is required. However, in a democracy, the need for tools to maintain safety has to be balanced with the principle that government should respect the rights of law-abiding citizens to privacy and that there is meaningful oversight of what governments are doing. Contemporary information privacy matters are typically framed in terms of liberty versus security. As we saw in Chapter 2, this is the attempt to balance individual rights with the powers we give to the state. There are multiple problems with this. The first is that few would argue we do not need surveillance. What critics are concerned about is the type of surveillance and whether indiscriminate surveillance of entire populations is necessary, or even a good idea. After all, why not spend money on tracing links between bad people rather than surveilling everyone? This debate is not easily resolved because we simply do not know how many plots are foiled because of application of indiscriminate surveillance. What we do know about, however, are the plots that were successful. Recent attacks in Europe for example show that those involved were already known to security services:

- July 2012: the suspects of the Bulgarian attack in Burgas, Malid Farah (also known as Hussein Hussein) and Hassan al-Haj, are linked to Hezbollah.
- May 2013: Michael Adebolajo and Michael Adebowale who killed an off-duty British soldier were known to British security services.
- May 2014: Mehdi Nemmouche, the gunman who opened fire at the Jewish Museum of Belgium in Brussels had known links with radical Islamists.
- January 2015: Chérif and Saïd Kouachi, the *Charlie Hebdo* gunmen, had criminal records and known links with terrorist organisations.
- February 2015: following release from prison two weeks before, the Danish authorities knew the Copenhagen attacker, Omar el-Hussein, was a potential threat.
- November 2015: intelligence services in France and Belgium knew about attackers' jihadi backgrounds (some had had records identifying them as radicals) and others (at least five) had travelled to fight in Syria and returned to homes in France or Belgium.

This is not proof that indiscriminate surveillance is irrelevant or does not work, but what it does suggest is that there is strong value in monitoring known individuals and that few (if any) perpetrators have no record of suspect activity. What this points to is need for improved policing, co-operation, data sharing across borders, pooling of files and sharing of insights known to security services. The key difference is that this requires better human intelligence of known suspects.

GOOGLING FOR ANTHRAX

Following the revelations by Snowden, the American Civil Liberties Union (ACLU) filed a legal case against the US government over the *chilling effect* of mass surveillance on Americans. Although the chilling effect certainly connects with questions of what we are willing to search and say online, and the ways by which the Snowden leaks have inhibited people's willingness to search for anything they deem sensitive, the term is actually an older one originating in 1952.[20] The 'chilling effect' is based on *inhibition and discouragement* of free speech by individuals and groups due to fear of punishment (such as fines, imprisonment, imposition of civil liability or deprivation of a governmental benefit). The nature of a chilling effect has two factors in that it is an act of deterrence, and when people are deterred we can speak of an activity as being chilled. To push this slightly further, and in a US context, a 'chilling effect occurs when individuals seeking to engage in activity protected by the first amendment are deterred from so doing by governmental regulation not specifically directed at that protected activity' (Schauer, 1978: 693). This means that a person may feel deterred even when the activity they are engaging in is not the one a government seeks to stop. For example, people may feel deterred from innocently Googling their favourite rock band (Anthrax) for fear of being suspected of having an intention to build bombs or engage in biological attacks. This goes beyond searching for music content and digital media to more fundamental political matters of the ability to say what we want without fear of reprisal. In other words, it is about democracy and the right to freedom of expression. In the US this is addressed by the First Amendment to their Constitution that prohibits impediment of freedom of speech.

Research from the US is showing that since the Snowden leaks, there has been a decrease in searches of potentially sensitive terms. A Google Trends study after the Snowden leaks of June 2013 found that people were less likely to search using terms that they believed might 'get them into trouble' or 'embarrass' them with their family, their close friends, or with the US government. They found a drop of 2.2 per cent in traffic for search terms that were rated as 'high government trouble' search terms (Marthews and Tucker, 2014). This is an effect of potential surveillance that inhibits or discourages legitimate behaviour. For example while searches of words such as 'anthrax' dropped in frequency so did words such as 'eating disorder' that clearly has nothing to do with terrorism. The study admits it only examined Google (and people may have moved to other, more privacy-friendly, search engines), but the point is an illustrative one in that it demonstrates the risk-aversion aspect of the chilling effect. Here risk is not about what is clear and known, but uncertainty, what-ifs and lack of confidence in the surveillance assemblage to differentiate between an innocent and threatening search query. The Google Trends study also connects with a report from PEN America (2013)[21] that highlights self-censorship of writers in the US after the Snowden leaks. It states that 16 per cent of writers polled by PEN said they would not do certain Google searches in case it piques the government's interest. Twenty-five per cent say they regularly self-censor in email and on the phone. Many are less willing to write about certain topics that includes military affairs, the Middle East and North Africa regions, mass incarceration, drug policies, pornography, the study of certain languages and criticism of the US government. This is understandable because, for example, UK journalists and even comedians have been placed under surveillance and listed as 'domestic extremists'.[22] Similarly, the critical online news publication *The Intercept* has been engaged in a Freedom of Information battle with the UK's Metropolitan Police Service to find out if it is investigating journalists. In July 2015 the police confirmed that they are.[23]

This invokes another characteristic of the chilling effect in that when daunted by the fear of punishment, people may refrain from saying, studying or publishing that which they lawfully should be able to. In times of social uncertainty, this is exactly when authors *should* feel free to express criticism, controversial opinions and assess uncomfortable subject matter (such as videos produced by ISIS/Daesh). To clarify, the problem is that democracy is undermined because citizens are fearful of voicing dissenting opinions in public, or even finding out more about what is taking place. In 2016 other US research demonstrated that the NSA's capacity to monitor the online activities of US citizens 'can contribute to the silencing of minority views that provide the bedrock of democratic discourse' (Stoycheff, 2016: 1). What this means is that majority opinion is able to dominate without challenge, but also that the majority is able to take control of online spaces (such as Facebook and other social media) where discussion and deliberation takes place. Inhibition and the chilling effect thus does not just impact on individuals who feel dissuaded, but society, as authors, academics and journalists worry about reprisal. The fear of reprisal is exacerbated by uncertainty, particularly when we know what we are doing is legal, but we fear that surveillers will come to another conclusion about our actions and motives. In the case of electronic surveillance this is intensified by: reach of the aforementioned security programmes; mistrust in the effectiveness of machinic analysis of key words that do not take into account context and motive (false positives and misidentification of threats); and direct fear of dissent from governmental arguments (as in the George W. Bush aphorism, 'if you're not with us, you're against us').

CONCLUSION

This chapter has outlined some of the privacy implications of the Snowden leaks of 2013. Having detailed the background context to the leaks and presented an overview of what information is being collected, it progressed to consider the effectiveness of surveillance and the social effects. Due to the fact that so little is published about its effectiveness, it is difficult to make the case for mass surveillance. What we do know, however, is that perpetrators of atrocities are typically already known to security agencies, which calls into question the need to monitor the communications of entire populations. This point perhaps becomes more convincing if we consider the testimony of William Binney, the ex-NSA employee of 36 years turned whistle-blower, who argues that the data presented by bulk data collection makes the work of analysts harder, and hinders comprehension of a target's intentions and capabilities. He even goes as far to suggest that mass surveillance has cost lives. If Binney is right, far more preferable is greater reliance on community and human intelligence, rather than big data processing (and its generation of false positives that tie-up analysts). One might respond that we need better mass surveillance, but the onus is then to answer how much is enough, where is the line, what are the limits and what forms of oversight should we have. This is perhaps the biggest surprise from the Snowden leaks: that oversight of mass surveillance activities and accountability to the public has been so sorely missing.

Although the connection between privacy, surveillance, media and personal technologies is self-evident, this chapter has focused on the chilling effects of mass surveillance. This is when people feel inhibited to speak publicly, and in our case use media technologies to search for information. The principle of chilling effects has legal origins in the US and the 1950s. It is less a direct threat than a vague fear of reprisal, potential negative outcomes, incursion of further monitoring and a risk-based decision to desist from a line of action. In our case, this is a decision not to search for information through a search engine we know to have been under surveillance by national security agencies. This inhibition and discouragement is pervasive and has risen since Snowden's disclosures. This is deeply undesirable because a person will feel deterred even when they are not doing anything wrong. The net result of this is distrust of the web, a sense of being out of control (low privacy), lack of willingness of citizens to research and inform themselves, and even avoidance of reading up about personal matters unrelated to terrorism.

Research and challenges

1 This chapter has only begun to detail the extent and nature of contemporary surveillance activities. Explore the sources given early in this chapter and also find two more high quality sources about modern surveillance. Discuss points of interest with your peers.

2 How satisfactory do you find the premise that mass surveillance is necessary to create a backdrop against which deviancy might be discerned. What are the problems with this, if any?

3 Is it mass surveillance if human eyes do not see most of the data collected? Explore both sides of the argument and come to a conclusion.

4 Governments and their security agencies should be accountable to citizens but a degree of secrecy is necessary for these agencies to function effectively. How can accountability and meaningful oversight be built in? Also see David Anderson's report for the UK government, *A Question of Trust*. This is available online.

NOTES

1 Audio file available from www.theguardian.com/world/interactive/2013/nov/01/snowden-nsa-files-surveillance-revelations-decoded#section/1.

2 Available from www.washingtonpost.com/world/national-security/edward-snowden-after-months-of-nsa-revelations-says-his-missions-accomplished/2013/12/23/49fc36de-6c1c-11e3-a523-fe73f0ff6b8d_story.html.

3   Available from: https://twitter.com/snowden/status/659408231794610176?la
    ng=en-gb.
4   Available from www.theguardian.com/world/interactive/2013/nov/01/snowden-
    nsa-files-surveillance-revelations-decoded#section/1.
5   Available from https://snowdenarchive.cjfe.org/greenstone/cgi-bin/library.cg
6   Available from http://ojs.library.queensu.ca/index.php/surveillance-and-society/
    issue/view/Intelligence.
7   Intelligence services have a foreign mandate and focus on external threats
    while security services have a domestic mandate and focus on domestic threats.
8   The Federal Bureau of Investigation (FBI) has a useful list intelligence types
    available at www.fbi.gov/about-us/intelligence/disciplines.
9   Article available from www.economist.com/news/united-states/21651817-
    america-argues-anew-over-how-much-snooping-nsa-can-do-reviewing-
    surveillance-state?frsc=dg%7Cd.
10 See www.theguardian.com/us-news/the-nsa-files.
11 See https://theintercept.com/search/?s=snowden.
12 See www.aclu.org/nsa-documents-search.
13 Note, however, that in Canada and Australia, some form of judicial authorisation
    is required before the police may access metadata. In the US, the FBI may access
    metadata without judicial authorisation, but state police forces ordinarily require
    a subpoena or a court order in order to do so (Anderson, 2015).
14 This is a chat and instant messaging service.
15 Article available from www.theguardian.com/world/2013/jul/31/nsa-top-
    secret-program-online-data.
16 Quote available at www.theguardian.com/uk-news/2014/oct/29/gchq-nsa-
    data-surveillance?CMP=EMCNEWEML6619I2.
17 Big Brother watch available from www.bigbrotherwatch.org.uk/wp-content/
    uploads/2015/05/Big-Brother-Watch-Report-Police-Communications-Data1.pdf.
18 William Binney worked for the NSA for 36 years and oversaw the develop-
    ment and construction of the first technologies used for the bulk collection
    of Internet communications. He left the NSA after the 9/11 attacks when the
    agency greatly expanded its surveillance programmes and began surveilling
    the US population.
19 Available from www.youtube.com/watch?v=Xeo1e_T_USI.
20 The United States Supreme Court first uses the term in the context of the
    United States Constitution in *Wieman v. Updegraff* [1952]
21 PEN America is a fellowship of writers, editors and translators that works to
    advance literature and defend free expression.
22 See the article from the British newspaper the *Independent* that highlights that a
    number of journalists and the comedian Mark Thomas were placed on watch lists:
    www.independent.co.uk/news/uk/crime/six-journalists-sue-the-british-police-
    over-spying-revelations-9874795.html.
23 Letter of confirmation from the police force at: https://s3.amazonaws.com/s3.doc-
    umentcloud.org/documents/2178930/uk-met-police-snowden-investigation-foi-
    response.pdf.

5
ENCRYPTION
SIMULTANEOUSLY PUBLIC AND PRIVATE

There's another attack on our civil liberties that we see heating up every day – it's the battle over encryption [...] If you put a key under the mat for the cops, a burglar can find it too.[1] (Tim Cook, Apple CEO)

I think in the current situation, it doesn't matter if he's being honest or dishonest. What really matters is that he's obviously got a commercial incentive to differentiate himself from competitors like Google. But if he does that, if he directs Apple's business model to be different, to say 'we're not in the business of collecting and selling information. We're in the business of creating and selling devices that are superior', then that's a good thing for privacy. That's a good thing for customers.[2] (Edward Snowden, former NSA employee)

Key questions

- What is encryption?
- Can technology be part of privacy solutions as well as problems?
- Should governments have backdoor access to networked communication?
- To what extent can values such as privacy be 'baked' into technology?

Key concepts

- Encryption
- Hashing, pseudoanonymisation and anonymisation
- Privacy-by-design and privacy-enhancing technology

Following the Snowden leaks of 2013, mobile phones and web applications began to arrive on the market that made use of encryption. Most notably, this included handsets from both Apple and Google. When successfully implemented, encryption means that meaningful communication cannot be understood by prying eyes. This means that citizens can communicate securely and confidentially, but it also means that criminals and terrorists can communicate confident that security services cannot discern what is being said. In essence to encrypt means to encode, which in turn means that information is sent so only authorised parties can read it. It does not stop others from intercepting encoded information, but rather it will be meaningless without the keys to decode the encrypted communication. The backdrop to consumer-level encryption being offered by Apple, Google and other technology behemoths is Snowden's revelation that the US National Security Agency mined data in possession of Google, Apple, Facebook and Skype, among others. Now Apple and Google encrypt users' data by default, this means that the meaningful content of the communication is not only hidden from governments, but the companies themselves. They do this so they cannot be coerced again and to rebuild consumer faith in their products. What this tells us is that privacy is being baked into the design of media technologies. Phrased otherwise, this approach to online communication makes use of *privacy-by-design* in which privacy, a social principle, is embedded into the technology itself. Although the subject of this chapter flows from the last in that I am interested in encrypted online communication in the post-Snowden era, the theoretical dimension is different because here we are interested in engineering solutions to privacy matters.

WHAT IS ENCRYPTION?

From the point of view of understanding privacy today, the use of encryption in our personal devices and favourite apps raises thought-provoking observations about privacy. Encryption comes from the study and practice of cryptography that essentially is about creating and solving codes by means of complex mathematics and computer science.

It works by means of *ciphers*, which are algorithms used for encryption or decryption. For example, a basic cipher is a substitution cipher. Here each character of the plain text (or the message which is to be encrypted) is substituted by another character. Each character could be shifted along by three places, so the character 'A' is replaced by 'D', 'B' by 'E', and so on. Related techniques of encoding information include 'hashing' and 'pseudoanonymisation'. Hashing entails mathematical algorithms applied to data. A highly simplified example of this is if we have an *input* number of 31,222 and apply the hashing algorithm input# x 999 we have a hash value of 31,190,778. It is very difficult to work out that 31,190,778 came from multiplying of 31,222 and 999, but if a recipient is able to know that the multiplier was 999 then it is easy to calculate the original message (which in our simple example is 31,222). Pseudoanonymisation is the more straightforward procedure of replacing identifying fields within a data record with artificial identifiers, or pseudonyms. This is not encryption per se, but a means of disguising identity. Importantly, this is done by an algorithm (or other additional information held separately) which means a person who has been pseudoanonymised can be re-identified by those who know how identity has been encoded and which features of a data record are real and which are not. Pseudoanonymisation is typically associated with health records where practitioners and researchers seek to protect an individual's privacy, but still make use of data about bodies. As explored in greater depth in Chapter 9, there are concerns that even if a person's name is removed, additional information that an attacker may come into possession of might identify a person (Ohm, 2009). For example, a string of numbers, birth date and disease record cannot give a person's identity away. But, if the string of numbers also appears next to a geography area code and gender in another document, and an attacker now has both documents, this vastly increases chance of identification. This contrasts with anonymisation where all person-related data that could allow inference of identity has been removed or encrypted.

Success in encryption is defined in terms of how hard a code is to crack. Today, digital encryption essentially locks data with a key, and allows the message to be transmitted and unlocked at the other end with another key. Thus, Ali types a message, turns the key, encodes and sends across a network. Helen receives the encrypted message, turns her key, decodes, unlocks the message and reads it. What is actually transmitted is relatively open and public, but incomprehensible without a key to unlock the communication. This means it is both *simultaneously* public and private. The mass growth of apps and software that use encryption occurred in the wake of global controversy over government surveillance after the Snowden leaks. Although interest in online encryption has existed for some time – perhaps most notably since 1991 and the rise of Pretty Good Privacy (PGP), a program used to encrypt and decrypt email – popular US technology companies led the way from 2013 onwards in developing and offering users ubiquitous encryption. This is end-to-end encryption of data with only the sender and intended recipient possessing decryption keys. Encryption worries governments that want access to information about our communication because whereas strong encryption was once only available to the military and intelligence services, it is now freely available and relatively easy to use to secure email, voice communication, images, hard drives and website browsers. The reason why the big tech platforms have done this is to win back trust from consumers following the revelation that they were coerced into sharing information with governments (most notably the US government).

THE BATTLE OVER ENCRYPTION

People who believe that communication should be private and encrypted argue that governments should not have keys to our communications. This in part is an ethical and political position, but it is also a practical one in that more keys equates to weaker security. This may not matter too much if the content of the communication is a short message about meeting for coffee at Starbucks at 1 p.m., but when one thinks of business, banking, health and other sensitive information that flows across the internet, the case becomes more convincing as extra sets of keys, or a master key, weakens security across the internet.[3] One should also consider the desirability (if not necessity) of secure communications in countries with truly repressive governments.

The political response has been mixed across the world. In a report delivered in 2015 for the United Nations (a transnational organisation founded to promote international co-operation), the author David Kaye declared that encryption and anonymity must be protected to 'enable individuals to exercise their rights to freedom of opinion and expression in the digital age and, as such, deserve strong protection' (2015: 1). The report argues that the capacity for anonymity grants means to protect privacy. It allows people to browse, read, develop and share opinions and information without interference. It also enables 'journalists, civil society organizations, members of ethnic or religious groups, those persecuted because of their sexual orientation or gender identity, activists, scholars, artists and others to exercise the rights to freedom of opinion and expression' (ibid.: 3). The value of encryption is vividly depicted when we consider that it protects free speech in locations where states seek to censor political and religious discussion. It also allows us to search for information, communicate, test and explore parts of ourselves. For example, growing up gay, as around 1.7 per cent of us do,[4] entails difficult self-revelations, self-acceptance and peer-acceptance. The web provides an invaluable means of exploring matters not easily discussed elsewhere. The same applies to questions of religious identities, gender, disability and more issues, where the capacity to ask questions and express thoughts without being identified is cherished. People who believe in high levels of privacy point out that the capacity to be anonymous grants freedom to explore a wider range of ideas and opinions than a person would do if forced to use actual identities. To feel stifled is to undergo what we referred to earlier as the 'chilling effect'.

ARGUMENTS AGAINST ENCRYPTION

There are powerful counter-arguments against encryption. Although this book sees privacy as positive and that which allows space for intimacy, experimentation and free expression, the abuse of privacy rights involves child pornography, criminality, terrorism and, closer-to-home, cyber-bullying and online harassment where anonymity may hide deeply undesirable behaviour. The moral debate over encryption is not clear-cut or straightforward, but there are both legal guidelines and existing ethical agreements in Article 12 and Article 19 of the United Nations Universal Declaration of Human Rights, agreed in 1948, that respectively say:

- No one shall be subjected to arbitrary interference with his privacy, family, home or correspondence, nor to attacks upon his honour and reputation. Everyone has the right to the protection of the law against such interference or attacks.
- Everyone has the right to freedom of opinion and expression; this right includes freedom to hold opinions without interference and to seek, receive and impart information and ideas through any media and regardless of frontiers.

Supporters of encryption and the ability to communicate without surveillance argue that if encryption were banned, this would be a victory for terrorists who seek to destroy the freedoms we enjoy. Although the Declaration does not address encryption (or the internet), it does say that everyone has the human right to privacy and family life (along with freedom of expression and thought). Today this takes the form of communication through email, apps, online video calls and other messaging services. Although undoubtedly encryption may be misused, it provides a means of providing anonymity in our modern online world so we can enjoy a private life.

UK POLITICAL SITUATION

The UK provides a very good case study because, as noted in the previous chapter on the Snowden leaks, it possesses a highly active surveillance apparatus. In early 2015 the promise of encryption came under threat from the UK government. For example, in January, pre-election mode, and against the background of the attack of the *Charlie Hebdo* office in Paris, David Cameron, the Conservative British Prime Minister (2010–2016), sought to ban encrypted online messaging apps, unless the UK government is given backdoors. He asked, 'Are we going to allow a means of communications which it simply isn't possible to read? … My answer to that question is: No, we must not.' The fear for intelligence agencies, expressed in multiple reports and public speeches, is that the internet would 'go dark' (ISC, 2015: 9; RUSI, 2015: 14). At the time of writing it is unclear how the UK will proceed with regard to the legality of encryption. The concern is that companies will be legally obliged to assist and bypass encryption. Companies such as Apple have argued: 'The creation of backdoors and intercept capabilities would weaken the protections built into Apple products and endanger all our customers. A key left under the doormat would not just be there for the good guys. The bad guys would find it too.'[5] This is a reasonable argument in that any backdoor into an encryption system will make the whole system vulnerable. If our own security agencies can use a backdoor, this means it exists for foreign intelligence agencies, criminals or terrorists themselves.

Apple's is both a moral and strategic business stance, because Apple are effectively being asked to hack into computers they have sold to customers on behalf of governments. This presents a crisis of trust – something they have fought hard to regain since Snowden revealed that the PRISM programme included tapping into the central servers of Apple (among other companies). Although the US is a key architect of the global surveillance apparatus, the Obama administration reluctantly backed down from a dispute with companies in Silicon Valley (such as Apple, Google and Microsoft) over encryption of communication. However, the government's wishes are clear, as Obama in January 2015 said: 'If we find evidence of a terrorist plot ... and despite having a phone number, despite having a social media address or email address, we can't penetrate that, that's a problem.' The key reason the government relented is that they concluded that it is not possible to give American law-enforcement and intelligence agencies access to encryption keys without also creating weaknesses that can be exploited by other states, cybercriminals and terrorists.[6] There were other factors too in that if the US attempted to insist on backdoor access to communications to US platforms such as Apple and Google, other countries around the world could reasonably insist on the same. Further, we can speculate that given the budget the NSA has dedicated to getting around digital encryption, it is plausible that it has the tools and means to work around companies' encryption methods.

TECH INDUSTRY REACTIONS

Although leading companies were implicated in the Snowden leaks for providing access to people's information and communications, many have come out strongly pro-privacy in the post-Snowden leak era. This is important for two reasons: first, because they are best positioned to provide privacy-friendly technologies; second, because they lend considerable heft to the argument that their customers/citizens should not have to make a trade-off between privacy and security. This marks a change in the privacy landscape. After all, champions of the data industry, such as Facebook's Mark Zuckerberg, have argued in the past that people no longer should have an expectation of privacy, and that privacy was no longer a 'social norm'. Given what Snowden revealed many data companies now seek to win privacy credentials. This is quite remarkable because, paradoxically, the internet business model is based on extracting as much information from people as possible (generally to better understand users to target advertising). Rather than turning to government to provide secure communications for citizenry, we have effectively turned to companies whose businesses are based on mining financial value from consumer tracking (I have Google especially in mind).

Following the Snowden leaks many of these businesses have reformed and fought back against state incursions into their businesses. Politically and culturally, this should be seen against the context of US libertarianism and dislike of governmental interference in affairs of the people. For example, in 2014 Microsoft went head-to-head with the US government over its insistence that Microsoft should allow it access to emails held on the company's servers in Ireland.

The significance of this is two-fold in that 1) it involves corporations fighting back against governments; and 2) the principle of privacy is very much back in play. Whereas post-'9/11' many businesses, such as Microsoft, were seemingly complicit in assisting the US government in their surveillance programme, the situation is different now. Indeed, there is something of a standoff between the two. The lack of willingness of businesses such as Microsoft and Apple to engage with governments led Robert Hannigan, the head of GCHQ (a UK intelligence agency) to chastise US tech firms for failing to co-operate enough with 'Five Eyes' agencies. In response to Apple and Google's introduction of strong default encryption in mobile operating systems launched in 2014, he even went as far as to call them 'the command and control networks of choice' for terrorists.

Apple and others are responding to their own libertarian impulses, but also a market opportunity where consumers are keen to have more control over who collects their information. Speaking at an event in 2015 hosted by the Electronic Privacy Information Center (EPIC), a non-profit research organisation in Washington, Apple's Tim Cook highlighted that people have a fundamental right to privacy; and, in addition to moral arguments, US laws demands it. On encryption, security and stifling of expression, Cook said:

> Now, we have a deep respect for law enforcement, and we work together with them in many areas, but on this issue we disagree. So let me be crystal clear – weakening encryption, or taking it away, harms good people that are using it for the right reasons. And ultimately, I believe it has a chilling effect on our First Amendment rights and undermines our country's founding principles.[7]

Apple was again tested in 2016 following a shooting in San Bernardino, California in December 2015. Here the FBI demanded that Apple unlock an iPhone 5C recovered from one of the shooters. Apple refused on the basis that compliance would have consequences that would reach beyond the case at hand. Indeed, in a letter to Apple's customers they explained that they refused because compliance would equate to 'a backdoor to the iPhone' and that weakening encryption 'would hurt only the well-meaning and law-abiding citizens who rely on companies like Apple to protect their data'. They also explained that even if a backdoor were built into the iPhone, criminals and bad actors 'will still encrypt, using tools that are readily available to them' (Apple, 2016).

Underpinning this political stance is, at least in part, a business motive because Apple is using privacy to differentiate itself from other technology companies. This is a very significant development for both privacy and Apple because while their competitors continue to mine their users for personal information, Apple is building its business around the idea of how little it knows about each of us *personally*. This point is subtler than it appears in that Apple wants the devices it manufactures to have deep familiarity with our lives, but the key difference is that data is stored locally on *our* devices and not centrally in cloud servers. However, despite this, Apple has undergone privacy scandals, perhaps most notably in 2014 when private photos of celebrities (many nude) were posted online and re-circulated through Reddit and other social media channels. These were obtained through hacked iCloud accounts. Apple defended itself by saying that it was not the system that was hacked, but 'a very targeted attack on user names, passwords and security questions'.[8] The case highlights, however, that Apple and its users are not immune from attack.

When Apple say they are not interested in collecting personal data because they both provide encryption and do not use personal data for advertising, they put others (such as Facebook and Google) in the position of having to defend why using personal data is morally acceptable. Indeed, at the aforementioned EPIC event, Cook went on to say that, 'some of the most prominent and successful companies have built their businesses by lulling their customers into complacency about their personal information'. This is most certainly a salvo aimed at Google, Facebook and Amazon, among others. This presents an interesting situation for privacy campaigners because historically they have been sceptical of the motives of corporations who, after all, exist to generate revenue for shareholders. What Apple did was strategic in they sought to both win consumer trust and outflank competitors. Privacy has effectively become a commodity, or that which has market value. Although perhaps not the way campaigners sought to win the 'privacy war', the phrase 'by any means necessary' comes to mind.

LIBERTARIAN PRIVACY

Encryption and denial of state access to the public's private communication is an expression of the libertarian ethos that drives many Silicon Valley companies. Libertarianism is a modern-day exaggeration of liberal values defined in Chapter 2 that provides a theoretical background to privacy. It is a conviction that society is best served by the promotion of personal autonomy, freedom and private property, but libertarianism also promotes unbridled capitalism, distrust of authorities (particularly governments) and dislike of regulations. Some of this may have appeal, but it also has tendencies towards being anti-democratic, monopolistic and self-focused (at the expense of others). A counter-factual example may help make the point about libertarian approaches to privacy. BlackBerry, for example, sought a 'balanced' approach to encryption by incorporating intercept capabilities into their devices. In contrast to Apple who purposefully cannot decode and unscramble encryption, BlackBerry hold the algorithms that encode communication and are able to co-operate with law enforcement if the situation warrants it (Inside BlackBerry, 2015). They say this is achieved without a backdoor, but instead that a government or agency should present a lawful access request. In both cases, what is becoming abundantly clear is that in the post-Snowden era, corporations play a larger role than previously in defending private communications. I will leave it to the reader to decide whether Apple's pro-privacy stance is informed by a) libertarian politics; b) a wish to do the right thing; c) strategic business acumen as Apple hones in on the home; or d) a combination of all of the above. I tend towards the latter option. Overall this is a welcome development, but we should not abandon the principle of government because regulations are also required to keep the reach and ambitions of businesses in check.

PRIVACY-BY-DESIGN AND THE SOCIAL CONSTRUCTION OF TECHNOLOGY

Apple's embracing of privacy is notable on two fronts: a) it embeds privacy-by-design principles throughout its products and services; b) the Apple brand is a very good ally for privacy activists. If privacy is about habits, social norms and practices, Apple's strategic manoeuvring towards a pro-privacy stance is good news. However, it is also worth considering what is on the technological horizon line. As addressed in later chapters, there is a renewed interest from the large technology platforms in artificial intelligence, personal assistants, ambient sensing and use of ever-larger sets of joined-up data. This manifests in concentration on expansion into the financial sector, health, insurance, wearable technologies and the home. These developments will be more intimate and important than traditional web- and app-based technologies we have grown up with.

Software and hardware that makes use of encryption utilise what has come to be known as privacy-by-design (PbD). This fits within wider discussions of what are known as privacy-enhancing technologies (PETs). These function in face of privacy-invading technologies (PITs), or what Schmidt and Cohen (2013) phrase as systems that are invasive-by-design (IBD). As you might have noticed, technologists are keen on acronyms! The latter recognises that the current state of the web and internet is invasive because it collects our photos, comments, tweets, friend-lists, preferences, likes and behaviour, and converts this into information that can be either used for profit (typically through marketing and advertising) or surveillance. The design of technology can be marshalled in a number of ways and both aid in regulating privacy as well as exploiting it. This means that technology may be part of privacy solutions as well as problems. Encryption is perhaps the best example of this principle because it factors anonymity into communications systems. What this allows us to see is that hardware and software that goes into our devices, and the broader network of computers that makes up our global digital infrastructure, are not simply indifferent material objects. Technologies have significance and can even be said to be political because they contribute to specific states of affairs and social arrangements (such as being able to communicate in private). Although it is routine to say that technologies themselves do not care about human affairs, the ways in which technologies are created, made and implemented means that technologies always have biases and dispositions as they embody values and sets of social interests.[9]

Indeed, PETs are also able to act as policy devices because human values and standards may be embedded in the technology. This is another key point because when we think about how to improve privacy standards, embedding values in technology complements other elements within the privacy toolbox. This also includes *legislation* (making privacy friendly laws), *regulation* (the specifics of how these laws are applied in practice to industries), *public education programmes* (these may be initiated by governments, pro-privacy campaign groups or by industries seeking to make themselves appear more privacy-friendly) and *incentivisation* (where companies see reputational and financial reward for better privacy behaviour and doing more than the bare minimum to comply with the law).

As we can see with encryption, this privacy situation involves a blend of legislation, incentivisation and privacy-enhancing technologies. It entails legislation because we need lawmakers to agree to it and financial incentivisation, as businesses such as Apple brand themselves as privacy-friendly. Ultimately however this is a matter of privacy-enhancing technologies and privacy by design, because privacy is safeguarded by taking privacy considerations into account at the design stage of systems which process personal data (Lieshout et al., 2011). Rather than trying to make existing leaky technologies safer, the idea is to avoid the problem in the first place.

What we see through this process is the deeply socio-technical nature of privacy-friendly systems. By linking 'social' and 'technical' I mean how human values (such as the wish to be able to communicate without anyone else listening in) are inextricably linked with the constitution and design of media technologies. Again, in addition to Google and Apple, one might consider, for example, Whatsapp, Snapchat and lesser-known services such as Signal and Telegram. The latter two are generally held to have stronger encryption techniques, but the point remains: they are imbued with social values and these technologies inform our social practices, behaviour and what we say, post and do. This technical approach to social questions does not just apply to encryption and privacy. Michel Callon (2012 [1987]), for example, refers to 'engineer-sociologists', and the ways in which engineering is intimately connected to social knowledge, study and decision-making. In general however, engineer-sociology, privacy-by-design and privacy-enhancing technologies means that cultural and human factors (preferences, beliefs, values and biases) are factored into design and the formative and creative stages of technology.[10]

CONCLUSION

This chapter has considered the nature of encryption technologies, their social dimensions, connection with privacy and the debates surrounding their use. I conclude that encryption and anonymity are necessary to ensure freedom of opinion and expression in an age defined by digital communication. However, we should also be mindful that anonymity and privacy is not the same thing. As described in Chapter 2 and alluded to in other chapters, this book prefers a positive account of privacy. This has less to do with seclusion than the ability for a person to decide whom to be open with. Although encryption technologies certainly do 'hide', we should keep in view that overwhelmingly most people do this to enjoy intimacy with friends, peers, loved ones and family without unwanted observation. This means anonymity can serve privacy, but they are not the same thing.

We began by defining encryption as that where the meaningful component of communication is only available to authorised parties. This means that government approved encryption algorithms, or situations where governments may possess third-party keys, misses the point. Although we should be mindful that state employed hackers and other hackers are constantly working to breach encryption algorithms, at the time of writing the fight appears to have been won over whether citizens should be afforded privacy through encryption. In large part, we have the big US technology companies such as Apple to thank for this. While their motives may be mixed (combining moral stance, reputation-building, branding, market positioning and need to build trust so we are amenable to using their payment systems and health kits), the net result is a win for encryption. Encryption is an excellent example of what privacy scholars refer to as privacy by design (PbD) or privacy-enhancing technologies (PETs). This bakes privacy into networked communications, notwithstanding active attempts to attack the system. The principle behind this is that our technologies are imbued with values, norms and principles defined in terms of their capacity to shape and participate in social life. From the point of studying privacy and media this is a useful observation because it allows us to consider how emergent technologies impact on privacy and society, what they allow or deny, and whether they enhance privacy, erode it or possibly even do both.

Research and challenges

1 Do you think governments should be able to break encryption if specific conditions apply?

2 How comfortable are you with balanced approaches to encryption?

3 To what extent should we rely on technological solutions to safeguard privacy? What other factors from the privacy toolbox should we consider, and why?

NOTES

1 Available from https://techcrunch.com/2015/06/02/apples-tim-cook-delivers-blistering-speech-on-encryption-privacy/.

2 Available from https://techcrunch.com/2015/06/17/but-bring-the-hammer-if-it-betrays-us/.

3 Cyber-crime is already a global problem. For a sense of the scale, form and speed of cyber-attacks I suggest the reader has a look http://map.norsecorp.com/#/ which shows attack origins, types and targets taking place in real-time.

4 See article by *The Economist* on counting how many people are gay: www.economist.com/blogs/economist-explains/2015/05/economist-explains-3.

5 Reported by the *Guardian*. Article available at www.theguardian.com/technology/2015/dec/21/apple-uk-government-snoopers-charter-investigatory-powers-bill.

6 *The New York Times* has coverage of this story at www.nytimes.com/2015/10/11/us/politics/obama-wont-seek-access-to-encrypted-user-data.html?_r=0.

7 Reported by TechCrunch. Available from http://techcrunch.com/2015/06/02/apples-tim-cook-delivers-blistering-speech-on-encryption-privacy/#.p1ugga:kVGu.

8 Apple's response available at www.apple.com/pr/library/2014/09/02Apple-Media-Advisory.html.

9 This point was best made by Langdon Winner in his 1986 book *The Whale and the Reactor: A Search for Limits in an Age of High Technology*, University of Chicago Press.

10 There is an entire academic discipline dedicated to this named Science, Technology and Society (STS) that examines how social, political and cultural factors impact on scientific research and technological innovation. See, for example, the journal *Science, Technology & Human Values*.

PART 2
COMMERCIAL DIMENSIONS OF PRIVACY AND MEDIA

6

PLATFORMS

DISRUPTION, CONNECTION AND NEW SOCIAL ACTORS

Key questions

- What is a platform?
- Why are platforms different from businesses?
- How should we assess the culture of a platform?
- What are the problems with a control-based account of privacy?

Key concepts

- Platform as institution
- Network effects
- Platform cultures
- Social versus institutional privacy

Over recent years it has become clear that platforms will play an increasingly greater role in all forms of life affected by data. What are 'platforms'? Strictly speaking they are software foundations upon which services and applications can be constructed. Google's Android, Linux, Apple's App Store, Apple Pay and the Bitcoin distributed ledger are good examples of these. A key characteristic of software platforms is *network effects*. This means that the value of a platform should be judged in terms of the number of people and organisations that use that platform. The more users there are, the more valuable the platform becomes to the owner, and its users, because of increased access to the network of users. The success of social media platforms are based on this positive feedback loop in that as more people adopt and use a service, this equates to higher revenue and a better end-user experience (and thereafter more interest from other potential users). Another way of seeing media platforms is as walled gardens where the platform provider has control over applications, content and media that are carried on its services. Platform providers include companies such as Airbnb, Google, eBay, Facebook, Etsy, Wikipedia, Amazon, PayPal, LinkedIn, Apple and Uber, who each in their own way provide software *upon* which much of everyday life is carried out. Today life with platforms entails everything from taking a taxi, to health, leaving accommodation reviews (TripAdvisor), communication and how we pay for goods. One only has to look to Amazon and Alibaba (outside of the West) to see how platforms are not just affecting digital communication, but the very nature of consumer society and shopping. We should also note that platforms are not just commercial entities, but also political ones. Change.org and Avaaz are good examples of platforms used to collect voices for democratic political action.

Platforms are being discussed in a wide range of literature spanning business, logistics, economics, computer science and new media studies, but this chapter opts to see platforms as a new type of *social institution*. We will progress to unpack this term, but for now we should recognise the scale of these platforms, operations and institutions, and the ways in which they transform older institutions. Uber, for example, is an app that connects passengers and drivers, but it is also a service that has transformed public transportation. We can point to more cases: Airbnb, for example, redefines the nature of accommodation that we use when we travel and Yelp tells us where to eat. Another key feature is that platforms are dependent on a flow of stock or inventory from elsewhere. This may be personal updates, photos, news, second-hand items, accommodation, taxis or videos, or even hardback books (as with Amazon). Platforms also grant capacity for people to interact with each other, using software. The consequence of this is that platforms have no value unless people use them. Another key feature is that rather than selling goods at a profit, they make money by means of a transaction fee, by advertising, or by selling data about user behaviour. Of course it may be all three.

Due to the fact that platforms rely on new connective technologies that can entirely reshape how businesses and services function, and that they offer efficiencies and lower prices, this sees people make use of them. This in turn forces existing companies to work with the platforms and become part of it. Taxis and Uber is one example, and Amazon and bookselling is another. Taxi drivers may not like Uber because it is not regulated as heavily as taxi services and its drivers are paid less, but there is pressure on drivers to use Uber if that is where customer demand is. Similarly, even the largest and once powerful news agencies are now forced to distribute content through platforms such as Facebook. This is causing much crisis in news as distribution and advertising revenues plummet. Similarly for bookselling, merchants of second-hand books may dislike the way that it drives down prices, and that fewer people use second-hand book stores, but they are effectively coerced into using Amazon. This has consequence because it creates very powerful institutions that are monopolistic and in effect swallow up older businesses. This grants power, scale and financial opportunity to use the vast amounts of data travelling throughout the platform.

Information captured through platforms can be used for what are undoubtedly good causes. For example, medical researchers use health data collected by Apple's Healthkit. If switched on, this is able to collect data from all relevant apps and wearable devices a person uses. This provides big data opportunities that, as we will see in Chapter 7, entails capacity to both access large amounts of information, but also to be able to monitor a wide variety of information types in real time. However, as the chapter will progress to discuss, the monopolistic and sheer size of platforms brings with them a need for critical interrogation of privacy practices. This fact has not been lost on political authorities and governments around the world. Both the European Commission[1] and the UK Parliament, for example, see the potential for platforms, but harbour concerns about their scale. This interest reflects an awareness that these organisations are important, but also that they are not easy to define. After all, an organisation that encourages more people to express their democratic voice is different from one that organises taxi rides. The task for this chapter is to more closely assess the nature of platforms and their significance. I do this by depicting platforms in terms of what can be loosely termed social institutions. We will then explore ways by which platforms can be analysed, particularly in terms of their status as a social institution. Paying specific attention to Facebook, this will lead us into a discussion of how Facebook thinks about privacy and how this squares with academic theories about privacy.

ON PLATFORMS

Platforms are organisations of the internet age. Platform businesses do not make or even own things (be this physical objects or media content) and push them at us, as historically has been the case with consumer capitalism. Instead platforms are *intermediary* companies in that they link, connect and serve as conduits. To convince other businesses to use the platform and thereby create revenue for it, the platform must serve a function that the business could not otherwise achieve. This tends to be the capacity of platforms to reach a large user-base and to execute a particular task more simply, elegantly, efficiently and easily (whether this be booking a taxi or advertising plumbing services to a specific location). However, platforms are not static. They develop so to offer both business and consumer users more services, but also to react to external threats. Google is a good example of this in that it started life as a web-based search engine but progressed to provide a free toolbar that could be integrated with a user's chosen web-browser. To expand, they subsequently created a range of tools such as email, maps, applications and storage. Each of these told Google a great deal about its users that allowed it to more effectively target ads and create revenue. Likewise, as mobile media have overtaken desktop media, Google bought and developed the Android operating system and created the Chrome browser. This helped them lead mobile computing, searching and advertising.

Primarily discussing YouTube (which is owned by Google), Gillespie (2010) argues that the term 'platform' has four dimensions that contribute to its overall meaning. The first is *computational* in that a platform is an infrastructure that allows particular things to happen (such as running games, applications, online television and software more generally). The second is *architectural* in that we can see platforms as human constructed things that people and objects can stand on. This connects with the *figurative* character of platforms, whereby we may speak of platforms for action, or the basis by which something can happen. The last is *political* in that we can see platforms as stages by which people may be addressed. Each of these in their own way has a positive sentiment to them, perhaps under-pinned by egalitarian words such as 'supportive' and 'empowering'. This connects with the rhetoric of user-generated content, participatory culture and Web 2.0 that typically assess how content is mostly created by a platform's users, rather than media owners or traditional publishers (Bruns, 2006; Jenkins, 2006; Shirky, 2008). However, the word 'platform' is both suggestive and vague enough to serve end users, advertisers (whose money frequently funds the platform) and professional content producers. For example, the top ten YouTube videos at the beginning of 2016 is all professional pop music content (Psy's Gangnam Style, Taylor Swift, Mark Ronson, Justin Bieber, Katy Perry, Enrique Inglesias and Meghan Trainor all feature). As Gillespie notes, platforms are often able to use the same language they employ to appeal to users, amateur producers, professional producers and advertisers alike. This typically includes words such as awareness, innovation, engaging, connecting, experience and opportunity.

Despite their increasingly important roles in society, the expression 'platform' has a neutral character. Arguably unlike other public systems that have common carrier status (such as telephone, mail and the internet), platforms are *keenly* profit driven (although telephone and mail systems need to be paid for and require sur-plus value for shareholders). Although today's platforms facilitate communication and interactions, they are not neutral. They both seek to avoid liability yet also create extraordinary levels of revenue through our use of these platforms. We see this on Twitter and Google as they complain that their systems are not set up to stop ISIS's videos, hashtags and accounts getting online (as soon as they take one down, another appears). Uber has also denied being liable for its drivers. This was illustrated when a six-year-old girl named Sophia Liu was killed when an Uber-contracted driver struck her in a San Francisco crosswalk. In its statement, Uber denied liability and said that 'this tragedy did not involve a vehicle or provider doing a trip on the Uber system'.[2] Gillespie concludes his article by asking what is the shape, and what are the edges, of platforms? By this he means what are their limits, how does egalitarian rhetoric collide with need for profit and will professional media producers colonise space professedly for amateurs? We can also read his point about edges in terms of responsibility. When does the platform take responsibility for things taking place in its own domain?

Platforms sometimes make their money through a transaction fee, and on other occasions by means of donations and publicly spirited individuals, but typically they use data to create value. The word data is abstract and unlike oil, gas, electricity or even soil in the ground, it is difficult to understand why data is deemed so valuable. We understand that good fertile land helps grow crops (thus helping with agrarianism) and that fuel drives machines so we can make more stuff and transport people and things around, but data is less clear. The answer to why data is so important is because it is about people, what they do, what they buy, how they feel, and what their habits and interests are. Each time we connect to the internet, we are wittingly and unwittingly sharing data and insights about ourselves. Why does this matter? The answer, if you have not guessed, is advertising. This becomes clearer when we see that a company such as Google (owned by Alphabet) makes roughly 96 per cent per year of its revenue from advertising. In real terms, in October 2015 Google reported yearly revenue of $18.67 billion and a profit of $4.7 billion. Data generated from platforms is clearly valuable.

WHAT IS A SOCIAL INSTITUTION?

There are all sorts of social institutions, but they might best be defined as

> a complex of positions, roles, norms and values lodged in particular types of social structures and organising relatively stable patterns of human activity with respect to fundamental problems in producing life-sustaining resources, in reproducing individuals, and in sustaining viable societal structures within a given environment. (Turner, 1997: 6)

The reason why this long definition may appear somewhat vague is because social institutions encompass language, hospitals, governments, businesses, laws and more. The key part is to recognise *these systems organise human activity*. We see this with platforms in that each of them in their own way 'disrupt' (a favourite word of the technology industry) and alter the ways in how fundamental activities are done. Be this democratic processes such as expressing public feeling, healthcare, transportation, police forces, trading and even governments themselves, platforms are new social institutions. It is readily arguable that the concept and phenomenon of traditional institutions as we know them are being overturned by the rise of networked online platforms. These platform-based institutions are organisations that, as we are beginning to understand, are potentially transgenerational deeply and certainly transnational. As widely reported, this is reflected in tax practices. For example, in the UK in 2015 Facebook paid £4,327 in UK corporation tax, while paying their staff £35 million in bonuses. This is achieved by complex, bespoke tax arrangements and shifting profits around different countries. Google UK similarly pays an extraordinarily low portion of corporation tax. While it does business in Britain, it processes most of its sales in Ireland. Reports in the press[3] (drawing upon a report by Deloitte) estimated that in 2014 Google has been legally diverting nearly £3 billion, or more than 80 per cent, of its British revenues offshore to avoid tax.

What is perhaps more interesting, for the purposes of this chapter, is how Google defended itself. It argues that Google did not just profit from the UK, but that it contributed £11 billion to the UK economy in 2014 due to businesses using its products. They have a point when one considers YouTube vloggers, Android app developers and money made by start-ups (and larger companies) using their AdWords services. This led Eileen Naughton, the Google UK boss, to claim that it supports 210,000 jobs and that 'Google is a growth engine for British businesses large and small'. Google may be a catalyst and engine, but what this shows is that it is also a platform core to the UK economy. Phrased otherwise, they are a social institution that sees itself as being beyond the UK's standard tax principles. To underline the point, Google believes itself to be more than a business, yet not a political organisation. This is new territory.

As well as being important to individuals and businesses that make use of the Google platform, it increasingly has a trans-generational character. Although many businesses from the dot.com era have long since faded, Google and Facebook still have no challengers. Although other social networks have joined the scene, these are typically used alongside Facebook (Ofcom, 2015a). This becomes important when we think that so much of our life is lived out through these platforms. Think, for example, about baby photos, the child's life and the later adult's death, performed through social media. Platforms are most certainly businesses and should be subject to the same regulations as smaller actors, but they are something more than that because they interact, make use of, and affect core parts of our life (in the case of social media, this entails life chronicles and memory).

PLATFORM CULTURES

It is useful not just to consider the prevalence of platforms, but also the make-up of platforms. When analysts study social institutions, they pay attention to the structure, size and form of organisation, but they are also interested in the culture of organisations. This means understanding behaviour, attitudes, values and norms. In practical terms, we can assess today's platforms by considering:

- what the primary function of the platform is;
- what the goal of the platform is;

- how the platform makes revenue;
- what the apps, website and public face of the platform looks like (what brand name, semiotic cues, symbols, colours, images and language are used, and to what effect);
- what the structure of the platform is (how elements of the business fit together, what job titles are there, which people fulfil key roles);
- public statements about values (such as in reports by the platform, responses to events and crisis, and accounts from participation in public events such as conferences);
- its terms and conditions of use;
- how the technology works, ease of use and the degree of control one has over it (particularly in regard to managing how and in what contexts information is transmitted, and whether information sharing is the default option);
- treatment of individuals and businesses who are required to use a platform to survive, grow or simply generate income;
- treatment of customers (do they respond to complaints either privately on email or publicly on social media such as Twitter);
- legal disputes (these are useful because businesses are forced to state and defend stated values);
- the platform's patents (these are much under-appreciated, but provide a very good sense of what a company would like to do) – Google's patent search tool can be invaluable (https://patents.google.com);
- ideally too, we would be able to access the company to comprehend it in ethnographic terms and understand the points of view of actors working for the platform, what the interior of the headquarters looks like, product development, corporate ethos (and whether employees abide by this), how meetings function and how people interact.

From the point of view of privacy and media studies, this is useful, because it allows us insight not just into the technicalities of how a company treats our information (such as abiding by laws), but their intentions and beliefs. By understanding both the structure of the business, and its function, products, behaviour, self-image, negotiation of laws and regulations (and tax arrangements), statements and aspirations, this grants convincing insight about the *culture of a platform*. What is valuable is not just knowledge of culture for its own sake, but the fact that culture (norms and values), and the collective intention of the platform, dictates the direction and activities of the platform. In sum, by understanding form, structure and intention, we have a much better sense of how a platform will treat, manage and care for our information.

WHAT OF PRIVACY?

What we typically see with platforms is a tendency to circumvent the state, a willingness to push regulatory boundaries, disruption of the traditional way of doing things and what can be broadly seen as libertarian logic (briefly accounted for in Chapter 5). This philosophy has immediate appeal because it is based on freedom, choice and lack of interference from others. This is echoed in discussion of privacy. For example, platform owners such as Mark Zuckerberg (Facebook) tend to talk of privacy in terms of personal control. Writing for the *Washington Post*,[4] Micheal Zimmer, from the University of Wisconsin-Milwaukee, created the Zuckerberg Files. This is an archive available from zuckerbergfiles.org that contains all the public utterances of the Facebook creator. It includes blog posts, letters to shareholders, media interviews, public appearances and product presentations. What Zimmer (2014) found is that when discussing the principle of privacy, he uses the word control instead. Zuckerberg is right in the sense that people want control about how much or little they wish to reveal to others. Privacy is not about hiding things, but control over what and with whom information is shared. Zuckerberg's position is not wrong per se, but by focusing on interpersonal and *social privacy*, this only considers one facet of privacy – typically the sort about control and visibility of social media profiles. This is important, but so is *institutional privacy*, or the sort that protects people from organisations that abuse their position and require unreasonable amounts of personal data about people and peers within their network (Young and Quan-Haase, 2013).

The sheer scale of these institutions means there is even more need for means to keep the behaviour of these new corporate actors in check, especially given their natural inclination to generate more data about people and their behaviour. For example, Facebook has historically pushed boundaries of how it uses people's data and, as Zimmer points out, behaved in ways that denies users control over what happens with their information. Indeed, the US Federal Trade Commission forced Facebook to comply with regular privacy audits for 20 years because it 'deceived consumers' with its privacy promises. It said that Facebook deceived consumers by telling them they could keep their information on Facebook private, and then repeatedly allowing it to be shared and made public.[5] An article from *Time* magazine[6] synthesises some of the controversial ways that Facebook has used people's data:

- It has tried to keep people's data for ever, even if they leave.
- It told friends what a person buys online.
- It tracks movements across the Web (and not just on Facebook).
- It used a person's 'Likes' in ads.
- It has forced people to make themselves more searchable (by increasing the amount of information a person is required to make publicly viewable).
- It uses facial recognition software to spot people in photos.
- It gave and made money from giving user's data to the US government.

THE PROBLEM WITH A CONTROL-BASED ACCOUNT OF PRIVACY

Although this book broadly (but not entirely) agrees with the idea that privacy can be read in terms of control over information, we should be wary of saying they are synonymous. If we jettison the word 'privacy' in favour of personal 'control', this shifts the debate from one of ethics, principles, norm, and how we as a society would like things to be, to one where people fend for themselves to maintain control over their personal information. Libertarianism has attractions (who can say they do not like freedom, autonomy and agency?), but it has consequences too (lack of clear meaningful laws and absence of regulatory power to curtail powerful actors). As detailed in Chapter 2, I have sympathy with the liberal outlook (control grants autonomy, it requires respect for selfhood and others, and typically means that high levels of consent are required if one person wishes to appropriate something from another). However, by focusing on individuals, it forces them to take responsibility for processes that are difficult to manage. It is well understood, for example, that most people do not read terms and conditions due to time and complexity (Cranor et al., 2014), but less obvious is what a person can do if they disagree with parts of them. Leave or avoid the service is one option, but this is not always possible for a number of reasons. We may be required by our university degree courses to sign up to processes that generate data about us for advertisers (such as the online learning platform Blackboard). The net effect of focusing on individuals' control over data is the downplaying of structures that serve to defend privacy. While I very much agree that control over one's information is important, so is the fact that we must have collective power. One way this is achieved is through regulatory actors with legal power and civic interest that are capable of taming the emerging class of social institutions.

CONCLUSION

Materially speaking, platforms are businesses built on software that facilitate connections, sharing of content, flow of information, financial transactions, business activity by actors other than the platform owner and a multitude of digital services (such as the many apps that sit on our smartphones). Some go further than being a way to track calories or send photos to being social institutions. These are businesses that 'disrupt' existing ways of doing things, whether this be booking taxis, renting accommodation, delivering news or selling second-hand books. What conjoins them is that they are digital and *connective* technologies. They are indivisibly digital, networked and reliant on economies of scale (in our case, lots of users).

As Google and Facebook are demonstrating, successful platforms have potential to be powerful as well as lucrative. Governments and transnational European bodies recognise the potential for platforms, but harbour concerns about their scale and interests. Although the word itself has neutral characteristics, platforms are not benign or blank conduits for their users or businesses that make use of these platforms. Similarly, the rhetoric of transparency, openness, conversation and building connections should be treated with deep scepticism for the simple reason that platforms do not apply these principles to themselves. Even the most attentive privacy scholars do not know precisely what happens with personal information collected by these companies. The philosophy and logic behind platforms tells us privacy lessons. Facebook is illustrative of platform-based approaches to privacy that promote a control-based account of privacy. On the surface this is laudable and accords with liberal ideals we discussed in Chapter 2. With closer attention (particularly on applying the suggestions in the platform cultures section), we see that a control-based account of privacy actually entails a weakening of privacy by means of unclear laws and reduced regulatory safeguards. As libertarian-inspired platforms continue to ascend in scale and value, we need good clear laws, and willingness to apply these, to ensure socially healthy growth.

Research and challenges

1 What is the political significance of platforms? That is, what role do you see them playing in society?

2 To what extent do you agree that platforms-as-social institutions marks new political territory?

3 By means of the tips provided in the *platform cultures* section assess a platform of your own choosing.

NOTES

1 See, for example, http://ec.europa.eu/digital-agenda/en/news/public-consultation-regulatory-environment-platforms-online-intermediaries-data-and-cloud.
The House of Lords has taken a special interest: www.parliament.uk/business/committees/committees-a-z/lords-select/eu-internal-market-subcommittee/news-parliament-2015/online-platforms-inquiry-launch/.

2 Background to story available at http://techcrunch.com/2014/01/02/should-car-services-provide-insurance-whenever-their-driver-app-is-open/.

3 See, for example, the *Evening Standard*: www.standard.co.uk/business/gideon-spanier-google-talks-up-its-role-in-the-uk-economy-but-try-searching-for-its-tax-details-a2953181.html.

4 Available from www.washingtonpost.com/lifestyle/style/mark-zuckerbergs-theory-of-privacy/2014/02/03/2c1d780a-8cea-11e3-95dd-36ff657a4dae_story.html.

5 See www.ftc.gov/news-events/press-releases/2011/11/facebook-settles-ftc-charges-it-deceived-consumers-failing-keep.

6 See coverage from *Time* magazine: http://time.com/4695/7-controversial-ways-facebook-has-used-your-data/.

7

BEHAVIOURAL AND PROGRAMMATIC ADVERTISING

CONSENT, DATA ALIENATION AND PROBLEMS WITH MARX

Key questions

- What is consent?
- How useful is consent as a mechanism to safeguard privacy?
- What are third parties and what do they do?
- How has media theory contributed to criticisms of behavioural advertising?

Key concepts

- Consent
- Personal data
- Audience-as-commodity
- Data alienation

It is an under-appreciated fact that money generated by advertising is the primary sponsor of newspapers, magazines, television, radio and digital media. Online, it helps fund some of the most popular activities such as searching, social networking, reading news, researching purchases, checking weather, streaming content, getting travel information, watching videos, using forums, visiting adult websites, blogging and downloading entertainment. We should keep this in mind as we progress through this chapter. The reader may be surprised to know that online advertising is, by some margin, more popular with advertisers than any other medium – including television, newspapers, magazines and billboards. Thus, when we think about what advertising is, the first thing that should come to mind is not images from television or content seen on the street, but sponsored Google links, Facebook ads and banners at the top of our favourite webpages. This helps answer why our favourite social media platforms are worth so much money,[1] even though we use them for 'free'. Of course, there is a cost to using these services, because the revenue model is utterly based on profiling users on their sites and beyond, and serving behaviourally targeted ads. Google is an especially good case because although we typically see it as a technology company, in essence it is an advertising firm. We should also recognise that we also pay with money when we buy goods because the cost of advertising is factored into the ticket price of the item or service.

The point about advertising, platforms and online profiling is summed up well by James Whittaker. As an engineering director at Google he led teams working on Chrome, Google Maps and Google+. He subsequently left and re-joined Microsoft. In interview with a Microsoft feature writer, he commented

> As a Google employee, the work is interesting, and there are all these cool toys and free food, but eventually you wake up and realize what you're doing […] In a nutshell, Google's business model is to attract as many users as they can by producing useful stuff, surveilling the hell out of them and then selling that information to advertisers so they can monetize it. At Google their product is literally their users. They hide it well. (Warnick, 2012)

Most will recognise that there is no 'something for nothing' when it comes to online media. As the adage goes, 'if you're not paying, you're the product'. What people are less likely to be aware of is the scale of the data-tracking business and that the commercial internet functions by logging behaviour every time we interact with the connected world. Even the most ardent and well-resourced scholars struggle with this because the data industry is purposefully opaque about what it does. In the past advertising has been targeted on the basis of publication (such as aftershave in men's fashion magazines), but today it is increasingly targeted on the basis of who is reading the content, and what people have clicked on, looked at, bought, posted, who they have communicated with, what friends are interested in and where people happen to be. This invites questions about privacy, control over data and digital experience, and the adequacy of data-protection law, particularly in regard to the principle of *consent*.

This chapter unpacks the mechanics of behavioural advertising and what is known today in industry circles as programmatic advertising. It will account for these developments in relation to what in media studies is known as 'critical political economy'. This means consideration of the political and economic dimensions of media, and scrutiny of how their power is maintained and challenged (Hardy, 2014). In particular, we will consider what media scholars phrase as the 'audience-as-commodity' and the argument that the principal output of the media industry turns out not to be content and services, but audience attention time that is sold by media companies (be this television, newspapers, social media or search engines) to advertisers. Having unpacked how this works, the chapter will explore this in relation to consent. This is a key element to privacy debates today because consent is simultaneously an ethical, practical, philosophical, legal, technological and industrial principle that guides how people and organisations can collect and use information about us. Quite arguably, consent sits at the heart of modern media culture.

PRE-CHAPTER SUGGESTION

Behavioural advertising tracks users' browsing activities between websites over a period of time for the purpose of serving advertising tailored to what advertisers assume are users' interests (McStay, 2011). The idea behind behavioural advertising is to display ads according to *who* is looking at a particular webpage, rather than according to the content of the page itself. I will define the techniques below, but the principle behind behavioural advertising is essentially the same as wearing a t-shirt that says 'I'm from the UK, between 37 and 40 years old, spend quite a lot on technology and like holidays in the French Alps. Target me with ads for related products whether I like it or not.'

Before we get into the detail of how behavioural targeting works, where it is going and what the privacy implications are, it will be useful to obtain an idea of *who* and *what* is tracking our activities online. On the assumption that the reader has either an internet-enabled phone or a computer nearby, there are apps and services that can help identify these. On your phone, tablet or computer, load one or more of these applications:

- *Lightbeam* (formerly known as Collusion): this Firefox add-on enables people to see who is tracking their activities on the web without being seen. It does this by means of listing trackers, and visualising how trackers and websites visited link together. When kept on throughout the day, it is very enlightening to see the proportion of websites with which we knowingly share data compared to tracking businesses that we would otherwise be unaware of.
- *Ghostery*: this counts how many trackers there are on websites people visit. In a workshop I had my students compete to find who can find the site with the most trackers. The Perez Hilton homepage was the winner (with 146 trackers). Have a look at your favourite sites to see if you can beat this figure. Don't forget to click through and see what type of companies they are.

- *Disconnect*: this also tracks the trackers, identifies who they are and tells the user what happens to the data that is being tracked. Importantly, this works with phones and tablets, and not just desktop computers.
- Another useful activity (best done on a computer rather than a phone) is to download the data that Google holds about individuals. When we consider that Google, and the advertising companies it owns (most notably Doubleclick), is responsible for most of the world's digital advertising,[2] the reason for this becomes clearer.

TECHNIQUES: HOW BEHAVIOURAL ADVERTISING WORKS

If you do not have an internet-enabled phone or computer nearby, not to worry, but do download one of the apps when you have the opportunity. What they show is which *third parties* collect information about us. For example, when we log on to our favourite news sites (be this Buzzfeed or *The New York Times*), our devices do not just share information with these news sites, but other actors too, who serve ads on their news sites and collect data about our online behaviour. The mechanics of this is that web publishers (who publish websites and online services where advertising is placed) mostly allow web users to access content without paying for information or services. Instead they generate money from advertising and selling data about us to survive and profit. They typically employ *advertising networks* (a third party) to handle the advertising process. These companies have access to ad spaces on publishers' websites and act as an intermediary to marry available stock from web publishers with demand from advertisers for spaces in which to place their advertising. The reason why publishers often prefer to let a third party do this is because it saves them having to find advertisers, format their ads, serve the ad on the website and collect data about interaction with the ad (to assess its effectiveness). In addition to serving ads, the third party ad network will also place a tracking cookie on our computer. Due to the fact that ad networks have so many sites and publishers in their portfolio, this means they get to know what our interests are by means of other sites we visit and how we interact with them.

Online cookies were first created in 1994. They are small text files residing on a user's web browser and computer. They register information that identifies each session between a browser and a server (the computer that a browser 'talks' with to receive information) and the interactions between a user's computer and a given website (such as when we log onto Facebook). A useful way to think about them is that cookies provide the web with a memory because they allow computers to remember and identify a user. Sometimes they are simply used to remember our website preferences, personal details, from information or items we have saved to a 'basket'. Due to the fact that cookies remember us, they are also used to target users with advertising.

For example Figure 7.1 shows a list of cookies for a range of sites I have visited in recent months. Some such as discountcyclesdirect.co.uk remember my preferences so I do not have to log in each time. These are first-party cookies. Other cookies in the list, such as doubleclick.net (the advertising network owned by Google), are third-party cookies in that they collect data as I visit websites that do not belong to Google. As explained in more depth below, ad networks such as Doubleclick generate revenue by serving ads for websites and simultaneously collecting data about us. They collect and use information when a user visits a website participating in that particular network. Third-party ad networks have access to thousands and millions of sites. Google's Doubleclick for example reaches over 90 per cent of websites worldwide. As such, third-party tracking to serve behavioural advertising is the principal revenue tool for internet companies. What this means is that while in theory I might not use Google's services because I prefer not to be tracked by them, they still are tracking me on 90 per cent of the sites I visit.

If you inspect your own cookie folder you will find that many have nondescript names. Although not listed in Figure 7.1, my own folder contains a cookie titled 207.net. I have never been to a website with this name and on searching online to find who this third party is that has placed their cookie on my computer, I find that it was put there by Adobe Digital Marketing Suite. Interested in what

Cookies and site data			✕
Site	**Locally stored data**	Remove all	Search cookies
dirtmountainbike.com	1 cookie		
www.discountcyclesdirect.c...	1 cookie		
dlvr.it	1 cookie		
www.domo.com	Local storage		
doubleclick.net	1 cookie, Channel ID		✕
	Channel ID id		
selfesteem.dove.co.uk	6 cookies, Local storage		
dronejournalism.org	3 cookies		
www.dronejournalism.org	2 cookies, Local storage		
dropbox.com	2 cookies		
www.dropbox.com	5 cookies		
dropboxusercontent.com	1 cookie		
www.dsmelite.com	1 cookie		
easyjet.com	6 cookies		
net.easyjet.com	1 cookie		

Figure 7.1 Screen-grab of cookie list

data they are collecting about me, I go deeper into the site to the Adobe Privacy Center. This is where I find out what data they are capturing. They say that their analytics services collects data on: website addresses and the time I spent on them; the link that took me to the site that contains the cookie; searches I have performed, including searches that led me to that company's website; information about my browser and computer (device type, operating system, connection speed and display settings); my internet protocol (IP) address that Adobe uses to approximate my general location; information I provided to the company's website (including information on registration forms) where I was given the cookie; whether I clicked an ad; items I have either bought or placed in the shopping cart; social network profile information, including photos, fan and like status, user IDs, age and gender.[3] Adobe's webpage continues by telling me that some companies using Adobe's services may send them information that allows them to identify users personally. Further, some companies may also buy additional information about users (first-party information) and then add that additional information to the information collected by Adobe's products on their websites (third-party information). This additional first-party information may include things like email addresses, account information and Facebook profile information, including photos and usernames (Adobe, 2015).

PROGRAMMATIC

We now know that third-party web-based behavioural advertising involves advertising that changes according to the profile of the person looking at the screen. For example the *Guardian* newspaper uses this type of advertising on its website and ads will vary according to who is visiting. This is done by publishers outsourcing advertising spaces on their website to advertising networks. Further, due to my use of the Ghostery app recommended above, I can see that trackers on the *Guardian* website include Audience Science (an ad network), DoubleClick (the ad network owned by Google that serve the *Guardian's* ads[4]), Facebook Connect (that allows Facebook to see what Facebook users are doing on other sites) and Scorecard Research Beacon (owned by ComScore). Whereas behavioural advertising is oriented to desktop computers using the web, programmatic approaches are based on understanding always-connected people who use a *variety* of screens and technologies.

Programmatic includes and develops web-based behavioural techniques. Whereas behavioural techniques are typically about the web, programmatic entails capacity for advertisers to target consumers across a range of devices and displays. Although all forms of behavioural advertising are interested in the identity of users, the programmatic method takes this a step further because it tries to understand behaviour across different formats, apps and devices so to know us more intimately. Given the rise of smartphones in the last ten years, this endeavour is not just about the devices themselves, but where and when we use them.

After all, our smartphones help us navigate real as well as virtual life. This is done by generating usage information from apps, maps, social media, web browsing, video watching, stores visited and physical location. The objective is to be able to reach the right people with salient messages when they are most likely to spend, and understand which stimuli were influential in getting us to click or buy. This requires sensitivity to our behavioural and demographic profiles, geography, time of day, and the extent and means by which we engage with advertising.

WHAT DATA DO THEY COLLECT?

Programmatic approaches make use of a more diverse range of data than behavioural advertising. As discussed in McStay (2016), this includes:

- *First-party data*: this is the most valuable information because it is collected directly from websites that we use. This includes location, purchase histories and how people behave on a company's websites (what we click, read and linger on). These reveal clear expressions of interests in products and brands for advertisers.
- *Second-party data*: this is a more unusual form of data sharing that occurs when companies collaborate to achieve mutual interests. Information is generated when a partner (company X) shares customer data with company Y (and vice versa). For example, a person interested in expensive mountaineering clothing might visit the partner company's site about adventure holidays and be tagged with a cookie. They are not competitors so interests can align without harming either company.
- *Third-party data*: this is information bought, sold and traded on an open data market. In programmatic advertising this includes cookie data (as with behavioural advertising), but also information from apps, social media, website registration data, public records and offline transaction data such as loyalty cards. Companies that collect and organise this information are known as data management platforms (DMPs). A browse of the websites of leading marketing companies, such as eXelate, Lotame and Bluekai, is very revealing. I strongly suggest that readers familiarise themselves with these data companies to understand in more detail how they function and what their aims are (they are quite bald in their assertions to know people in the most granular terms possible).

WHAT DOES THIS DATA MEAN?

Although we now have a good grasp of what and how data is collected, the significance is still missing. We can appreciate this by considering some of the cluster headings DMPs use to categorise us. eXelate, for example, segment people into clusters such as 'men in trouble' (established by buying flowers or chocolates online). Another category, utilised by the marketing firm IXI Services (a division of Equifax) has the charming category 'burdened by debt: small-town singles' (*The Economist*, 2014). What we see with these clusters is that they are not simply demographic factors (such as age and income), but the conversion of real life into data that can be combined with other incoming data to make assumptions about us. The objective is to use quantitative means (pattern recognition) to serve marketing content that is meaningful to us (quality). In an article for *Wired* magazine, Madhumita Venkataramanan (2014) illustrates this with her experience and analysis of the personal data economy:

> I'm a 26-year-old British Asian woman, working in media and living in an SW postcode in London. I've previously lived at two addresses in Sussex and two others in north-east London. While I was growing up, my family lived in a detached house, took holidays to India every year, donated to medical charities, did most of the weekly shopping online at Ocado and read the *Financial Times*. Now, I rent a recently converted flat owned by a private landlord and have a housemate. I'm interested in movies and start-ups, have taken five holidays (mostly to visit friends abroad) in the last 12 months and I'm going to buy flights within 14 days. My annual income is probably between £30,000 and £39,999. I don't have a TV or like watching scheduled television, but enjoy on-demand services such as Netflix and NOW TV. I passed through Upper Street in north London every day last week. I can cook a little but tend to eat out or get takeaways often; foreign foods (Thai and Mexican) are my favourite. I don't own any furniture and don't have children. I've never been married. I often eat with my university friends on weeknights. I don't care for cars or own one. I dislike any form of housework, and have a cleaner who lets herself in when I'm at work. I shop for groceries at Sainsbury's, but only because it is on my way home. I am not attached to my neighbourhood, and have no contact with my neighbours; I like the idea of living abroad some day. I prefer working as part of a team rather than alone; I'm ambitious and it is important to me that my family thinks I'm doing well. I often go to the pub on Fridays after work. At home, I am far more likely to be browsing restaurant reviews than managing my finances or looking at property prices online. I am rarely swayed by others' views.

This is not a personal profile written by Madhumita on a dating website, but it is her account of what she found when she followed up what information data-tracking companies were holding on her. As she highlights, the principle behind the commercial internet is that behaviour is logged every time we interact with the connected world. If we break down the insights into her life that were collected by the data industry, the information includes personal characteristics, histories, desires, thoughts, hopes, wishes, emotions and attitudes. To list in no particular order the sorts of data in play, these include: gender and ethnicity, film and entertainment preferences (television or on-demand), holidays (how often, when, where and probability of when the next flights will be booked), income bracket, home and past addresses, whether or not a cleaner is employed, geo-location and mobility throughout the day (where a person is), cooking versus eating out, who a person dines with, whether a person has children, marital status, education, car-ownership history, supermarket preference, working preferences (alone or with a team), degree of contact with neighbours and charity-donation habits. This information was collected from a range of trackers (and not just one firm), but it is illustrative of the intent and reach of the market research and data industry. There are multiple reasons for companies to analyse people online, but these break down into two categories: the first is to improve usability and our experience of online media, but by far the most financially important is to generate data about us for advertising.

PERSONAL DATA AND CONSENT

Behavioural advertising techniques typically do *not* collect names, email addresses, telephone numbers or other information that we normally think of as personal. Instead they generate strings of letters and numbers that identify unique website visitors and users. This is personal information because the techniques generate codes that are unique to individuals and can in theory be traced back to living individuals. This final point about traceability back to real living people is enough for regulators to deem behavioural (and programmatic advertising) as dealing in personal data. The consequence of what appears to be a technicality is that the advertising industry should gain *meaningful consent* from people to legally collect and process their personal data. This is an important point to consider because so much of the data industry (services we use) are predicated on the fact that we are aware of what is taking place and that we agree to have data collected and processed about us. The problem is this is a sham. Although consent accords with liberal privacy values accounted for in Chapter 2, in practice it is difficult to meaningfully give or withhold consent. The difficulty that both privacy defenders and industry alike recognise is that it is a tall order to tell computer and smartphone users who is collecting data, what is being collecting, why it is being collected, where the information will go and how long it will be stored for. The problem is two-fold in that simple plain-language cannot adequately convey what takes place with the data (to legal satisfaction), yet existing terms and conditions are difficult to read (and, of course, mostly unread) (Cranor et al., 2014).

In principle, people should have a proper choice that reflects a person's intentions about whether or not to receive personalised advertising generated by tracking digital behaviour. The standard of consent is supposed to be that consent cannot be assumed by inaction, or not clicking either agree/disagree. Although we are asked to give our consent to many data processes online, the extent to which this is 'real' consent is very questionable. Do people click 'agree' because they have read the details and thereafter offer informed consent, or do we blindly click 'agree' with a vague sense that we should read them, yet do not have time or inclination? What is clear is that informed consent is problematic online. Even the most benign and legally compliant businesses face an inherent problem with online consent in that they can either be detailed and explicit about what happens with personal information (which no one will read) or they can be brief and potentially read by people (but the notice will be light on important detail about collection, processing and whom data is shared with). This phenomenon is so widespread that in 2013 there was even an award-winning movie about the topic called *Terms and Conditions May Apply*.[5] Also, in the UK in 2010, as an April Fools' joke, Gamestation, a video-game store, buried a clause in its terms and conditions that read:

> By placing an order on this Website on the first day of the fourth month of the year 2010 Anno Domini, you agree to grant us a non transferable option to claim, now and for ever more, your immortal soul. Should we wish to exercise this option, you agree to surrender your immortal soul, and any claim you may have on it, within 5 (five) working days of receiving written notification from gamestation.co.uk or one of its duly authorized minions.

The number of souls captured was 7,500 or 88 per cent of people who bought from the site on the first day of the fourth month of the year 2010. This highlights what we all know: *very* few people read terms and conditions of online services.

This is indicative of a larger problem – that is, the connection between people and their digital environments. The problem goes back to the origins of online behavioural advertising in the mid-1990s when companies began depositing cookies on users' terminals to track them. This set a precedent whereby users had to become aware of their existence if they were to opt out (if they knew how). Particularly in the US, where behavioural advertising originated, policy-makers were keen to support fledgling industries so they did not regulate industries too heavily. As a principle, most governments do this to nurture growth and new economic activity. The idea is that as industries mature, they become more resilient to change and able to deal with more vigorously applied regulations. Although the behavioural advertising industry (that gave rise to programmatic approaches) has existed since the 1990s and received a great deal of regulatory attention, even in Europe where regulation is hardest for businesses, it has still not fully addressed core concerns. This is the extent to which we consent to online tracking.

Research by the advertising industry shows that people care about online privacy and have concerns about data practices by the advertising industry. In the

UK that has a very successful online advertising industry (judged by spend on digital versus other media) the Internet Advertising Bureau (a trade association that represents the interests of the industry) found that 89 per cent of people 'want to be in control of their online privacy' (IAB, 2012). This is not surprising (why would 11 per cent want to be out of control?), but their finding that 62 per cent 'worry about online privacy' is notable. This data is from before the Snowden leaks of 2013 when data privacy discussion increased in prominence in the mass media. Post-Snowden, UK data from TRUSTe (2014) highlights even higher levels of concern about advertising, with 89 per cent of British internet users worried about their online privacy. This has resulted in a generalised mistrust of the online advertising industry as Britons are less likely to click on an online ad (91 per cent), use apps they do not trust (78 per cent) or enable online tracking (68 per cent).

RESISTANCE AND ADBLOCKING

In addition to surveys, dissatisfaction with the status quo is demonstrated by use of adblockers, such as Adblock Plus. I address this challenge to the advertising industry in chapter length elsewhere (McStay, 2016), but in summary the most effective protection and disruptive response to behavioural advertising is use of adblockers. These are apps and programs employed to remove ads placed by third parties. These are increasingly popular with 22 per cent of people in the UK using them (IAB, 2016). However, while certainly employed for privacy reasons, a small majority (52 per cent) reports they use them to block *all* ads (IAB, 2015a), although as mentioned they only block ads placed by third parties. More detailed reasons for blocking ads are: they are interruptive (73 per cent); the design can be annoying (55 per cent); ads slow down the browsing experience (54 per cent); ads aren't relevant (46 per cent); and privacy concerns (31 per cent). Bandwidth and battery life (on tablets and phones) are also concerns for people. Resistance to online advertising by means of adblockers has also given rise to anti-adblocking companies such as PageFair, Sourcepoint and Secret Media. These detect use of adblocking and serve users with messages encouraging them not to use adblockers.

SETTING A TOUGH GLOBAL STANDARD: CONSENT IN EUROPE

When it comes to tracking people online to serve tailored online advertising, consent is a fundamental issue to consider. As an illustration and example of the importance of consent we can look to Europe, which has what is generally considered to be the toughest standard for data protection and privacy rules in the world. Countries that want to collect data about citizens within the European Union (EU), or conduct business with companies in member states, must have legislation or special arrangements to adequately meet EU standards. Data privacy regulations and 'directives' are made in Brussels because the majority of European countries are part of the EU. Over the last twenty years, two directives in particular have shaped privacy and how information is handled in Europe, and arguably further afield.

The first, created in 1995, is called Directive 95/46/EC, which addresses the collection and processing of personal data (the Data Protection Directive). The second is Directive 2002/58/EC on Privacy and Electronic Communications (or the e-Privacy Directive), which, for our purposes in this section, deals with how consent is gained for placing cookies or similar tracking devices on user's computers. For consent to be valid, it must be informed, specific, freely given and be a genuine indication of a person's wishes.

The General Data Protection Regulation (GDPR) is set to replace the Data Protection Directive in 2018 and, at the time of writing in 2016, the e-Privacy directive is also in line to be revised to harmonise with the changes laid out in the General Data Protection Regulation. The latter, GDPR, recognises that although the original Data Protection Directive was intended to be 'technology neutral' (to avoid regulations becoming quickly obsolete as technologies that make use of personal data develop), technology and society have progressed so far since 1995 that a new data protection instrument is required. It is important to understand that Directives prescribe certain results that must be achieved by each member state of the European Union, but each is free to decide how to transpose directives into national laws. In effect while the desired outcome of the Directive should be met, this gives some interpretive licence to each country. Regulations are stronger and have binding legal force throughout every member state.

Before we get into some of the detail, it is worth noting that these new and forthcoming pieces of legislation attempt to balance privacy rights with economic growth in the digital sector, create meaningful guidelines for organisational treatment of personal data, foster trust in commercial uses of personal data and give users greater control over their personal data. Also, while new, they are revisions of earlier laws rather than an overhaul, although there are some significant big changes. Perhaps foremost is that the new rules apply to non-EU businesses (such as Google, Facebook and other behemoths) that want to monitor the behaviour of EU residents, even if the data processing takes place outside of the EU.

On the conditions necessary for personal data processing, Article 7 of the new regulation discusses consent. The key characteristics of consent include:

- The minimum age at which an individual can consent to their data being processed will range between 13 and 16 years old across member states (each can choose).
- Companies will not be allowed to divulge information that they have received for a particular purpose without the permission of the person concerned.

- Consent can only be given for a specific purpose and it can be withdrawn at any time.
- Consumers will have to give either their *unambiguous* or *explicit* consent to the use of their data (more on this below).
- Information provided should be done in a concise, transparent, intelligible form, using clear and plain language so for consent to be meaningful, freely given, specific and unambiguous.

The fact that from 2018 onwards businesses will only be able to collect data with either unambiguous or explicit consent is significant. Although consent seems like it should be relatively straightforward, in practice it is more complex. Please bear with me as I unpack this. Directive 95/46/EC (which came before GDPR) effectively allowed implicit (silently granted) consent or what is otherwise known as opt-out consent. There is much debate around this that is too detailed for this chapter, but in essence it boils down to whether the cookie settings on a person's web browser can be taken as a valid expression of consent (see McStay, 2012; Clifford, 2014). In practice, if a person's browser is set to 'accept' then in theory this is a signal they are OK with having third-party cookies placed on their devices. As we read earlier the problem is this: do people really have comprehension of what tracking cookies are and how browser settings work?

Instead, GDPR requires people to signal agreement by 'a statement or a clear affirmative action'. This is horribly unclear and at the time of writing in 2016 the way that industry and legal experts will interpret it has yet to be clarified. For sensitive personal data (such as about racial or ethnic origins, political opinions, religious beliefs, trade union membership, physical or mental health, sexual life, offences or details about court proceedings), the status of this is clear: a person must give their informed and *explicit consent* before data processing can start. Consent in this case will require affirmative action in that a person should be presented with information about the choice they are making and then have to actively respond (such as by a clearly explained tick box).

Things are less clear when it comes to more routine personal data used for advertising purposes. In relation to advertising my assessment[6] of the unfolding situation is that the GDPR requirement of *unambiguous consent* means that non-sensitive personal data will be collected if a person has been exposed to a 'By using this site you consent to cookies' type of note on a webpage (which is what happens now). The thinking behind this is that, although nothing has been clicked or explicitly agreed, the nature of the context in which the person is in (such as a social media site or news site containing ads) would mean if such a privacy notice were given there is *conceivably* a reasonable expectation that a person understands and affirms collection of personal data. In addition to the site or app they see the notice on, the user's device will also be set to allow collection of personal data. This is suspicious and one could make a strong case that this is simply an implicit and opt-out approach based on user inactivity as a means of providing consent (for a more extended discussion of consent logic also see Kosta, 2013).

Another factor to consider is that collection of personal data may take place without these conditions if there is a 'legitimate interest' and that fundamental rights and freedoms of the individual are respected.[7] Although this may appear as a backdoor to use personal data, there are onerous tests that need to be met before the legitimate interests argument can be applied. It is doubtful that advertising meets these. In summary, this messy and illogical approach to consent is the result of conflicting pressures from: those who support industry in easing the conditions on how non-sensitive personal data can be used; and those who believe that consent is meaningless if a person neither understands what is happening and has not actively given their consent before data collection starts.

AUDIENCE-AS-COMMODITY CRITICISMS

Critical media work on advertising that targets people by means of their behaviour focuses on how people's data is *commodified*. Inspired by Marxist thinking, this is based on the observation that capitalism tends to turn all aspects of life into a tradable commodity. Put otherwise, commodification is the process of giving economic value to something not usually considered in economic terms. This essentially sees privacy erosion as exploitation because it entails converting personal information into money.

The online truism that 'If you're not paying for something, you're not the customer; you're the product being sold' has early roots going back to the 1970s. In *Communications: Blindspot of Western Marxism*, Dallas Smythe (1977) suggested that critical scholars of media should focus on the economic dimensions of media industries in capitalism, and recognise that audiences are the main commodity manufactured by these industries. Smythe's work generated the phrase 'audience as commodity' to refer to the generation and circulation of information about audiences as a means of generating revenue. Whereas historically media studies has typically analysed the content of what the media industry produce, Smythe drew attention to the ways by which audiences and attention time is traded by media companies in exchange for advertising revenue. This leads Smythe to argue that the principal product of the media industry is not content, but audiences that translate to income and profit. Seen this way, content (such as television shows, newspapers, social media and search engines) is a means of baiting consumers so to expose them to advertising. With behavioural and programmatic advertising the audience as commodity is truly realised. This is because the *recursive* nature of digital systems expands the commodification process in that companies may package users in a variety of means depending on the needs of prospective purchaser. What is more, with programmatic techniques, this happens in real time. This means that whereas non-digital media audience research companies had to conduct surveys with samples of an audience to understand their make-up and interests, digital media gives immediate feedback to publishers and third-party advertisers so our interests, locations and habits can be acted upon in the time it takes to click to another page and for our screens to refresh.

Underpinning this is a more general argument about the commodification of people by the media industry. Inspired by Marx, Christian Fuchs has explored critical approaches to media and capitalism in great depth. Echoing the arguments of Smythe, he argues that our use of social media is a form of work, or labour, because ultimately it generates value for others. For Fuchs (2016), this is digital labour because our attention and online activities on social networking platforms creates data that is sold as a commodity to advertisers. The connection between clicking webpages and labour is still questionable, although if labour is to be defined as the production of value for others, then so be it.[8] What is clear, however, is that both basic and more nuanced facts about our basic existence, movements, behavioural patterns and our location on both the internet and in physical environments are traced, registered, analysed and used to generate insights to target advertising. More generally, beyond social networks, Fuchs is right in that every time we go online we are generating data and insights for others. The extent to which we are aware of this and consent to these processes is dubious.

Arguably a more useful term than labour is the critical notion of *data alienation*. I have dealt with this elsewhere (see Chapter 10 of McStay, 2014), but in general alienation is a more exact fit to diagnose how our actions become 'congealed' and used as a means of selling ourselves to ourselves. It involves taking something we have contributed to producing (such as data) and using this against us for the interests of others (such as personally targeted ads to sell us things we do not need). The translators' notes in Marx and Engels' (2011 [1844]) *Economic and Philosophic Manuscripts of 1844* highlight that the word 'alienate' has roots in the sense of loss of something that remains in existence, of making external to oneself and to be estranged from. This reflects online activities well in that connected life involves ongoing externalisation and registration of interests, preferences, life moments, emotional states, location, purchases and communication with others. The notion of alienation is also useful in that it reflects the sense of a lack of control and that the world is not our own, but rather someone else's system. To this end we accept situations in connected life that we would not usually. For example, if we walked into a store, picked an item up, put it back and left the store, we would be surprised, spooked and irked if a shop assistant followed us around the town trying to sell us that product. This is what happens with re-targeting, a form of behavioural advertising.

SQUARING AUDIENCE-AS-COMMODITY IDEAS WITH PROPERTY-BASED VIEWS OF PRIVACY

Critical scholars of a Marxist disposition have a difficult relationship with privacy because privacy tends to be connected with property and ownership (where X is mine, and Y is yours). In other words, it sees an interest in privacy as a self-interested one. For those with a penchant for Marx, property entails accumulation and, as a result, social separation and division. Liberal citizenship for Marx is to be self-confined to private interests and caprice, and to be separated from the possibility of real community because property generates self-interest rather than public contributions (McStay, 2014). Liberal ideals for Marxists represent a philosophy of individualism, separation and ultimately inequality that undermine the possibility of emancipation, which can broadly be taken to mean economic and political equality. Marx's argument is that real freedom is found in collectives and more positive relations with others. This entails common rather than private ownership.

There is an argument to be made here because seeing privacy as property is expressed in a range of liberal writing that says privacy ultimately derives from property rights. Judith DeCew (1997), for example (drawing on Thomas Scanlon, Jeffrey Reiman and William Parent), makes this argument saying that property rights are a much older set of established rights in liberal societies. Privacy is simply a late second-order expression of this. This line of thinking can lead one into a market-based conception of privacy whereby we treat it as a stock that can be traded or exchanged. There is an attractive simplicity to thinking of privacy this way, particularly when we are discussing media content whereby we exchange data for content (notwithstanding flawed consent mechanisms discussed above). However, to test whether a property-based view of privacy works, we should ask: does property adequately cover all privacy matters and outcomes? Further, do we even own our behaviour and electronic traces? Indeed, does it make any sense to say that we own ourselves? While it may be correct to say that others do not own us, is it not absurd to define ourselves in terms of ownership? Thus, when we consider our thoughts, pin numbers, birth dates, website visits or past illnesses, does it make sense to say that we own these? Also, if ownership of property comes about through gain, theft, exchange, finding, making, purchasing or receiving bestowments, does it make sense to think of our birthdays, being gay, or that I was in Starbucks last Friday as property? There is perhaps more to privacy than a market-based analysis of stocks and trade suggests.

MARX: NO FRIEND OF PRIVACY

However, beyond property-based critiques of privacy, Marxists have another problem with privacy. As established in Chapter 2, privacy connects with ideas about respect for selfhood, autonomy and personal control. These are individualist rather than collectivist. Indeed, as discussed in McStay (2014), Marx (2012 [1844]) was scornful of the idea that rights could be useful in establishing a political community seeing 'human rights' as accentuating an individual's egoistic preoccupations. This is a step further than property-based criticism. It also asks questions of the entire media studies enterprise that is deeply influenced by cultural studies, which in turn is informed by Marxist politics. The problem is this: what value does privacy have when there is no need for rights because the interests of the collective are bound together? Marx's vision was a society of free individuals where the interests of individuals and the collective are the same. In theory this is good, but we should ask whether dissent, difference and freedom to develop ideas that run counter to the collective aim are acceptable.

Thankfully Fuchs, a leading Marx-inspired media critic, takes a more sensible line and points out that it would 'be a mistake if we were to fully cancel privacy rights and dismiss them as bourgeois values' (2012: 140). Although Fuchs continues to connect privacy with property, he highlights what he sees as a larger crime than personal self-interest: this is corporate and state surveillance for the purpose of capital accumulation. In developing this, he tries to develop a socialist account of privacy. This is uncomplicated and 'aims at strengthening the protection of consumers and citizens from corporate surveillance and other forms of domination' (ibid.: 141). This connects privacy with ideas of struggle, class, resistance, wealth, power, hierarchy and economic differentiation. In tangible terms, for Fuchs, on social media, this means that Facebook should tell their users what data the platform stores about them and they should be protected from exploitation of that data.

CONCLUSION

The aim of this chapter has been to provide understanding about the most important revenue model for the internet: advertising that targets us by our online behaviour. Although I suspect all readers of this book will already appreciate that 'if you're not paying, you're the product', this chapter has accounted for the technical, industrial, legal and critical detail behind this online truism. This has been a complex chapter that has required the reader to get to grips with the mechanics of cookies, tracking, online identity, muddled laws that guide consent and data processing, and critical media theory about the significance of these.

The difficulty today is that while consent is perfectly rational in that someone should ask before taking something from us and explain what is to be taken, many scholars have identified this as problematic (Acquisti and Grossklags, 2006). There are multiple reasons for this; not least, how are people to know what happens to personal data? How are they able to know with whom it might be shared/traded? How might they guess the life cycle of their data? How are they to know its value? There is then the question of the time we have available to make such decisions, our ability to comprehend legal notices and our media habits (I imagine most of us quickly click things away to get to the content we want). In sum, is consent meaningful? As it stands, the answer seems not. It remains to be seen how in Europe this will develop in light of new legislation. On behavioural advertising, identity, commodification and critical media theory, this tends to be discussed in relation to Marx-inspired thinking about labour and generation of value for others (the 'audience-as-commodity'). Here I argued that data alienation may be a more useful explanatory term, perhaps foremost because it entails the feeling of being out of control and that the world is not our own, but rather someone else's system. The chapter concluded by examining Marx in relation to privacy. This is not an easy relationship given Marx's dislike of human rights although, as explained, more recent invocation of Marxist criticisms of advertising have rejected the notion that privacy rights are simply bourgeois values to express property ownership.

Research and challenges

1   Install one or more of the suggested apps to appreciate the scale of the tracking economy.

2   Inspect your own cookie folder: do an online search and find out who placed them and what data is being gathered. Understand in practical as well as theoretical terms how this works.

3   By means of this chapter and data protection regulations, assess whether unambiguous consent is opt-out consent. What are the consequences for the advertising industry and privacy?

4   To what extent do you agree/disagree that the principal output of the media industry turns out not to be content and services, but audience attention time?

NOTES

1   Google's revenue from advertising for the third quarter of 2015 was $18.7 billion and Facebook's revenue for the second quarter of 2015 was $4.042 billion. Note: US companies file quarterly reports detailing their performance. This means these figures represent three months of trading.

2   Complete individual histories can be downloaded from https://support.google.com/websearch/answer/6068625?hl=en.

3   At the following link to Adobe's analytics page, scroll down to 'What type of information is collected when a company uses Adobe's analytics and on-site personalization services?' at www.adobe.com/privacy/analytics.html?f=2o7.

4   Established by viewing the source code of the webpage.

5   Details available from www.imdb.com/title/tt2084953/?ref_=nm_ov_bio_lk2.

6   This is informed by close following of the legislation as it developed, examination of the final May draft of GDPR, discussion with the Internet Advertising Bureau (IAB), and attendance of workshops on GDPR with European Commission data protection regulators and representatives of the UK's Information Commissioner's Office.

7   This is in Article 6 of GDPR and carries over from Article 7(f) of the Data Protection Directive whereby processing of personal data must be necessary for the purposes of the 'legitimate interests' pursued by the controller or by the third party to whom the data are disclosed, except where these interests are outweighed by the interests or fundamental rights and freedoms of the data subject.

8   Other accounts of media and labour acknowledge this. Kücklich (2005), for example, introduces 'Playbour' in relating gaming, modding, leisure activity and play that equates to unpaid labour.

8
THE RIGHT TO BE FORGOTTEN
MEMORY, DELETION AND EXPRESSION

Key questions

- What is the right to be forgotten?
- What is the significance of the legal case, particularly for people who cannot afford lawyers?
- Why does the right to be forgotten jar with Google's corporate philosophy?
- To what extent is online media a-historical?

Key concepts

- Consent
- Collective memory
- Forced openness
- A-historical tendencies

In a May 2014 ruling, *Google Spain v AEPD and Mario Costeja González*, the Court of Justice of the European Union found that individuals should have the right to ask search engines to remove certain results about them. The ruling applies to all search engines but given Google's dominance of the business (which hovers around 90 per cent), this chapter focuses on Google.

The capacity to have content de-listed from search engines has emerged because search technologies that crawl and sift data from the web means that personal information that might have naturally faded into the background in previous decades ends up hanging around longer than it otherwise would. Compare search engines with newspapers and television: although press clippings could be kept and television programmes recorded, interest in stories tends to disappear unless the salacious topic is reported about again. Today stories are less easily obliterated from social memory, which begs the question: should people have a 'right to be forgotten' or what is otherwise known as 'right to erasure'? Underpinning this are questions about memory, time and temporality, privacy, expression, corporate ownership, power and who decides what should be publicly known.

LEGAL CONTEXT

The background to the court ruling is (once more) the Data Protection Directive and the forthcoming General Data Protection Regulations (GDPR) that will replace the Data Protection Directive in 2018. Both of these reflect an interest in protecting personal data rights as established in Article 8 of the Charter of Fundamental Rights of the EU. Without going into excessive detail, the key article of GDPR is Article 17 which is titled 'Right to be forgotten and to erasure'.[1] In summary, it says that if a controller (an organisation that deals with personal data) has no reason to further process personal data, or the data processed is in breach of the Regulation, the data subject (the person who the data is about) is entitled to have the data deleted. This is a very pro-privacy stance geared towards arming people with rights to have data deleted about them. Reflecting the fact that search engines and the web provide greater permanence of one's past, it grants people greater rights over erasure of personal data relating to them and the abstention from further dissemination of such data.

As we have seen in this book multiple times, privacy rights are not absolute but they are subject to competing rights – in this case, freedom of expression. We discussed this distinction in Chapter 3, but in the forthcoming Regulations it finds expression in Article 17(3) that protects the processing of personal data for journalistic, artistic or literary purposes. It says that: 'The controller shall carry out the erasure without delay, except to the extent that the retention of the personal data is necessary… for exercising the right of freedom of expression in accordance with Article 80'. Article 80 of the General Data Protection Regulations (that Article 17 refers to) is titled 'Processing of personal data and freedom of expression'. With my emphasis it says that:

> 1. *Member States shall provide for exemptions or derogations from the provisions on the general principles* in Chapter II, the rights of the data subject in Chapter III, on controller and processor in Chapter IV, on the transfer of personal data to third countries and international organisations in Chapter V, the independent supervisory authorities in Chapter VI and on co-operation and consistency in Chapter VII for the processing of personal data carried out solely *for journalistic purposes or the purpose of artistic or literary expression in order to reconcile the right to the protection of personal data with the rules governing freedom of expression.*

This regulatory background sets the context for the ground-breaking legal case that resulted in Google (and other search engines) being required to remove links. The overall result is that if stories are deemed to be inaccurate, irrelevant or excessive, Google and other search engines must remove data from past results if requested to do so by a member of the public. Importantly however, it is only the search engine that has to comply. The news outlet to which the search engine linked is not required to take the news item down. This means that those who know where to find the information can still access the news item, or they could search the website of a given news outlet. Although the removal of links may not seem especially significant, when we consider that regular people without access to expensive lawyers are now able to have a strong say over how their private past is presented to the public world, we begin to appreciate the significance of the ruling.

THE CASE AND THE COURT OF JUSTICE RULING

The full title of the 'right to be forgotten' case is *Google Spain SL, Google Inc. v Agencia Española de Protección de Datos, Mario Costeja González*. González's dispute began in 2009, when he found that when he searched his name on Google the results listed legal notices from 1998 when *La Vanguardia*, a Spanish newspaper, published two announcements about the forced sale of properties arising from debt. One of these was his repossessed home. The announcements were subsequently posted online as the newspaper digitised its library. This pointed to a period of insolvency and the fact that he had his property seized. Eleven years later in 2009, González contacted the newspaper to complain that when his name was entered into Google's search engine, it showed the announcement containing personal information. He requested that the newspaper either remove or alter the story to remove personal information; and that Google also remove personal data so that it no longer appeared in the search results. González argued that any reference to these events were irrelevant and damaging. In 2010 the Spanish data-protection authority agreed that Google should remove the link, although it disagreed that the newspaper should be forced to change or remove the story. Both Google Spain and its parent, Google Inc., brought legal cases against the Spanish data-protection authority. The Spanish court referred the case to the Court of Justice of the European Union and asked:

1 Whether the EU's 1995 Data Protection Directive applied to search engines such as Google's;
2 Whether EU law (the Directive) applied to Google Spain, given that the company's data-processing server was in the United States;
3 And whether an individual has the right to request that his or her personal data be removed from accessibility via a search engine (the 'right to be forgotten').

On 13 May 2014, the Court of Justice of the European Union ruled that internet search engines must remove information deemed inaccurate, inadequate, irrelevant or excessive for the purposes of data processing, thus upholding a right of erasure and to be forgotten. This is because although the physical processing of a person's information may take place outside of the EU, the fact they are doing business and selling advertising in Europe means they must abide by EU rules. This is an important ruling as it sent a signal saying that no matter where data is processed, if a company is operating in Europe it must abide by European rules. Further, as 'data controllers', this means they have a responsibility to abide by EU data-protection laws. This means that the 'right to be forgotten' principle applies. In the ruling itself, the court highlighted that the right to be forgotten is not absolute but will always need to be balanced against other fundamental rights, such as freedom of expression and the media. Centrally, the court stipulated that search engines operating in Europe must find a balance between offering information in the public interest, and protecting people's personal data and rights to privacy. When an agreement cannot be reached, the ruling said the matter should be brought before a local judge or regulator (which in practice is each country's data regulator).

The consequence of the ruling is that an internet search engine must consider requests from individuals to remove links to freely accessible webpages resulting from a search on their name. This goes against the grain of Google whose stated intention since 1999 has been 'to organize the world's information and make it universally accessible and useful'.[2] To get a full sense of this aim it is illustrative to have a look at Google's corporate philosophy page[3] that promotes the value of collecting more information of all types (and archiving news) for people seeking answers. Indeed, until relatively recently, Google placed great stock on being the company that could archive, preserve and index all of the knowledge in the world. Although Google's efforts have moved from archiving to exploration and experimentation with mobile, the Internet of Things, vehicles and the capacities of AI, the idea that archived information might be deleted still goes deeply against the corporate ethos.

IMPLEMENTATION

Whether we like it or not, Google, a corporation, is now a default means of searching for information. Indeed, 'to Google' is even a transitive verb appearing in multiple dictionaries. This means that in regard to the question of whether it is proper to have 'a right to be forgotten', for many practical purposes Google now acts alone as the judge of what is and what is not available. In one sense Google would prefer that this is not the case and that they do not have to de-list content, but the outcome of both the decision of the European Court of Justice and Google's implementation of the ruling is that to a real degree Google decides what is removed from society's collective memory. This assertion comes with a large caveat in that links are removed from Google, not the web itself. In most cases the original story will still exist on the host publisher's site meaning that, for example, newspapers can publish information but search engines cannot link to it.

Of all the search engines, Google publicly respected the court ruling and complied quickly. On implementing the court ruling, Google said that they would assess each individual request and attempt to balance the privacy rights of the individual with the public's right to know and distribute information. As of 13 November 2015, the total number of URLs that Google has evaluated for removal was 1,214,061 and the total requests Google had received was 342,378. They removed 42 per cent of the URLs. Again, it is important to recognise that by removing a link from Google's search results, this does not remove the link from the web, but only the search results of a Google search. For up-to-date statistics visit 'Google Transparency Report' – 'Requests to remove content'.[4] The application to have links de-listed begins by aggrieved individuals filling out a web form. Properly titled 'Search removal request under data protection law in Europe',[5] this asks for personal details, links and provides opportunity for 1,000 characters (including spaces) for the applicant to explain why they want content de-listed. Although in theory Google might use automated decision-making processes, one or more people from Google manually assess applications. When decisions are made, they do not share details about requests with web masters, but simply tell them their link has been de-listed. Factors in the decision-making include whether the results contain outdated information about a person, as well as whether there is a public interest in the information. Examples given were information about financial scams, professional malpractice, criminal convictions or public conduct of government officials.

PUBLISHER PERSPECTIVES: GOOGLE AND 'IMPARTING' INFORMATION

Although requests for de-listing of Facebook posts outweigh any other publisher,[6] news publishers have taken a keen interest in right to be forgotten matters. As the public defenders of what is in the public interest and freedom of expression, this is as it should be. On discussions about the court ruling (and journalism in general), news publishers draw attention to Article 10 of the European Convention on Human Rights, that states:

> Everyone has the right to freedom of expression. This right shall include freedom to hold opinions and to receive and impart information and ideas without interference by public authority and regardless of frontiers.[7]

This is an important point because, as we saw in Chapter 3, freedom of expression is vital for democracies to function. Although we may not like what others express, diversity of opinion and controversial ideas help to inform social and political debate. The key word that has application to this chapter's discussion is the capacity to 'receive and *impart* information'. Although Google is not defined as a media company (they are legally and technically defined as a data controller), their role as a platform and news conduit arguably makes them responsible in part for enforcing these rights to impart information.

Publishers have also complained that although Google informs them that a link has been de-listed, they do not know the search terms de-listed, or detail of the complaints. Perhaps foremost, they are most upset about not having scope to challenge the decision, offer arguments why they should remain, or add context and provide evidence on why the link should stay. This is the principal argument from news publishers in that Google are making decisions about what to de-list with only scant evidence. Greater engagement with the publisher would allow them to give detail about the reporting and further evidence about the cases. They call for more transparency over de-listing methods and decisions because Google has a great deal of power over what people are exposed to and the ways by which a publisher's content is seen. Although the Google platform does not create or report news, it is increasingly a primary channel for news. This means it raises concerns in relation to what is in the public interest. The situation is looking increasingly worse for publishers because the new General Data Protection Regulation, that in broader terms better protects the privacy of European citizens, suggests that publishers should not even know they have been de-listed. The problem with this is less about the case of people who have valid reasons for wanting information removed from Google than people who abuse this opportunity for removal from living memory on issues that have nothing to do with privacy protection (whether this be celebrities, politicians or relatively unknown people guilty of a misdeed). Although Google may work hard to stop this happening, the net effect is an asymmetry of knowledge whereby the publisher has no idea they have been de-listed.

PRIVATE INTERESTS

The rules about what can be de-listed are tipped towards everyday individuals rather than people who play a role in public life.[8] This has helped allay concern that the ruling could have a negative impact on the public's right to know relevant information about those who have influence over their lives and society. On why people want links removed, there are a wide variety of motives. Some are very reasonable and others not as ethical. High-ranking public officials, for example, do not want old criminal convictions haunting them; business people do not want Google to show articles about their lawsuits against the press; priests do not want material about their child sex abuses online; people convicted of business fraud and financial crimes do not want this information to be accessible; media professionals have asked for embarrassing content to be de-listed; others have requested removal of links to articles that referenced dismissal for sexual crimes committed on the job; and a welfare claimant asked for links to be removed showing that he abused the system. All the above are real cases that Google refused to comply with.

Conversely, an activist was stabbed at a protest and asked to have content de-listed (presumably because of trauma); a teacher had coverage of a minor conviction ten years ago deleted; a crime victim had a link removed with her name in; a woman had a result showing her home address removed; another woman whose husband was murdered had a page containing her name removed; a rape victim had a page containing their name removed. Some of the cases are less binary in that they are not simply 'keep' or 'de-list'. For example, a UK doctor requested removal of more than 50 links to newspaper articles about bungled procedures. Google says that on this occasion, three pages that contained personal information about the doctor, but did not mention the procedure, have been removed from search results for his name. The rest of the links to reports on the incident remain in search results.[9]

The crime issue is an important one. Another case that Google responded to was a news summary of a local magistrate's decisions that included the man's guilty verdict. Google deemed that under the UK Rehabilitation of Offenders Act, this conviction has been spent, so removed the page from search results for his name. Unlock, for example, a charity that provides advocacy for people dealing with the ongoing effects of criminal convictions, highlights that there are over 10.5 million people in the UK with a criminal record. Given that in 2013 the UK population was 64.1 million, this is an eyebrow-raising figure. Most offenders put their mistakes behind them and live law-abiding lives, but Unlock argue that discrimination can be suffered even many years after the offences for which they have already served their sentences in full. This is particularly pertinent in employment. This raises a mild conundrum in that it would be preferable that society could recognise and accept that many people have a record of mild infractions. If this fact were more open, then it is possible that discrimination would lessen. Conversely, as Unlock point out, to reach this point means that many people have to undergo discrimination.

FORCED OPENNESS

This issue has arisen in privacy studies. Richard Posner, a privacy and law scholar details this problem. He controversially argues that allowing people privacy is *not* defensible because people use privacy to conceal and selectively disclose information. Whereas academics that study privacy mostly agree that privacy is positive overall and has to do with autonomy, control over self-presentation, and the management and sharing of information, Posner takes privacy to task for precisely this reason. For Posner privacy is very much connected to the negative ideas of withholding and concealing, particularly in regard to personal uses of information. He argues that by attempting to manipulate the flow of information, this is tantamount to a wish to control others' perceptions. He says: 'It is no answer that people have "the right to be let alone," for few people want to be let alone. Rather, they want to manipulate the world around them by selective disclosure of facts about themselves' (1983: 234).

Posner's point is that if we want the world to be better and more accepting, we should tend towards openness and removal of barriers that impede the flow of information. His examples include full disclosure of early dealings with the law, but also sexuality and minor mental illnesses. Although these might cause irrational reactions by employers, Posner argues that it is wrong to withhold such information from public view. He argues that if informational transparency were the norm, in time irrational prejudices would be removed from society. When we consider the earlier statistic that 10.5 million of the UK's 64.1 million have a criminal record, one can see his point. There is an appeal to this argument. After all, who would not want to reduce prejudice? The problem is that this requires *forced openness*. This would create social risks for stigmatised groups and, essentially, calls for risk and a significant sacrifice by them to enlighten the rest of us. Further, although openness can generally be said to be a good principle, it is not clear what practical net positive results would be gained by forced openness.

Real world cases have a habit of complicating philosophical principles such as transparency and openness. Consider the following case study about a woman called Sonia. This was presented by Chris Stacey, co-director of Unlock, at a conference I attended in 2015, although it is also available on Unlock's website.[10]

> 8 years ago I was convicted of Arson. I set fire to my own home as part of being in an abusive relationship.
>
> As a result of having a very understanding boss, I had kept my job and just wanted to move on and concentrate on my career so I completed a degree. A fantastic job opportunity came up and I applied. I was totally honest and disclosed my conviction as I knew it was going to show up on my DBS which they requested. I was delighted to get the job and knew my life was now going in the right direction again and I was never going to look back.
>
> In the meantime I had met a 'nice' man and we married. The relationship seemed to be going well, but I eventually found out he was leading a double life. I told him to leave and I moved back in with my parents. I filed for divorce as I felt I couldn't ever trust this man again and that is when my life came crashing down again.
>
> He suddenly decided that he wanted revenge and told my employer that they were employing a very dangerous person who was a risk to others because of my conviction. He had also printed off the newspaper article he had found on Google about me and said he was going to post it around the city so everyone could read it and destroy me. His attacks on me were malicious and it was terrifying not knowing what this man could do and the

lengths that he would go to. I was advised by my solicitor and my employer to file for a Harassment Order and inform the Police of his allegations and intentions. My employer could see what this man was trying to do to me and supported me wholeheartedly. Despite having a spent conviction, that terrible newspaper article was being used against me again. It just wasn't fair and I felt that enough was enough. I had to fight to get the past 'put to bed'.

She made a request through Google's web form to have the links removed. Google agreed. She used this success to contact the newspaper directly and they also agreed to remove the story from their website. Also note that beyond questions of morality, by law in the UK, if a person has served the punishment for their crime, it is considered 'spent'. One implication of this is that if an employer finds out about the conviction, they are legally obliged to ignore it. Also, on recruitment, employers are legally required to not take into account convictions spent (unless for jobs considered exempt).

CONFLICTING RIGHTS: TOWARDS A PRAGMATIC VIEW OF PRIVACY

Critics of the European Court ruling argued that it impacts on freedom of speech, while on the other side privacy supporters highlighted that this is a win for individuals who are now able to request that unwanted content is removed. The right to be forgotten debate is divergent in character. By this I mean that whereas convergent problems have *a* solution, divergent problems have multiple solutions in that there is no single correct answer. Usually we have principles and ethics to express values that guide us towards an answer to a given problem. When there are competing answers tending towards different ethical directions, we are forced towards a more pragmatic approach. By 'pragmatic' I mean it both in the general sense of 'being sensible and realistic' but more importantly here, the philosophical sense of downplaying once-and-for-always ethics in favour of understanding the situation at hand, context and the specifics of a problem. As depicted in McStay (2014), Kegan (1992) uses the example of the decision to save someone drowning in a river. While this is the good thing to do, what if we have to steal a boat to do this? Philosophically we have two competing ethics in play (saving a life versus stealing), although one assumes that if the situation arose, most people would be able to assess the context of the situation and come to a humane decision. One might say this is easy in that we should always choose life over objects. We can complicate the moral question by changing the drowning human for a sinking bag of kittens, a leaking barrel of oil or a chocolate wrapper. The point is that moral decisions are not always clear and conflicting moral dimensions come into play during a decision. This is especially so with the question of whether we have a right to have control over how others see and perceive us (which means both to be forgotten

111

and to manage one's reputation), or whether our past should be transparent for all to see. Absolutes and principles are easily defended in theory, but day-to-day circumstances have a habit of providing situations that upset clear-cut philosophical axioms. Although Google could do more to keep publishers in the loop with what is happening with links to their stories, Google's case-by-case approach (as dictated by the court ruling) is the only sensible outcome so to balance sensitivity to a person's private life with the public's interest in information. Greater engagement with publishers would help, however, particularly when there is need for greater contextual information about a case.

IMPLICATIONS FOR UNDERSTANDING PRIVACY

As with much discussion in this book, the ways in which we regulate, manage and understand privacy is deeply affected by the development of new technologies. The connection between media, technology and privacy is found in the earliest modern writing on privacy. As discussed in Chapter 3, Warren and Brandeis (1984 [1890]) argued that new technologies employed to gather, process and disseminate news raise questions about privacy violations. Today we are right to ask the same questions because search engines (especially Google's because of its ubiquity), and their capacity to crawl and organise news and information residing on countless servers around the world, means that what has happened to us in the past, and what we have done, is more recallable than ever.

Whereas Warren and Brandeis decried how what happened in private could be broadcast to the world via photography, modern technology means we are less likely to forget. This provides modern life with *a-historical* tendencies. By this I mean that whereas news usually fades as time passes, the quest to archive the world's knowledge in principle removes the quality of disappearance through history. This is slightly odd because the recent direction of news has been towards evaporation of interest. Journalists, for example, typically work to news cycles (24 hours in the case of newspapers), hence the phrase 'yesterday's news'. As media technologies and content developed (such as television and thereafter rolling 24/7 continuous news), this sped up temporal rhythms, the news production process, and created ongoing need for new stories and more stimulating content. As a consequence news items became more forgettable, particularly small stories about unknown individuals. What search and internet technologies do is create a situation of instant recall for those with an interest in a niche area of news coverage (such as about me or you). This is a basic fact of life lived with digitally networked media, but from a theoretical point of view it is one worth noting, because news has always had a strong temporal character to it. To a real extent online life nullifies this because stories of today, yesterday and five years are equally recallable, meaning that recourse to the right to be forgotten is a valuable privacy success.

CONCLUSION

The right to be forgotten is at once an ethical, philosophical and legal assertion. As this chapter has detailed, it is also a principle that is subject to the gravity of other principles – most notably freedoms of speech and expression. The bombastic nature of the expression 'right to be forgotten' also hides an inaccuracy in that data remains accessible for people who really want to find information, but it is no longer ubiquitous or available to the casual search-engine user. The aim of this chapter has been to provide a sense of the legal dimensions that sit behind deletion, forgetting and digital memory. Those with a background in law reading this book because of an interest in privacy and media may be acquainted with the case details. Media students and scholars more used to theory, philosophy and social science may find the minutiae dry. This is reasonable, but this should not distract from the fact this legal detail shapes the nature of privacy and dictates the functioning of the world's most powerful companies.

The clash of principles at stake here are a pro-privacy viewpoint that arms people with rights to delete data, and protection of expression. Legally speaking, this applies to personal data for journalistic, artistic or literary purposes, but we have concentrated on the former. This was brought into sharp relief with the case of *Google Spain SL, Google Inc. v Agencia Española de Protección de Datos, Mario Costeja González*. Here we had an individual who had undergone insolvency and difficult times. Pre-search engines, his history would have been left in the past but the nature of our modern media environment lends towards recall of situations that occurred years and even decades ago with the same ease as that which occurred yesterday. Indeed, the mechanics of search engines means that what is recent needs not be at the top of the results. The result of the ruling by the Court of Justice of the European Union in 2014 is that internet search engines (most notably Google) must consider requests from individuals to remove links to freely accessible webpages resulting from a search of their name. Google have responded well to this, although publishers maintain that they should have greater input into the decision-making process that largely lies in the hands of individual companies (if applications are rejected, the complainant can turn to the member state's data-protection authority). A key argument is that the ruling impedes Article 10 of the European Convention on Human Rights that promotes the capacity to impart information without interference.

We also considered practical examples of people who have to live with a media environment that does not forget. Unlock, the charity that provides advocacy for people dealing with the ongoing effects of criminal convictions, have many case examples where discrimination can be suffered years after the conviction has been spent. In the UK, this is illegal. This raises philosophical questions of not just expression and privacy, but visibility and the possibility of forced openness. Although theory and philosophy are useful to characterise and diagnose conflicting principles, they are best solved by pragmatism. By this I mean the school of thought that asks we understand in detail the specifics of competing rights, context, stakes, harms and potential outcomes.

Research and challenges

1 Read Article 17 of the GDPR in full (it's less than a page) and discuss the ways in which the right to be forgotten clashes with freedom of expression.

2 To what extent do you agree/disagree with the principle of forced openness?

3 To what extent is morality a pragmatic matter?

NOTES

1 Full text of Article 17 (Right to erasure) at page 43 of the General Data Protection Regulation (use a key word search of 'Article 17'): http://eur-lex.europa.eu/legal-content/EN/TXT/HTML/?uri=CELEX:52012PC0011&from=en.

2 See Google's 'about Google' page at www.google.co.uk/about/company/.

3 Available from www.google.co.uk/about/company/philosophy/.

4 Available at www.google.com/transparencyreport/removals/europeprivacy/.

5 Available at https://support.google.com/legal/contact/lr_eudpa?product=web search#.

6 See section 'Sites that are most impacted' at www.google.com/transparency report/removals/europeprivacy/.

7 See page 11 of European Convention on Human Rights available from www.echr.coe.int/Documents/Convention_ENG.pdf.

8 The Article 29 Data Protection Working Party, which oversees the directive and other data protection issues, published a set of 13 criteria for search engines to make their decisions by. The principle behind these is that they uphold the right for individuals to have their privacy respected, but come down heavily in favour of keeping links that are related to people who 'play a role in public life'. Principles are available from http://ec.europa.eu/justice/data-protection/article-29/documentation/opinion-recommendation/files/2014/wp225_en.pdf.

9 Available at www.google.com/transparencyreport/removals/europeprivacy/.

10 Available from www.unlock.org.uk/unlock-speak-at-ico-policy-conference-the-google-effect-criminal-records-and-the-right-to-be-forgotten/.

9

BIG DATA
MACHINE LEARNING AND THE POLITICS OF ALGORITHMS

Key questions

- Why is 'big data' different from large amounts of data?
- What is the significance of Internet Protocol version 6 (IPv6)?
- What does it mean for algorithms to have politics?
- To what extent do labour metaphors developed in Chapter 7 apply to supervised machine learning?

Key concepts

- Big data
- Machine learning
- Black box
- Algorithmic discrimination

Through personal media and technology, we generate a large amount of information about ourselves and we are doing this at an exponentially increasing rate. Consider, for example, that 90 per cent of the data currently in the world was created in the last two years (House of Commons Science and Technology Committee, 2016). Each time we use a networked device, watch television online, visit an institution of some sort, pay for goods or are admitted to hospital, we are generating data. This is our *digital footprint*, or the traces we generate as we interact with our increasingly networked digital environment. The profusion of data coming from tracked behaviour, devices and sensors has led to what has been dubbed 'big data' although, as we will see, this notion does not simply refer to large amounts of data. The level of detail in big data applications can be astonishing. For a media example, consider Netflix. I assume that it is fairly well known that they recommend films based on analysis of customers' previous interactions. It goes further than this though as data informs the commissioning process (such as *House of Cards*), narrative development (*Game of Thrones*) and the design of covers for DVDs and Netflix itself (reactions to colour schemes).[1] When one considers that Netflix users collectively watch two billion hours of programming each month, one can see the interest in finding patterns and insights to progress the Netflix enterprise.

This chapter focuses on the human aspect of big data by considering what the exponential increase in data collection and analysis means for privacy. Some of the outcomes are immediately obvious in that a desire for more data invites potentially invasive practices, such as in the case of behavioural and programmatic advertising we explored earlier. However, there are also benefits, perhaps foremost in health and medical research (and good television!). Other factors of the debate are less obvious and require a bit more thought. These include the implications of how machines make decisions and predictions from data. To explore all of these matters this chapter first outlines the nature of big data techniques and the ways in which machines learn from data. I then progress to consider privacy and policy implications of big data. Finally, we shall consider the proposition that algorithms hidden from view in 'black boxes' are political and may even negatively discriminate. By this I mean that their decisions may be significantly influenced by all-too-human human cultural biases. As we will see, the consequences of this are significant.

BIG DATA

Although the epithet 'information society' tends to be associated with the 1960s and the rise of data warehousing in the 1980s, it was in the late 1800s and early 1900s, mainly in the USA and Europe, that we saw the rise of interest in how data can be leveraged to create new commercial opportunities. It was in this period that media, advertisers and brands professionally recognised that consumers are not a single audience, but multiple groups with different outlooks and interests. Dedicated firms were avaricious for data from consumers and audiences to understand what people thought about their products. The significant factor is the principle of *feedback*. Need for this continues today, not least through the non-stop requests for reviews and information about what we think of services, visits and merchandise.

To understand the origins of feedback practices, consider techniques employed by the Audit Bureau of Circulation (ABC) that was formed in 1914. Set up by the Association of National Advertisers in the US and still an industry leader today, they ensure that when advertisers spend money on advertising in newspapers, they actually reach the promised audiences. In the early twentieth century they employed a battery of market research tools to get feedback from people, such as house-to-house calls, attitudinal and opinion surveys, retail sales, audience monitoring, statistical-sample surveys, testing effectiveness of ads, assessing in-store retail trends, and other approaches to identifying audiences and recording feedback (McStay, 2011). These methods became more popular within the early data industry and led James Beniger (1986) to say that the transformation from industrial to information society was essentially completed by the late 1930s. This insight tells us that commercial obsession with data far precedes the rise of computers and digital warehousing in market research. Further, while we tend to think of feedback loops in engineering and technological terms, the principle is broader as the market research industry collects data from people, this feeds into production of goods/ads/services, more data is collected about people's responses, this feeds into product development, and the loop begins again.

Although corporate interest in data is not especially new and the early data industry was dealing with sample sizes collected across whole nations (and relatively complex subgroups therein), this still does not qualify as 'big data'. This is because the term refers to something practically, technically and qualitatively different. Big data is best thought of *not* in terms of size, but a type of processing and the means by which information that has been collected can be searched, aggregated, correlated, cross-referenced and used to find unexpected relationships. These *analytics* can assist with everything from understanding the spread of disease to marketing by Amazon. In addition to finding relationships of value through *patterns* and *correlations*, big data is also based on analysis in *real time*. Indeed, the person who coined the term says that big data entails a large *volume* of data from a *variety* of sources used at extreme *velocity* (Laney, 2001).

The last point is perhaps the most important and forgotten element because this is the speed with which data can be processed so people can receive feedback that is meaningful in some way. Although certainly about scale and size, big data is perhaps better seen in terms of reactivity, especially when we remember that size is a very relative idea. On reactivity, advertising for example is increasingly relevant to time, place, interests and what we are doing at a particular moment. Similarly, online news outlets are increasingly using big data audience analytics to enable better understanding and targeting of readers with news as it becomes available. This includes knowing where people are reading (which cities/regions), what they are reading, the success of headlines in baiting readers and how far into stories they are reading. It also grants tracking of 'shares', segmentation of viewers into groups and understanding of the profiles of people reading. By means of this data news outlets can use the degree and type of attention to story to test theories about journalism, optimise headlines, personalise content, show editors how stories are performing online, track devices news is being consumed on, understand advertising on their sites, count social media mentions and interaction, and in general listen to the conversations taking place online and understand how their content is performing. All of this takes place in real time. This is possible because so much of our activity takes place through devices and technologies that are networked and connected to the internet. Beyond journalism and media, big data processing affects *all* sectors of life, including:

- *banking*, e.g. decisions about markets and customers, and new payment ecosystems;
- *communications*, e.g. understanding flow of content across new technology infrastructures and communication streams, who and what is connecting, decisions about product launches, opportunities for collaborations and alliances between brands;
- *consumers goods*, e.g. supply chains (weakness, vulnerabilities and strengths), marketing, social media as indicator of demand and opportunities;
- *energy*, e.g. extraction/distribution, supply risks, global pricing volatility and investment routes;
- *entertainment*, e.g. understanding audiences, movement of content, nature of attention and opportunities for cross-brand alliances;
- *healthcare*, e.g. questions about the nature of how care is delivered, patient data, clinician workflows and use of mobile health technologies;
- *insurance*, e.g. how risk is sensed and measured and how natural and human behaviour is understood;
- *manufacturing*, e.g. sourcing of supplies and raw materials, sensors, robots, and location of production facilities;
- *pharmaceuticals and life sciences*, e.g. manufacturing, population change, reacting to evidence and outcomes, and promotion of healthy lifestyles;
- *retail*, e.g. decisions about which markets to enter, cross-selling, responding to search, personalisation and creation of digital experiences;
- *technology*, e.g. software as a service, peer-to-peer, and the inception of Internet Protocol version 6 (IPv6) that will allow exponentially more IP addresses for new devices joining the internet. (PricewaterhouseCoopers, 2014)

The last point on IPv6 is not just a boring piece of technical information. 'Internet protocol' provides a means of identifying and locating devices connected to the internet (such as laptops and smartphones). Over recent years we have been running out of available addresses. As IPv6 norms are embedded into our existing internet that runs on IPv4, the scale and possibility increases. Whereas IPv4 allowed for around 4 billion addresses, IPv6 promises 340 trillion trillion trillion unique IP addresses for devices. At a practical level this matters because it allows an exponentially larger amount of devices to go online. This is not limited to familiar devices we use to access online content, but the potential networking of the smallest and largest objects derived from the most familiar and strange environments. For a better sense of the practices that IPv6 supports, this includes:

- *body and health management*, e.g. ranging from ingestible pill sensors, to activity tracking to monitoring of ageing family members;
- *the home*, e.g. connected ovens, fridges, lost keys, lighting, infrastructure (e.g. sensors on pipes);
- *the city*, e.g. sensors on street bins to indicate when they need emptying, traffic and pollution management, electricity grid management, street lighting and other civic services;
- *industry*, e.g. maintenance and repairing of hardware and machines, retailing and sensors in products and on shelves, in the fabric of buildings, in farming, in safety items (such as fire extinguishers) and in manufacturing;
- *the environment*, e.g. pollution, water management, wildlife (such as endangered species like bee populations), landslides and illegal practices (such as deforestation or slaughter of endangered species).

In sum, what IPv6 promises is *the connectivity and mediation of increasingly diverse aspects of human life, objects and environments* (the so-called Internet of Things, or IoT). There is no shortage of hype about IoT, but if eventually realised this will result in gigantic amounts of data that companies, governments and other organisations will be trying to make sense of. What this means is that big data is not just about lots of information coming from different places being acted upon in real time, but it has an epochal character in that automated data processing will increasingly play a role in shaping all dimensions of life. This understanding allows us to recognise the way in which computer and sensor-generated data is gradually assisting in policy and decision-making in business, health, social planning, government, academic research and more.

UNEXPECTED INSIGHTS: COLLECT IT ALL

Although there is no published agreed meaning on what the word 'insights' means among the business community, we can understand it as the generation of valuable thoughts, facts and analyses from data. These insights can affirm hunches, change assumptions or provide new unanticipated opportunities. With big data, this involves collection of seemingly irrelevant as well as predictably relevant information. This important point has not always been the case because historically data gatherers have sought to *reduce* the amount of information being collected and processed. The reason for this is that there were limited windows of opportunity to collect data (for example, one can only ask so many questions in a survey) and processing power was limited (it took people time to sort the incoming data and early computers were less capable of sifting data). Today's machines are not just employed to crunch numbers (or compute), and simply store large amounts of data, but with increasing degrees of awareness they may either make autonomous decisions, or provide people with insights so they can execute decisions. This typically entails financial decisions (such as credit and insurance), marketing

119

(who might be interested in X product) and surveillance (use of correlational profiling to judge likely targets), but the applications are wider.

This is increasingly achieved by *machine learning*, which is the capacity for computers to *adapt* as they encounter new data. Machine learning is a subcategory of artificial intelligence. The history of this goes back to the 1950s (for a digestible read about the history of artificial intelligence see Warwick, 2012). The key is that computers capable of machine learning do not have to be explicitly programmed, but can improve their algorithms by themselves, and 'see' and classify data from text, images, videos and other sources (Hinton, 2016). Machine learning can be used for all sorts of ends, such as fraud detection (banking), who may be in line to suffer a heart attack (health) or what books a certain type of person might be most interested in (online retail). Other well-publicised examples include Google's work on a self-driving car, recommendations by Netflix and programmatic advertising (what sort of ad a person may be most receptive to).

The essence of machine learning is akin to how people tackle problems in that we first draw on what we already know but, importantly, we are able to revise opinions in light of incoming information. We then carry this learning onto the next situation. Machines are able to do this if they are provided with large amounts of data so they can generalise, identify patterns and if need be revise 'opinion'. This is based on 'neural networking' that entails computer simulations of how biological neurons in the brain function (that develop through learning).

Machine learning takes two forms: 'supervised' and 'unsupervised' learning. For supervised learning we can use spam email as an example whereby we might provide a machine emails that are labelled spam and not spam (and, as you might imagine, a company like Google has quite a few of these). A human does not have to tell the machine what the differences between the emails are, but rather the application of deep learning techniques means the machine generates rules about what the differences are between the two. In generating it learns and is able to apply insights to incoming content to accurately identify what is spam and what is not. Related, the bigger the data set, the higher chance of learning and subsequent accuracy. The email/spam example matters less than the principle: the capacity of machines to analyse, create rules, learn, apply insights to new data and refine rules on an ongoing basis in relation to new incoming data.

On machinic 'seeing' and biometrics (or measuring bodily characteristics to identify people), we might consider Facebook's Deep Face that is able to recognise people, even in situations where the face is shot from a strange angle or in poor lighting. Similarly, Google's FaceNet can determine with 99.6 per cent accuracy whether two pictures show the same person, whereas humans score around 98 per cent. Although this may be useful and help with sorting messy personal photo albums, it is also very easy to see that a company's human-resources department may search for a person's face on YouTube when s/he applies for a job. Results will not only be what the candidate has decided to share, but all videos in which a person has ever appeared. Indeed, the candidate may not even know the videos exist.

We might also note that it is not just specialists who supervise machines, but *we* do it too. In Chapter 7 we discussed commodification, audience labour and the idea that 'if you're not paying, you're the product' (where platforms use services and content to build numbers of users, serve ads, generate data and thereafter revenue). Well, it applies to machine and supervised learning too because apps ask us to tag, organise and label data to help machines correct themselves and identity patterns. This also benefits from economies of scale. Consider, for example, apps such as Tinder, that ask users to determine the attractiveness of photos. On telling the machine what we find attractive, it is users who are doing the work of technologists and in the process making small teams of people very rich (in exchange for use of apps we presumably enjoy). This principle goes to the very heart of how platforms function in that it is regular people who indirectly supervise how machines learn.

Beyond Tinder, Facebook and Google, there are clear implications for loss of anonymity in public spaces because there is a very real possibility of biometric identification each time we are videoed by a digital camera. This raises all sorts of questions about differential treatment (such as by police, ads or shop assistants). While this might seem unlikely, consider an example from Russia where an app called FindFace lets users take photos of strangers and then determine their identity from profile pictures on social networks. This is significant because it entails nothing less than the end of *public anonymity*. While in theory FindFace may be used for harmless as well as creepy ends, consider that Russian police have already started using these techniques to identify dissenters, suspects and witnesses (*The Economist*, 2016). Advertisers are also interested in this technology because it grants retailers potential to target advertisements based on what individuals look at in stores. In general, what is now being done online is increasingly possible in physical space. This raises concerns along two axes: the first is horizontal and real time where people can be identified as they move throughout everyday life; the second less obvious one is vertical and historical as past footage and information may be recalled without difficulty. Indeed, we might also consider the theory of *a-historical tendencies* introduced in Chapter 8 whereby behaviour may no longer belong to the past as it once did, but may be called up with consummate ease by an interested person or machine. This raises questions of *forced openness* and transparency, a principle introduced in Chapter 2 (also see McStay, 2014).

The second 'unsupervised' version of machine learning is akin to learning without a training manual. For example, if a neural network is shown enough pictures that contain apples (without training or labelling by people), it may: a) note the occurrence; but also potentially b) data features that the picture of the apple coincides with. This means that without being asked, told or trained, machines are autonomously able to pick out features and generate previously unseen relationships within data. The key message is that machines can make sense of messy information in ways that people cannot. The reach and consequence of this possibility has yet to be fully understood. There are clearly positive outcomes (not least in pattern recognition in health and disease), but there are also obvious applications for mass surveillance, marketing and programmatic advertising (see Chapter 7). In general, any enterprise where understanding unexpected relationships may be of value will benefit from unsupervised machine learning.

POLICY AND BIG DATA

Whereas in the past privacy and surveillance scholars have been concerned about *mission creep* and the ways by which data collected for one purpose may be used for another, big data companies are now championing this possibility. This is because the value of big data and machine learning comes to be by mixing data sets and generating unexpected outcomes. There are clear legal and privacy concerns because this effectively means that data we allow to be collected for one reason may be used for another. This breaches the principle of consent whereby we agree to use of data for specific purposes (discussed in Chapter 7). The problem in a big data context is that information about what happens to a person's data is not always provided. Also, if opportunities and insights are unforeseen, how do processors realistically let people know what is happening? In Europe, the Article 29 Working Party[2] on 'purpose limitation' says that proper opt-in consent is required by an organisation that wants to analyse or predict the personal preferences, behaviour and attitudes of individual customers, which will subsequently inform 'measures or decisions' that are taken with regard to those customers. They make specific reference to direct marketing, behavioural advertising, data brokering, location-based advertising and tracking-based digital market research (Article 29 Working Party, 2014a: 47).

In addition to the breadth of unforeseen purposes that data might be used for, there is also the question of *retention*, or how long an organisation should be able to hold on to data. In reference to Europe's General Data Protection Regulation (GDPR), the UK's Information Commissioner's Office (ICO, 2014) states that if organisations wish to do this, they have to justify to data-protection authorities why it is important and what they expect to learn or be able to do by processing that data. Further, Europe's regulators say that finding unexpected correlations does not justify collecting and retaining 'all of the data all of the time'.

ANONYMISATION

Another key feature of discussion surrounding big data is that personal information is not always needed for it to be useful. This is because insights may be generated from data about people, even if individuals cannot be identified from that data. Actors ranging from health researchers to advertising companies make this point.

The argument is that if information can be stripped of markers that would identify a person, then it is fair game to put that data to work to help cure disease and target interest-based advertising. The principle is that by stripping, deleting or omitting names, addresses, phone numbers and other factors that would easily give away the identity of a person, this renders information *both* useful and harmless. Health researchers, for example, can correlate disease patterns, lifestyle and location, without knowing the names of people being referred to (thus rendering them anonymous). On the face of things, this is a win–win situation for data merchants and users of digital services. This is because it allows individuals to remain anonymous yet facilitates the extraction of value from networked behaviour (such as tracking what people do, say and buy). Seen more cynically, claims of anonymisation are an attempt to: 1) avoid data-protection regulations that are based on being able to identify people from data; and 2) make intensive information processing more palatable to citizens. The reason for scepticism is because it is questionable whether anonymisation is actually possible in a big data context.

SINGLING OUT

There are two factors at play here. First, when the data industry claims no personal information is being used, this is often not true. To target a device requires an address or code with which to communicate with that device. This comes under what we discussed in Chapter 7 as 'singling out'. This includes web browser data, mobile phone data, app information and IDs used for advertising. Related is the assumption that what bothers people are institutions gathering items of personal data. This again is not quite correct. The concern is less about the specifics of personally identifiable information, but what this allows an organisation to do. The point is not about possession of names and phone numbers, but how information can be used to affect that person in some way. Thus, a company may collect a large amount of information about a person's characteristics, without knowing their name. The important point is not whether the company has a name or not, but the level of tracking, profiling and combining of different data sets, to understand the significance of a person's behaviour. This then opens us up to the next potential problem in that although we might decline to be tracked, the insights gained from tracked people who are similar in profile (such as a rural cyclist who reads *The Economist* and subscribes to *Wired*) may lead to us receiving similar targeted advertising. Thus, for example, if I friend someone on a social network there is a likelihood we will have similar interests, and marketers can make inferences about my interests on the basis of my social network relationships. This is what Barocas and Nissenbaum (2014) phrase as 'the tyranny of the minority', because the few who consent to tracking affect the majority who may not consent. They draw upon a study by Mislove et al. (2010) who find that, from the attributes of a fraction of users in an online social network, we can infer the attributes of other users. Barocas and Nissenbaum quote that 'multiple attributes can be inferred globally when as few as 20% of the users reveal their attribute information' (Mislove et al., 2010: 255). In other words, you are who you know.

THE MOSAIC EFFECT

The next part of the anonymisation question is the matter of *re-identification*. Although data handlers may avoid collecting information deemed 'personal', when we begin to overlap references to where we live (such as postcodes), where we work, profession type, favourite coffee shop, income range and purchase habits, collectively this information can readily identify people. Ohm (2009) draws on Sweeney (2002) to illustrate the practical problems of anonymisation in relation to health data. For example ZIP/postal codes, birth dates (including year) and sex cannot in themselves give the identity of a person away, but when combined they will tell an interested party with access to this information the identity of a person. Sweeney brilliantly made this point with health data. The Group Insurance Commission (GIC) is a US government agency that purchases health insurance for state employees. In the mid-1990s, for purposes of academic research, they released abridged or 'anonymised' records of every state employee's hospital visits. On releasing the data the governor of Massachusetts placated the public by reassuring them that all personally identifiable information was stripped from the data. Sweeney knew that the governor lived in Cambridge, Massachusetts. This has 54,000 residents and seven ZIP codes. Cheaply and legally combining this data set with Cambridge's voter rolls (with name, address, ZIP code, birth date and sex of all voters) she identified and located the governor, and had access to all his hospital visits, diagnoses and prescriptions – that she subsequently mailed to him.

This example not only illustrates problems of releasing data to the public, but the potential impossibility of anonymisation. Note too, although it is unusual to have this type of health data publicly available, data brokers are in the business of obtaining the best and richest data sets, such as from banking, communications, purchase histories, search queries and so on. The principle is this: individual pieces of non-personal information will not reveal identity, but when there are more pieces of non-personal information the likelihood of anonymisation is reduced. This is not only the view of academics and privacy campaigners, but it is highlighted in a report on big data compiled for President Obama. It states:

> As techniques like data fusion make big data analytics more powerful, the challenges to current expectations of privacy grow more serious … Similarly, integrating diverse data can lead to what some analysts call the 'mosaic effect', whereby personally identifiable information can be derived or inferred from datasets that do not even include personal identifiers, bringing into focus a picture of who an individual is and what he or she likes. (Podesta, 2014: 8)

Political oversight of the information industries is founded on the split between personal and non-personal information. With assurances from industry, politicians and regulators have not intervened if data cannot identify people or single people out for different treatment. Recognition of mosaic effects and circumvention of anonymisation throws a spanner in the works. On 'what is the harm?' in being re-identified, Ohm states that almost every person in the developed world can be linked to at least one fact in a computer database that an adversary could use for blackmail, discrimination, harassment, or financial or identity theft (2009: 1748).

In response to criticisms of re-identification, Lafkey (2009) draws on a study by the US Department of Health and Human Services' Office of the National Coordinator for Health Information Technology to argue that re-identification is not as straightforward as critics suggest. Adopting the position of an adversary trying to merge health data with records that can be bought from data companies (in this case InfoUSA), accuracy on connecting people with health data was extremely low. Similar results were found when trying to merge open health data with social media profiles (0.05 per cent re-identified), with each taking multiple hours to find. However, while potential for identification is low it is still a significant figure, especially if applied to national populations or consumer groups. Also keep in mind too that it may be machines rather than people that are tasked with identifying people.

The UK's data regulator (the ICO) has provided detail about degrees of risk. They have argued for a relatively relaxed approach highlighting that security is never absolute. Notably, they have publicly stated that anonymisation techniques do not have to be 100 per cent secure (ICO, 2012). Instead they argue that the intention should be to minimise risk of identification until it is remote. This is also codified into the UK's Data Protection Act (1988) whereby data controllers should take into consideration 'other information which is in the possession of, or is *likely* to come into the possession of' other data controllers. The UK's ICO applies the 'likelihood test' as certainty of what data controller B may or may not have in their possession cannot be guaranteed. The ICO also suggests applying the 'motivated intruder' test. This is slightly different from the 'adversary' detailed above because although it assumes competence on behalf of the intruder who wishes to identify people by data, it does not assume that the person has prior knowledge of the data, is not a hacker and will not resort to burglary. Instead the motivated intruder will only be able to access public resources such as the internet, libraries and public documents.[3]

POLITICS OF ALGORITHMS

So far we have considered the nature and scope of big data, machine learning, difficulties with consent, singling out, the question of whether data can be truly anonymised, and that influential regulators argue that security of data privacy is a matter of degrees rather than absolutes. The next section is less about privacy than how insights from data are generated and the ways in which human biases find their way into machinic decisions.

On big data, the media scholar Mark Andrejevic remarks that it 'bypasses the vexed task of comprehension' (2013: 41). By this he means that data miners (who search data to find valuable nuggets of insight) are much more interested in patterns and correlations in data, rather than ideas about what caused the data to look the way it does. For Andrejevic an uncritical belief in technology and the seeming authority of big data is dangerous because it is being used in a range of sensitive sectors without adequate consideration of the terms by which machines are making decisions. Indeed, belief in the prominence, value and authority of machinic decision-making gives rise to what boyd and Crawford phrase as 'mythological' dimensions of big data. This entails the ways by which big data appears to be tinged 'with the aura of truth, objectivity, and accuracy' (2012: 663). As suggested in the activities list at the end of this chapter, an online search of the technology press typically shows highly optimistic attitudes to big data analytics.

Big data and technical answers to life's problems are deeply alluring because of the micro and macro scales that analytical technologies operate at. If we consider that the data industry is investing in being able to extract data from bodies, the home, cities, from industry (be this in retail stores, sheep in fields or the fabric of buildings) and the environment, data is everywhere. This gives rise to a somewhat *sublime* view of data (which means greatness beyond that which is calculable).[4] For a sense of what we might phrase as *big data mythologies*, consider this quote from an essay by Chris Anderson (2008), who is editor of *Wired*, a publication that provides news about technology, culture and start-up businesses. In his well-read and often cited piece, Anderson points to the death of theory or any inquiry that asks *why*, such as psychology, philosophy or even science itself. He comments:

> Petabytes allow us to say: 'Correlation is enough.' We can stop looking for models. We can analyze the data without hypotheses about what it might show. We can throw the numbers into the biggest computing clusters the world has ever seen and let statistical algorithms find patterns where science cannot.

Philosophically, we can phrase this as *correlationism*, which in turn is characterised by a somewhat technical mentality. Usually it is the sciences and the humanities, or the so-called 'Two Cultures'[5] that are cast head-to-head, particularly when it comes to questions of meaning and human experience. However, big data and the arguments laid out by Chris Anderson suggest a new actor that takes issue with the sciences and the humanities alike. Big data is arguably an engineer's approach to knowledge in that understanding is technical and functional, and opposed to theoretical knowledge. It is a rejection of both science (that builds testable theory through empirical observation) and the humanities (that investigates meaning, significance and quality).

Taken at face value, the belief in big data entails a conviction that all we need is data. As Kitchin (2014) points out, this is misguided not least because information is framed by the ways it was collected. This means that big data applications do not reflect the world, but construct a picture according to the strengths, sensing capacity, data provided, processing power and limitations of the technology. Again, they do not reflect but create and, as such, we should ask *why* machinic insights look the way they do. Next, as also developed below in relation to policing, it is risky to think that data is free of bias and outright dangerous for people to believe insights from data without asking questions about how they have been created. This is not to say that machines lie or intentionally distort but that it is often people who supervise, program computers, set parameters and give machines assumptions by which they will process and organise data. Even in the case of unsupervised machine learning, it is people that interpret results, comprehend and contextualise within their pre-existing outlooks on the world. The concern is that big data mythologies and the data sublime provide the illusion of irrefutable truth for what are often human judgements and biases. For Andrejevic and others[6] this reveals the truth behind big data: although seemingly indifferent and irrefutable, the decisions machines make are still grounded in the messy and imperfect domain of human culture, biases and stereotypes.

DISCRIMINATION

One important consequence is the potential for discrimination, particularly on gender, race and social class. A quick illustration of algorithmic biases in search engine results can open up the topic for us. For example, as depicted in Figure 9.1, if I type in 'black people are' Google automatically completes with the word 'rude' (search conducted 27 January 2016). Curiously, there is no autocomplete for 'white people are'.

The reason why Google is displaying this auto-completion is because it reflects what most people click after typing 'black people are'. The result essentially floats to the top by means of popularity ranking. The consequence is that algorithms (generated by user-based supervised learning) allow dominant trends to cause discrimination. One can go further and say that, in this instance, the Google search engine and its sorting algorithms are reinforcing racism. This is true to an extent but very regrettably it is people that are really at fault. However, this raises potential for interesting discussion: should Google's algorithms be tweaked so to challenge racism at every opportunity, just as people should? We can do a similar

Figure 9.1   Search entry for 'black people are'

test by typing 'CEO' into Google Images. Guess what we find: a very long list of white men (the first female comes in row 8 of the listed photos and is 'CEO Barbie' and a non-white man does not feature until row 7).[7] On gender, although it is true that more men are CEOs, what this result actually shows is that Google returns a finding worse than the fact that only 14.2 per cent of the top five leadership positions at the companies in the top 500 are held by women (statistically, a women should have appeared by the second row).

As Gandy (2009) highlights, these factors can stack the cards against sectors of society in terms of life options that are open and available to them. Rather than coolly cut through human errors, algorithmic culture has the potential to intensify discrimination. Thus, when we talk of life chances and opportunities, it really is a case of some people being born into the world with good odds, and others not. This is less about 'big discrimination' but 'small discrimination' and the ways by which algorithms and statistics have minor but ultimately significant biases built in. These can occur a lot. Gandy, for example, writes of discriminatory lending practices in the US. He highlights that skin colour can influence present and future valuations of property in US neighbourhoods, which subsequently impacts on the rate of bank loans (even though calculating race is meant to be illegal in the US). The problem is that the application of data mining, pattern finding, correlations and creation of categories is typically less restrained in political discrimination than in-person decisions against certain sectors of the population. Similar predictive digital judgements are being made in the area of policing. Again, in the US, this is especially acute because the rate of African American imprisonment is so high (with 60 per cent of inmates being of this origin, despite only making up 12–13 per cent of the American population). On the rise of predictive policing and systematic bias, Gandy goes on to argue that likelihood of imprisonment influences other factors, such as dangerousness and likelihood of offending. The problems here are multiple in that digital structural racism reinforces existing cultural biases (despite machines being seemingly indifferent) that in turn contribute to limiting of life choices, prejudiced job recruitment, maintenance of stereotypes and being wrongly assessed.

Today this takes the form of 'heat lists' of city districts, individuals and zones where there is the highest chance of committing a violent crime. Defenders (such as police forces) claim that the approach is unbiased, but we should keep in mind the earlier discussion of big data mythologies and correlationism. An article in *The Verge*,[8] for example, reports that the Chicago Police Department sent one of its commanders to Robert McDaniel's home in the summer of 2013. Although the black 22-year-old (who had dropped out of school) lived in a neighbourhood known for violence, he had not committed a serious crime or interacted with a police officer recently. He had no record at all of violence or gun violations. This did not stop him being placed on the city's 'heat list' of around 400 people in the city of Chicago who were deemed most likely to be involved in violent crime. This led to a knock at the door and a police commander delivering the unsympathetic message: 'If you commit any crimes, there will be major consequences. We're watching you.' Similar developments are under way to generate crime maps that highlight neighbourhoods that might soon be at risk of an increase in crime. Part of the logic behind this is that it is not just about committing a crime, but the relationships and networks that a person is part of. This means that a person can be targeted for being poor and living in communities where they know people who have been in trouble with the law. A comment by the press liaison for the US National Institute of Justice (NIJ) is illustrative: 'These are persons who the model has determined are those most likely to be involved in a shooting or homicide, with probabilities that are hundreds of times that of an ordinary citizen.' Again, note the fact that police intelligence is being outsourced to an algorithm that is purportedly indifferent, quantitative and unbiased. Ultimately, while machines may provide useful insights, these should not be uncritically employed nor trump human intelligence without scrutiny of how the machine arrived at the decision.

BLACK BOXES

Organisations that make use of big data techniques need to be able to easily see and comprehend what machines are telling them. A great deal of academic and industrial effort goes into data visualisation to help people see patterns and trends discerned by machines. This range from simple graphs to virtual reality in which people can immerse themselves in representations of data. However, as machines are required to make both data entry and comprehension easier so more people can make use of the data (thus lowering requisite expertise), as a consequence this removes from view the core functioning of the machine and how it works at a fundamental level. In other words, it tells a person what the results of analysis are, but not how the results are reached. This is black boxing, or that Latourian (1987) idea where the functioning of a technology works so well it becomes invisible. Use of these systems requires a high degree of trust because we take on faith that results and data insights are reliable. As we saw in the case of policing and discrimination, reliance on expert black boxes can lead to real-world problems. Black boxes are a good example of what the sociologist Anthony Giddens (1990) calls 'expert systems'. These are modern practices with societal impact that we rely upon, but again do not fully understand how they work. Black boxes and big data processing entails expert systems because they create distance between the expert and lay user of that technology. Centrally, as modern societies grow ever more reliant upon expert systems, this is founded on trust and faith (albeit tinged with dim comprehension of risk). In relation to big data practices, a consequence of this is that we only focus on what we enter into the machine and what we get back from it, but not on how decisions are made or how they are reached. Similarly, the advent of interfaces, menus and simpler means of data entry and access makes data more easily available, yet conceals the complexity of how a machine's insights are generated. It also hides our own lack of knowledge about how the technology works. This can be dangerous because we are less willing to challenge automated decision-making.

This is what Pasquale (2015) refers to as the social production of ignorance. Black box society (the title of Pasquale's book) has a paradoxical character because as people have more data communicated about them, the ways in which black boxes function are concealed. Pasquale (perhaps reflecting on the US rather than elsewhere) goes further and says that the law protects the secrecy of business, but remains quiet on people's privacy rights. Echoing earlier parts of this chapter, what Pasquale and other scholars and cultural commentators are noticing is that governance and decisions made by algorithms (and that were once made by people) increasingly shape important parts of our lives. This is diverse, but includes whether or not the bank will give us a loan, recommendations for jobs we should go for, predictions about health, who is likely to be a criminal, where in a city criminality might occur, surveillance, financial trading, and much more. While certainly due in part to human bias, on other occasions the problem is simpler and there are clear-cut cases where machines are making decisions with faulty information. For example, a US study of almost 3,000 credit reports belonging to 1,000 consumers found that 26 per cent had 'material' errors serious enough to affect the consumers' credit scores and therefore the cost of obtaining credit (Hoofnagle, 2013). Although people may also be provided with faulty information to make decisions, people are more easily challenged about how they arrived at a judgement. As decisions and technologies based on artificial intelligence and machine learning become the norm, this raises critical questions about the right to challenge automated decision-making. This is actually codified in the GDPR (Europe's aforementioned data-protection regulation that comes into force in 2018). Articles 15 and 22 for example say that people have a right to meaningful information about the logic involved in how decisions about them were made (just as one might ask a bank manager why they were turned down for a loan). Even for technology specialists, how one might explain the decision-making process of a neural network is a highly complicated task. The principles contained in the regulation (including suitable safeguards, the right to human intervention, explanation of decisions and ability to challenge decisions) are morally right, but it is currently difficult to see how this is possible in an automated context. However, this should not be impossible (Goodman and Flaxman, 2016) and the fact that GDPR recognises that algorithmic decision-making is not neutral or simply technical is a positive step forward. It is one that lays down the challenge for technologists to embed principles of transparency in all automated decision-making processes to make clear the terms by which determinations about life chances and opportunities are made.

CONCLUSION

We began by identifying 'big data' as a worldview, an orientation, a set of values, and preferences about knowledge that privilege patterns and correlations over theory. Although there is much hype around the term, big data refers to something socially important, particularly when we consider the increasing mediation of human life and our environment. The capacity for real-time decision-making (that is driven by machine learning and developments in artificial intelligence) is also significant. Although there are real social opportunities, perhaps foremost in health, there are privacy considerations too. As we saw in discussion of machine learning, it is not excessive to suggest that public as well as device-level anonymity is under threat. At the level of policies that guide what can and cannot be done with information about people, big data applications also raise questions of unwanted openness, forced transparency and mission creep. The use of data collected for one purpose but used for another is often justified by means of anonymisation and pseudo-anonymisation, but the problem is that security is a matter of degrees – not absolutes. Critics have pointed out the mosaic effect means that with extra sets of data, people can be re-identified. Defenders have retorted that success of these attacks is not as likely as critics suggest. We progressed to consider the consequences of automated decision-making. This is less about privacy than lack of critical scrutiny of how machines arrive at answers. The key concerns are the nature of human influences on how machines make decisions, the blind trust that people may place in automated decision-making and lastly what people do with insights derived from data. When these seemingly abstract matters are placed in the context of policing, discrimination and limiting life choices and opportunities, these intangible algorithmic biases become very real.

Research and challenges

1 In what ways will the profusion of data influence the development of media (pick your own examples)?

2 By means of technology news outlets such as TechCrunch and Engadget, find three recent examples of big data mythologies.

3 To what extent should we be concerned about correlationism? Give reasons for and against.

4 By means of online sources, examine your government's policies on big data, machine learning, data protection and privacy in light of ideas discussed in this chapter. How comfortable are you with them?

NOTES

1 See, for example, this article from *Wired* that details consumer responses to colour schemes on Netflix: www.wired.com/insights/2014/03/big-data-lessons-netflix/.

2 The Article 29 Working Party is composed of representatives of Europe's national data protection authorities, the European Data Protection Supervisor and the European Commission. It advises the European Commission on data-protection matters.

3 Specific sources include: libraries, local council offices, church records, general registry office, genealogy websites, social media/internet searches, local and national press archives and anonymised data releases by other organisations, particularly public authorities (ICO, 2012).

4 The word itself, sublime, goes at least as far back as the ancient Greek philosophers. However, another philosopher, Immanuel Kant (2004 [1764]), highlighted the mathematical and dynamic aspect of the sublime. The sublime for Kant is also a form of knowing and appreciation of that which underlies nature and thought. As we have explored, big data processes are based on numbers, correlations and movement of people, their activities, their body states, weather patterns, diseases and so on. For Kant the sublime is formless (data moves, circulates and flows) and it is boundlessness (data can be read of any phenomenon). It is highly notable that in semiotic terms 'big data' seems to equate to indefinite greatness (swirls and flows of incomprehensible yet affective information).

5 The expression comes from 1959 when the novelist Charles Snow delivered a lecture at Cambridge titled 'The Two Cultures and the Scientific Revolution' that discussed the gap that had opened up between scientists and 'literary intellectuals'. The expression 'Two Cultures' is now shorthand for the supposed stand-off between the sciences and the humanities.

6 See list complied by Tarleton Gillespie and Nick Seaver on critical approaches to algorithms at http://socialmediacollective.org/reading-lists/critical-algorithm-studies/.

7 Search conducted 27 January 2016 when signed out of my own Google account.

8 Available from www.theverge.com/2014/2/19/5419854/the-minority-report-this-computer-predicts-crime-but-is-it-racist.

PART 3
THE ROLE OF
THE BODY

10

EMPATHIC MEDIA

TOWARDS UBIQUITOUS EMOTIONAL INTELLIGENCE

Key questions

- Why are empathic media different from other media?
- Why might data about emotions be useful for the advertising industry?
- What critical questions does 'post-privacy' raise?

Key concepts

- Empathic media
- Hard versus soft biometrics
- Facial coding
- Intimacy

Today we hear a great deal about artificial intelligence, but less about artificial emotional intelligence. This is curious given the role that emotional understanding plays in day-to-day life. After all, when we meet both new and known people, we make judgements about how they are feeling and their intentions. We analyse faces, posture, gestures and voices to identify 'where they are coming from' – often before they have actually said anything of significance. Increasingly our technologies are doing the same thing. Although machines have for some time made use of what we say and click, machinic emotional intelligence introduces new critical questions for us to consider, especially about data collected through assessment and interpretation of facial cues, voice, gestures, gaze direction and other bodily signals.

This brings benefits in that we will be able to engage with our technologies in more natural ways, but information from this interaction is also valuable, perhaps most so for advertisers, marketers and retailers because emotions are deeply influential in consumer decision-making. We assume that we push the buttons on our devices, but maybe they will press ours? Recent interest in bodies and emotions have two primary sources: the first is that technologists and computer scientists increasingly understand that for interaction with technologies to occur more naturally, machines must be able to discern what we are feeling and what our intentions are. The objective of emotion recognition is for our machines to possess a modicum of *empathy* so as to bring to life human–machine relationships. The second is commercial awareness that emotions sway decision-making. The idea that we coolly and rationally weigh up the various merits when deciding which brand to opt for has, for the marketing and advertising industries, long since disappeared (if it ever really existed). This chapter presents an overview of emotion-sensitive technologies, or what I term empathic media. Paying special attention to facial coding of emotions in advertising, I outline the scale, characteristics and trajectory of empathic media. I then progress to consider critical questions for privacy and end the chapter by suggesting that some applications of these technologies entail *post-privacy* because, in some cases, although empathic media make use of intimate information, they do not always collect identifiable information.

PRE-CHAPTER SUGGESTION

To obtain a working sense of what facial coding technologies do, download an app called Affdex made by the company Affectiva. Available for both Android and iOS devices, this will provide you with a tangible sense of how facial coding of emotions works.

AFFECTIVE COMPUTING

Although in our minds the concepts of empathy, sympathy and compassion may overlap, this is not strictly correct. To understand the emotional states and intentions of others, or 'be in their shoes', does not require that we want the best for that person. This is a sad, true and necessary fact. In the worst cases, a torturer excels at their task because they are able to modulate mental and physical pain, or make threats that will hurt that person most (such as what they might do to the recipient's family). More commonly, we read the behavioural and communicational signals of others to help orient us to our inter-personal and social surroundings. As such, although empathy commonly signifies understanding the emotional states of others, responding appropriately and comforting others through distressing periods, sympathy is not a criterion for empathy. Instead empathy is simply an interpretive act to understand emotions and intentions. Empathic media represents the interests of affective computing, and academic and industrial research in user experience, emotional life and interpretation of human intentions. We do not have scope in this chapter to explore each aspect of empathic media in full (for this see McStay, 2017), but we might recognise they have implications for sectors including: insurance (well-being, health and risk reduction); recruitment (to test candidates for sensitive jobs where insincerity is intolerable); the workplace (to monitor workforce well-being); pharmaceutical research (testing authenticity of reactions from study participant reactions); fitness coaching (tracking athletes' emotional states); fashion (mood-sensitive wearables); child rearing (baby monitors); live events and festivals (creative use of face and voice recording, and feedback into event); online dating (enhancing online pre-meeting interactions); telesales (monitoring callers and optimising operators); automotive safety (driver stress levels); political strategising (monitoring sentiment/emotions on social media); and crime/security management (such as monitoring emotional states of police as they enter dangerous situations).

Empathic media are based on the observation that although machines cannot read thoughts, they *are* able to discern emotional behaviour. The curious term refers to the capacity for emergent media technologies to sense and discern what is significant for people, categorise behaviour into named emotions, act on emotional states and make use of people's intentions and expressions (McStay, 2014, 2016, 2017). The objective of this is two-fold in that it registers and recognises emotions, and entails the capacity for machines to give feedback to people that is emotionally correct. This facilitates more meaningful interaction with machines. I use the term empathy to classify this class of technology because it reflects what people do. We do not just comprehend the emotions of others, but we do this for a reason – to understand their intentions. Indeed, when we interact with people we often pay far more attention to the way something is said than the meanings of the words themselves.

Although machines cannot appreciate emotions in the same way as people (such as being able to appreciate the affective and visceral experience of anger), machinic understanding of emotion can be judged by the extent to which feedback is effective and integrates with the context of the communication we are having with that machine. A computer game for example may watch us (via a camera that measures facial expressions, or wearable input devices that record heart rate, skin responses or respiration) for bodily indicators of emotion. Having witnessed behaviour that correlates to what the machine understands to be an emotional state, it makes judgements by means of an algorithm (if person A is behaving in X pattern then do Z) so as to provide game content and meaningful player feedback. This might be a change in an avatar's behaviour, introduction of new gaming situations, speeding up the game, or other new game factors. This witnessing is done through assessment and interpretation of eye-tracking, skin conductivity, heart rates, speech, gestures, facial cues and electrical output from the brain.

Empathic media derives from a branch of computer science known as 'affective computing'. This is indivisible from the work of Rosalind Picard (1995, 1997). Today Picard continues her theoretical and practical work at MIT, yet she also commercialised her work by means of involvement with Affectiva – a facial coding emotional analytics company. The intention of affective computing is to improve human–computer interfaces and relationships with machines, and generate new modes of entertainment, home experiences, healthcare, retail opportunities, advertising, marketing, in-car automobile experiences, and more. Emotional interaction with our media technologies is a logical development because we spend a great deal of time interacting with them. Why should they not understand people better and what they are trying to achieve?

Although these technologies can certainly be used to identify people, this is not their primary objective because they are based on *soft biometrics*. Hard biometrics scans iris texture, fingerprints, faces, and voice and signature, amongst other means, to confirm the *identity* of a person. This happens when we pass through airports possessing hard biometric authentication that scans our eyes, but also on consumer level technologies such as Apple's iPhone that uses fingerprint identification. Soft biometrics are different because they are about enhancing interaction between people and machines.

The opportunity for wider use of soft biometric data will rise in tandem with both personal sensors and wearables (discussed in Chapter 11), and interactions with media technologies in our environments, such as home digital assistants, and in-store retail displays that judge age, gender and mood. Emotion-sensitive technologies should be seen in context of the push by marketing, retail and financial industries to stimulate consumer experience (that includes attracting, hooking, serving and maintaining customer–business relationships). The nature of this experience is both emotional and rational. Alongside emotion-sensitive technology, we should also consider intense personal data sharing to provide people with what they want when they want it (seamless service experience), extensive uses of sensors (particularly in retail environments) and deep learning (to collect volumes and varieties of data, and mine this for insights and commercial consumer opportunities). Although at the time of writing in February 2016, data about emotions was not being connected with personal data, the opportunity is there. In theory, this can be done through offers of free Wi-Fi (so to access smartphones), loyalty cards, store apps on mobile devices and transaction data, and offers by retailers to identify ourselves and consent to tracking (on the basis of offers, coupons, personalised services, tailored shopping and enhanced consumer experience).

CONTEMPORARY TECHNOLOGIES: THE CASE OF FACIAL CODING

There are various indicators that can be measured to infer emotions (such as heart rates, respiration, how we speak, what we say online and skin conductivity), but the method that is proving most popular is facial coding. This reads emotions by identifying features and muscles on a person's face, tracking their movement, and thereafter correlating the facial arrangement and movement with named emotional conditions (McStay, 2014, 2016, 2017). As will be developed below, this is being applied in advertising, although in 2016 Apple publicly declared their interest in emotion-sensitive media by buying a company called Emotient. The reason for this purchase was unclear, but presumably involves building emotion-sensitivity into personal assistants and interfaces. Emotient's system of analysing emotions works by clustering emotional expressions into one of seven possible emotions (joy, surprise, sadness, anger, fear, disgust and contempt).

The conceptual methodology of emotions derives from the psychological and anthropological work of Paul Ekman and Wallace Friesen (1971, 1978). Ekman now sits on the board of Emotient. He argues that there is a universal language of human emotion that can be discerned from people's facial expressions. Ekman and Friesen's studies included both developed countries and non-developed societies, such as New Guinea Highlands, which had not been significantly exposed to advanced media systems, television or photographs of people's faces from other countries. Along with Wallace Friesen, Ekman found that people in advanced and non-advanced media cultures connected concepts of emotion with the same facial behaviours, as do members of Western and Eastern literate cultures (Ekman and Friesen, 1971). This approach ultimately draws on Charles Darwin's (2009 [1872]) universalising and pan-cultural account of emotions and expression in people and animals. In *The Expression of the Emotions in Man and Animals* he writes, 'all the chief expressions exhibited by man are the same throughout the world' (ibid.: 355). Darwin connects this with his then still recent theory of natural selection, that all humans are derived from one parent-stock, that people are 'derived from some lower animal form' (ibid.: 360), and that emotional expression is shared with other primates and animals. This provides a phylogenetic and evolutionary view of emotions. Ekman and Friesen's work led to the development of the Facial Action Coding System (FACS). This is their formal taxonomy for measurement of facial movement and expressions in humans and connecting these to human emotions (Ekman and Friesen, 1978). FACS is made of seven facial expressions of primary emotion (joy, surprise, sadness, anger, fear, disgust and contempt) and three overall sentiments (positive, negative and neutral).

We should be wary of overly simplistic accounts of emotion, particularly because *arousal* and *emotion* are not the same things. For media theory that is strongly influenced by sociology, social theory, cultural theory and ethnocentric philosophies, this radical downplaying of signification, cultural, cognitive and mental life is controversial. In Ekman's introduction to Darwin's *Expression*, he distinguishes between emotions and other mental events (thoughts, attitudes and plans) and sees emotions as 'public leaks' whereas other mental events such as thoughts have potential to be private. Criticisms of this view are crystallised by Fridlund (1995) who argues that facial expressions are social. This means that rather than simply being external evidence of what we feel, emotional expressions

139

are also communicational. This social view of emotions even applies when facial expressions are made in private because the expressions we make on these occasions are implicitly social (Fridlund, 1991). However, Ekman's work has proven to be *very* influential, arguably because of its simplicity and that it provides an account of emotions that cameras and computer scientists can work with.

We can see how this functions in Figure 10.1. This is an example of Emotient's system that details a family (notably children too) and how cameras mounted on top of viewing screens collect facial responses. The pie charts below illustrate responses of each family member to the media content. The one on the right of the image shows the aggregated mean average of family emotion. In this case, it is 'Joy'. Other companies working in this field include Realeyes, Sension, Eyeris, nViso (partners with IBM), Intel (by means of their RealSense technologies) and Affectiva. Note too that many of these companies are making extensive use of machine learning to improve and refine their emotion detection technologies (see Chapter 9 for discussion of machine learning).

Figure 10.1   Demonstration of Emotient where a camera watches viewers emotional reactions to television content

Retail is another opportunity for empathic media companies. For some time we have been traced in stores by a multitude of cameras, but much of this information has simply been archived in case of theft. Analytics companies are lining up to make use of in-store camera information. Prism Skylabs for example is a 'business intelligence tool' that combines security camera video with software. This profiles people's movement within stores, how long they linger in front of specific items, how many times an object has been handled, and whether promotions and positioning are working as well as intended. However, Emotient (and others such as Affectiva) go one step further than assessing what, where and how often: for instance, Emotient assesses customers' moods as they enter and leave stores, and embed cameras on product aisles to understand customers' emotional reactions to products, packaging and placement.

ACTING ON IMPULSE: ADVERTISING

In addition to retail, rapid progress in mass-market roll-out of emotional analytics is being made in advertising. In advertising emotions are tracked via technical means for two purposes. The first is for in-house 'neuromarketing' research where market research companies such as Millward Brown use facial coding (provided by Affectiva), EEG signals and other intimate means of analysis to assess our bodies and brains for emotional reactions to advertising (also see McStay, 2013). The objective here is to bypass spoken responses of what we think about advertising to assess how our bodies react. This is done to understand how people feel about brands and to test the emotional impact of advertising before it is launched on the public. This entails ensuring that correct and appropriate levels of emotions are reached. In practice, this can entail changing parts of ads, altering music, amending the narrative or changing characters. The second way of tracking emotion is by sensors in our devices, homes and environments. For example, in London 2015 M&C Saatchi (partnering with Clear Channel and Posterscope) produced an ad that *evolves* unique ads based on people's facial reactions (see Figure 10.2).

Figure 10.2   M&C Saatchi, Clear Channel and Posterscope's ad for Bahio (a fictional coffee brand) on Oxford Street, London

This was a test for a fictional coffee brand named Bahio that, presumably, was produced to gauge public reaction to this novel emotion-sensitive advertising. It makes use of hidden Microsoft Kinect cameras to infer viewers' emotions by means of assessing facial expressions (also see McStay, 2016). Compared with the coding products offered by Emotient and Affectiva, the campaign used a very basic version of facial coding (to track whether people are happy, neutral or sad) versus the seven facial expressions (joy, surprise, sadness, anger, fear, disgust and contempt) offered by others. Each of these products function by identifying features and muscles on a person's face, tracking their movement, and thereafter correlating this movement with named emotional conditions. If the ad continues to receive sad or neutral responses, the ad is programmed to change its design (for example graphical elements and colour scheme) to win more smiles and positive sentiment. This is significant in that this is the first time that outdoor advertising has *optimised itself* so as to be more effective on the basis of viewers' emotional reactions. Importantly, it does this without using personally identifiable information.

INTIMATE, BUT NOT PERSONAL?

Other companies, such as Exterion Media and i2MediaResearch, are exploring this type of technology to improve 'retail engagement' (in-store reactive screens). Indeed, one industry figure I spoke to pointed to development of eye-level sensors on tags on hangers. These types of marketing activities raise critical questions. Some of these are regarding the social desirability of this, others are about ethics, but also important is the legal dimension. As it stands Europe's legal frameworks are based on privacy, consent and identification. For non-European readers, Europe has what is universally regarded as the toughest data-protection regime in the world (this is now crystallised in the General Data Protection Regulation, or GDPR). However, although this is true, empathic media currently have less to do with questions of privacy than intimacy. This is not accounted for in the GDPR, or other applicable directives and regulations (McStay, 2017), because in the case of advertising that tracks emotions in public spaces, no personal data or code (such as a string of letters and numbers) is generated to separate the facial reactions of one person from the next. As discussed in Chapter 9 and the General Data Protection Regulation itself, this goes back to the principle of 'singling out', whether a person experiences unique differential treatment in some way, and if a person can either be directly or indirectly identified.

If we do not have legal recourse, what are the ethical consequences of collecting data about emotions, even if they cannot be tracked back to an individual? I suggest that one cause for concern is about how these technologies may fundamentally alter our relationship with public spaces. Although we have lived with surveillance cameras for some time, the tracking of emotions for commercial (rather than security) purposes is a very different proposition. Sir Martin Sorrell,

CEO of the advertising conglomerate WPP, was asked by a journalist for BBC's technology programme *Click*[1] whether WPP would want to reach people with a marketing message through knowledge of their emotive state. He responded: 'Yes, one would like to do that but within the grounds of people knowing exactly what they're getting into so demystifying the process, simplifying the process, making people understand what they're letting themselves in for ... that's really important.' This is a good and positive answer in that if people know exactly what is happening they may well be OK with this. As it stands, however, our laws are not set up to deal with technologies that collect intimate (but not private) information. The consequence of this is significant because it means that, in essence, privacy laws have failed, which allows us to speak of *post-privacy* concerns. That is, given the fixity of privacy on identification (as expressed in laws around the world), we have a lacuna in data protection that the advertising and retail industries will exploit.

CONCLUSION

The roots of emotion-sensitive technologies are in the mid-1990s and the work of Rosalind Picard. Today these technologies are reaching the mass market. Interestingly industry leaders have strong academic involvement as Picard co-founded Affectiva, a leading facial coding company. The other leader, Emotient, that was bought by Apple, has Paul Ekman on its board who developed the conceptual principles behind facial coding of emotions. It is early days for artificial emotional intelligence and so far use of empathic media in advertising is limited. However, when seen against the backdrop of increased commercial use of artificial intelligence, neural networking, automated pattern recognition, machine learning, improvements in natural language processing, predictive analytics, increased use of personal biometric devices, continued use of sentiment analysis, emotional heat-maps of private spaces (such as stores) and public spaces (such as cities) and focus on 'consumer experience', there is a degree of inevitability about its use.

However, empathic media can be read in positive and negative terms. The capacity to interact more naturally with machines and mediated environments is progress. It promises new ways of interacting with media content (such as interactive films), extra immersion in gaming, assistance in maintaining physical and mental well-being, and much else we could deem positive. There is, however, scope for this technology to be used in ways that serve the few rather than the many. Further, even the pro-advertising industry lobby might pause for thought on considering the moral merit in using negative emotions to sell. Is it OK to target advertising by whether people are anxious, stressed, unhappy or even depressed? Are we OK with using negative moods to shape advertising and sell goods? If not, we have to be clear in our arguments and be willing to engage not just with the ethical, cultural and sociological dimensions, but also with industry and the policies that regulate its actions. Lastly, current use of empathic media in advertising forces us to consider post-privacy ethics as it challenges the adequacy of privacy law that is fixated on possibility of identification. What the use of empathic media in public spaces tells us is that intimate information can be used without consent (in both the personal and legal meaning of the term). Is this acceptable?[2]

Research and challenges

1 Should we be concerned about data practices that make use of intimate rather than strictly identifiable information? Assess in relation to regulations in your country about: a) what constitutes personal data/information; and b) what constitutes sensitive information/data.

2 Has privacy failed us?

3 Beyond the advertising examples given in this chapter, provide examples of other empathic media.

4 Should consent be required to use intimate information that does not 'single out'?

NOTES

1 First shown at 1.30 a.m. on 25 July 2015.
2 As discussed in McStay (2017), in 2015 I conducted a nationwide survey of what people in the UK think about this form of advertising (n = 2068). 50 per cent of people were against any form of data collection about emotions; 33 per cent were OK with use of data about emotions as long as it was not personally identifiable; 8 per cent were OK with use of data about emotions even if they were identifiable; and 9 per cent did not know.

11

RE-INTRODUCING THE BODY TO PRIVACY

INTIMATE AND WEARABLE MEDIA

What we call 'wearables' today, we'll call 'clothing' by 2030.[1] (Musician and entrepreneur, Will.i.am)

Key questions

- What is the quantified self?
- What is the difference between hierarchical and personal sousveillance?
- What can feminism tell us about privacy, data and the body?
- To what extent are people made transparent through use of wearables?

Key concepts

- Sousveillance
- Bodily objectification
- Coercion
- Transparency

As I wrote this opening section my Apple Watch gave me a gentle prompt to stand, stretch my back and move around. It did not do this with an alarm, but a warm haptic buzz on my wrist, and a wood chime-like prompt that is intimate rather than irritating. One picture of the future is based on hyper-connectivity, an internet of everything, connected clothing and a situation where networked technologies will become invisible as we are immersed in data. The sales pitch by technologists is the promise of new ways to see ourselves and others, take phone calls, manage health, pay for goods, entertain, keep fit, de-stress, track our bodies, watch individuals and organisations, play sports and avoid injuries. This is conceivable, but from the point of 2016 where many of us struggle to get Wi-Fi throughout modestly sized homes, one can be forgiven for some scepticism. However, doubt should be balanced with the history of new media that tells us that what was once outlandish can quickly become routine and ubiquitous.

The intention of this chapter is to chart the rise of wearable technologies and to reintroduce the body back into privacy matters. I begin by providing an overview of recent wearables and the history of wearables. I explore some of the reasons they are used, most notably the urge to self-track, quantify the self and ultimately make the body transparent to their wearers. One outcome of this is that our bodies also become more visible to service providers. There is a range of critical interests to address, but foremost is the principle of objectification. By this I borrow from feminist literature its interest in bodily ownership, instrumentality and commodification. The usefulness of feminist critique becomes apparent if we situate objectification within critical writing on the ways by which networked industrial processes put information about subjectivity and the body to work by converting subjective data into objective form (in our case, electronic data).

WEARABLE MEDIA AND THE INTERNET OF THINGS

After a long mountain bike ride, my house knows I have been cycling because of my heart rate, GPS and average speed. It knows this because it downloads wearable data from my Bluetooth-enabled phone. With this information the taps turn on and run me a bath. Music plays to reflect my post-ride cycling glow (generated by increased endorphins) and my coffee machine brews my post-bath coffee for some added pep to kick-start my afternoon book writing. This is not true, but it is possible. The question is: is it desirable? Painted by the technology and data industry, the big picture for the Internet of Things (IoT) is an invisible and ambient networked computing environment constructed out of 'smart' sensors, cameras, software, databases, massive data centres, and the efficient sharing of this data between multiple actors, applications and pieces of hardware.

Digital privacy studies is typically concerned about an individual's control over their personal data and communication. Desire for access to data and communication tends to be for two reasons: first, to know us better so to sell us things and services; second, for governmental surveillance purposes (social control through knowledge). In a pre-digital context this has roots in intercepting flows of communication such as letters and telephone calls, but contemporary digital contexts open up many other types of communication flows. These include the topic of this chapter – the profusion of sensors developed for the body. In 2015 Japan has the highest rate of wearables use at 12 per cent. In Europe, the UK rate is joint highest with Italy at 9 per cent (Ofcom, 2015b). While not yet a ubiquitous mass medium, wearables represent an entangling of commercial technologies and bodies in ways never seen before. This is being done to enhance awareness of self and human–technological interaction, but one key consequence of this is that a great deal of information is being generated by our bodies, brains, health, fitness, arousal states, moods and emotions. From the point of view of privacy and critical analysis, our object of inquiry is quite some distance from the information inferred through keyboards, mouse clicks and screen swipes.

The promise of wearables is to make life easier and 'frictionless'. The last word is an especially important one because the grand vision of technologists and service providers is a mediated environment where (paradoxically) the prominence of technology fades into the background so for the internet and its devices to effectively disappear. The goal is an environment where our technologies know our preferences, and are able to engage us in a cognitively and emotionally aware manner. Companies such as MasterCard for example are keen to add contactless payment credentials not just to Apple phones and watches, but also car key fobs, smart rings and even clothing. General Motors' proposed contactless key fob is a move towards an 'integrated commerce experience' so, for example, if a driver needs to order a pizza on the go from their car, they can order and pick it up on the way home for dinner. Banking companies say that a key benefit of wearables as authentication devices is that biometric data (such as heartbeats) can be used to authenticate payments. The principle behind this renewed version of consumer society is one in which all difficulties in interactions, finding goods, and paying for products and services is removed. This is facilitated by both hassle-free and frictionless payment systems, but also programmatic advertising (discussed in Chapter 7) that offers moment-by-moment recommendations and gentle nudges towards brands and products potentially of interest to us. This is much less about hard sell than an attempt to improve and understand 'consumer experience', or trackable interactions with companies understood in rational, emotional, sensorial and physical terms.

BACKGROUND TO WEARABLES

There are some wonderfully strange and weird wearables. These include the 'selfie hat' from Acer that quite literally is a sombrero with a screen hanging off the rim. Only slightly less unlikely, there is Sony's patent for a SmartWig. Worn in addition to natural hair, this can communicate with other wireless devices, help navigate roads, collect data on health and blood pressure, and even allow the wearer to move PowerPoint presentations to the next slide by simply raising their eyebrows. There is also a smart bra from Microsoft that claims to detect the wearer's emotions (by heart rate) and then assess whether the wearer eats more when stressed. If you have not seen these in stores, there is good reason. And then there is Sexfit from Bondara that, inspired by FitBit, does not collect steps but men's 'thrusts'. Worn at the base of the penis, the wearable connects to a mobile app via Bluetooth to track performance during sex. Further, as with most wearables and trackers, the wearer can share their 'workout', and compare their favourite sessions and 'impressive' individual milestones via the accompanying app on social media.

Other wearables may seem outlandish, but on reflection *may* be considered useful. These highly intimate wearables include the KGoal Smart Kegel Trainer from Minna Life. Again, this is akin to a FitBit that tracks 'Kegels' (pelvic muscle exercises that strengthen the muscles around the vagina and anus), which help women avoid or reduce incontinence, and improve vaginal stimulation.[2] Acer (in addition to its sombrero) has also developed sensors that sit inside nappies (or diapers in the US) to detect moisture, methane, body temperature and sleeping position. All of this information can be relayed to an app. Another intimate wearable by Loon Lab Inc., named Looncup (based on the Mooncup, a re-usable period cup), is a menstruation-monitoring device that texts women while located inside their bodies. This lets women know the rate of their flow by smartphone updates and when the device is reaching 59 and 70 per cent capacity. By means of an app, women can track their period and receive information on the colour of the fluid that is indicative of factors such as sleep deprivation and stress. Indeed, if this is not sufficiently personal or intimate, Verily[3] have developed ingestible (as opposed to wearable) intravenous devices at nanoparticle scale that, taken in pill form, will be able to travel the body and scan for a range of phenomena, such as cancerous cells, plaque in arteries or for too much sodium. They have also developed contact lenses that can track diabetes (by means of measuring the levels of glucose in tears).

Other examples may make sense on first consideration. Disney Park for example sells MagicBands that customers buy to get through queues quicker because it contains their reservation data. It also tells them which parts of the park are busy and when the best time is to visit a ride. Inside each band is an RFID chip. This connects wearers to a network of environmental sensors inside Disney's parks. This allows in-Park personalisation so a host may greet the visitor by name. The band contains credit card information that allows people to pay for meals, snacks throughout the park and Mickey Mouse paraphernalia without them taking their wallet (and when payment is easier, we spend more). In addition to identification and payment, the band also collects data for marketing by information about which characters a visitor has interacted with. For example, if a visitor hugs Donald Duck, but walks by Pluto, Disney can tailor its marketing messages.

Increasingly media are something that we wear. As we can see from the examples above, this is potentially a strange understanding of media because we typically think of it in terms of content and entertainment. However, if we approach media as a verb – that is, to mediate – we recognise that wearable technologies contribute to the mediation of the body and human life. Wearable technologies are not a new phenomenon, not least because of MP3, Mini-Disc and cassette players before those. For the roots of wearables we can even go back much further to 1286 where, in Pisa (Italy), eyeglasses were invented that 'make for good vision'. The first recorded mention of these was in a sermon delivered by Giordano da Rivalto in 1306 (Ilardi, 2007: 5). By 1505 in Germany we had the Pomader Watch that was worn around the neck, shaped like an apple, and recognised as the first invented portable timekeeping device. The first computational wearable comes from circa 1660 during China's Qing Dynasty in the form of a ring with a usable abacus on it. Although simpler than the clockwork mechanism above, the fact it is a wearable computational device is worthy of special mention. By the 1860s watch production had gone into mass production by means of the Waltham Watch Company. This is significant because although clocks in towns had existed for centuries, wearable timepieces contributed to a common temporality (or sense of time). This was important in the industrial age when time measurement was critical. We might also signal forward to today's wearables where watches produced by Apple also contribute to a commonality of experience with fellow wearers (such as being able to send messages and intimate haptic buzzes).

Although early computers were huge (often the size of rooms) the possibilities of wearable computers were explored surprisingly early. For example, by 1961 Edward Thorp and Claude Shannon had constructed a single-purpose computerised timing device to cheat at roulette. One of these was worn in a shoe.[4] On entertainment, by 1979, we had the first mass-market portable music player in the Sony Walkman (the aforementioned cassette player). However, perhaps more than any one person, Steve Mann – the engineer, inventor and theorist – has realised both the technological and social promise of wearable computing. Since the 1970s he has experimented with new ways of mediating the self and his environment by means of sensors, transducers and other body-worn devices controlled by a wearable computer. Although many of his inventions presaged devices such as Google's Glass, it is the principle of using computational devices to self-track that is perhaps more remarkable. This is what Mann refers to as sousveillance.

QUANTIFYING THE SELF AND PERSONAL SOUSVEILLANCE

Steve Mann developed the word *sous*veillance to account for when we are doing the watching. This contrasts with more usual discussion of surveillance, which is when we are being watched. Mann's idea for the expression derives from the French words for above and below (*sur* and *sous* respectively). Thus, sousveillance may also be understood as watching from below. For Mann, this typically entails wearable and personal technologies. Sousveillance has two dimensions. First, it refers to the capacity to watch and hold power-holders to account (Mann calls this *hierarchical sousveillance*). Second, it refers to the capacity to watch ourselves (Mann calls this *personal sousveillance*). While Mann has invented a range of sousveillant technologies that record and sense, we can also see mass adoption of such technologies in, for instance, camera-enabled smartphones. What is refreshing about Mann's premise is that it allows us to see that acts of watching and holding to account are not uni-directional (or aimed at us). Instead we have fields and regimes of watching, holding to account and exercising of power (if people feel they are being watched, they behave differently).

Hierarchical sousveillance refers to resistance to surveillance societies (accounted for in earlier parts of this book) through politically or legally moti-vated sousveillance (Mann et al., 2003; Mann, 2004; Bakir, 2010). Types of technologies include aforementioned smartphones used to observe corporate and state observers, but also how they carry out operations. For example, any-one who has recently attended a political demonstration will be aware that many participants are recording events in case of excessive police behaviour and potential brutality. An early example of hierarchical sousveillance is the video camcorder footage recorded in 1991 that showed Rodney King, a black man, being repeatedly beaten by four Los Angeles Police Department officers (Bakir, 2015).

Mann's (2004) *personal sousveillance* is less overtly political in that it refers to mediated watching and recording of the self. By 1981 he had designed and built a backpack-mounted computer that was able to record and disseminate video data. As Bakir (forthcoming) depicts, from 1994 to 1996, while a student at MIT, Mann logged his life and continuously transmitted every waking moment of his life's experiences, in real time, to his website for others to experience, interact with, and respond to. These *CyborgLogs* were an early forerunner of today's impulse to share insights about the self with others (a key attribute of social media) and the Quantified Self[5] community. They believe in 'self-knowledge through self-tracking' and quantify their bodies and minds to learn more about themselves. In relation to health, for example, tracking and analysing trends can reveal useful patterns and thereafter insights into the self.

The technical and social logic established by pioneers such as Mann is manifested today in devices like *Narrative Clip*, a tiny always-on geo-tagging wearable camera, and better known devices such as Google's *Glass*. Now retracted from sale, this was first to grant web access, augmented reality, and pho-tos and video sharing when instructed to do so by the wearer. In 2016 Snapchat launched Spectacles, a set of connected sunglasses that record 10-second snippets of video. It remains to be seen whether people will take to being 'always-on' and see enough personal value in wearables to reach ubiquity. What is clear, however, is that we certainly have an appetite for increased life-sharing (demonstrated through social media) and use of a range of wearable devices is certainly increasing (also see Lupton, 2016).

Before mass adoption of the web we had a litany of self-help books to help us get into shape, eat better and live healthier. Today sensors play a similar role in that we use them as a means of self-help and to provide extra impetus to make a positive difference to our lives. In addition to standalone apps, wearables integrate with software platforms and Apple iPhone users may already be familiar with Healthkit. This provides its users with the opportunity to track from one interface an extraordinarily diverse set of states and activities. This includes body measurements, fitness, and basic data about the self, nutrition, results, sleep, vitals and reproductive health.[6] In general, if a wearable device can measure bodily output, it can be logged with Apple's Healthkit. However, although many of these devices and technologies are new, in many ways it is an extension of longstanding ownership of bathroom scales and the rough proxies we hold in mind of our exercise activity. Today, the logic of wearables promotes intense self-disciplining, self-monitoring and maintenance of the self as a productive unit (what have I achieved today, have I reached my targets and how can I do better tomorrow?). This echoes what Marwick (2010) phrases as 'self-work' and while her focus is the ways by which we construct self-hood on social media, the argument is similar in that we seek to refine, improve, enhance, augment and perfect the self. The quantification of the self through wearables also reflects Silicon Valley discourses of personal optimisation and 'self-knowledge through numbers' (the Quantified Self motto). This in turn reflects an attitude to health and the self based on self-reliance, self-improvement and self-governance. This is highly neoliberal in character and contrasts with healthcare found in clinical settings and expert/patient relationships.

We might note too that self-tracking is much easier than it used to be. When Steve Mann was developing and experimenting with wearables, they were comically big and ridiculously shaped. Today we have both tiny and soft sensors that are millimetres in diameter and able to move with the contours of the body. This means technologies have potential to fade into the background so to be far less distracting. This provides opportunity for unobtrusive use (and a higher chance of devices being used) and improved levels of tracking and wearable performance. For wearables to become a mass-market phenomenon, what is required is the 'socialisation' of wearables. This is an expression used by businesses (and in some policy circles) to refer to normalising what was once strange. This is done by embedding in everyday routines, making customary and thus rendering a given activity as ordinary. For wearables this requires big brands to get involved. Levi Strauss for example teamed with Google who have developed touch-sensitive textile that can be tapped and swiped under Project Jacquard (see Figure 11.1). The principle of this technology is to lessen distraction to better balance real-world interactions with our digital lives.[7]

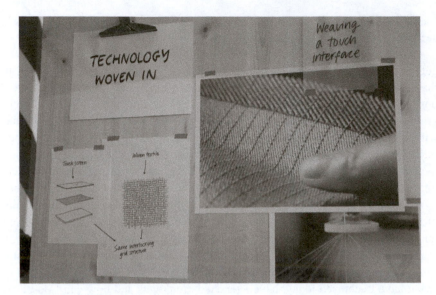

Figure 11.1   Google's Project Jacquard

WORK

Wearables have received most interest from professional and recreational sports. This is followed by workplaces. Businesses see an opportunity to better understand where workers are, what they are doing, measure workflow and productivity, engage in hands-free virtual meetings as people move, and to reduce the number of sick days. Increasingly this takes the form of 'encouraging' employees into healthier lifestyles. Otherwise known as 'corporate well-being', while people may be happier when healthy, we should also consider the possibility of *coercion*, or even being forced to self-track. This is reflected in programmes offered by well-known companies such as Virgin (and their software platform, Pulse). Other companies include Kronos that offer 'human resource solutions' that tell employers who is doing 'what, when, where, and why' (Kronos, 2016).

From the perspective of privacy, the coercion and consent point is key because even if an employer has the best of intentions for its workforce, it is likely that those who reject the offer of wearables will feel they have been placed on a real or mental list of non-participative employees. They may also believe that this may hinder career progression and opportunities. The concern here is that positive aspects of personal sousveillance become a means of conducting surveillance (that we described in Chapter 4 as collection of personal data to manage people). Although workplaces require management and some understanding of workers, the desire for increased workplace efficiencies needs to be balanced with respect for privacy and the right to a private life.

Surveillance through wearables entails time-and-motion insights into where people are, what they are doing, monitoring of workplace habits and behaviour, and charting the health of employees. The background to this is an industrial logic that emerged from the rise of the factory system in the late eighteenth century. This was not just about technology but an approach to management founded on controlling every aspect of production. This included seeing workers as components in production processes rather than free individuals exchanging labour for reward. The suggestion that people should wear wearable technology at work to monitor their performance should not be an easy sell (not least to professions with trade unions) because tracking devices give power to the employer. However, it may work the other way too because wearables can conceivably protect workers by revealing hidden hours and stresses.

What both positive and negative readings of wearable devices indicate is a renewed interest in the body. Indeed, one thing that conjoins most forms of work is the body; that is, there is quite literally 'some body' fulfilling a given action and role. Work is situated and, even in knowledge-based industries, employers seek to understand how bodies are performing, if only to track sick days. The role of bodies becomes even more pronounced when we consider that management structures typically address many people, possibly whom managers have never met. This distance from the subjective dimension of individuals gives rise to treating people as objects and statistical abstractions.

INSURANCE

Insurance companies are in the business of measuring risk. To do this they require as much information as possible to make decisions about the degree of risk and likelihood of having to pay out. The role of insurance in privacy matters is less pronounced in the UK (with its national health system) than with other countries, notably the USA (where health is a privatised industry). What wearables grant is insight into the health of wearers. Factors that can be assessed include exercise rates (steps, running and cycling) that can be balanced with body mass index information, but also more detailed information on heart rates (that change by age, fitness and stress levels). There is also the potential to collect data on mental health. From a personal sousveillance point of view, this is a liberating possibility. They quite literally assist in improving and better understanding both our bodies and minds. After all, our bodies are our own, and while we pay into systems to receive expert care and attention, there is merit in taking care of what is nothing less than our actual self.

However, sousveillance can tip back into surveillance. For example, health insurance companies such as Aetna, Humana Group, Kaiser Foundation Group and United Health are keen to obtain information from wearables. The incentive is clear, perhaps foremost to existing wearables users. Early adopters of wearable technologies tend to be people with a pre-existing interest in fitness and staying well.

The motivation is to demonstrate how fit you are and reduce premiums. There are two outcomes in that those who are fit and use wearables will reduce their premiums, but also that those who can afford the best health tracking devices will obtain lowest rates. This creates a two-tier system in which people who are not keen on wearables are (again) effectively coerced to wear them. Should this seem a little far-fetched, we only need consider the apps and devices we can currently equip our cars with to gauge whether we are careful drivers. In the UK, for example, the mass-market insurer Aviva provides an app that monitors a person's driving skills. Once they have driven 200 miles, they will get an individual driving score out of 10. Safer drivers scoring 7.1 or more can save an average of £150 on their car insurance.

The matter is less about exploitation, but unintended outcomes. When we are fit and well, our wearables reward us. There is a degree of 'gamification' as Apple Watch, for example, sets daily challenges for us to meet (steps, exercise, standing up and calories burnt). When things are going well (such as when I am not travelling with work, when I do not have a cold and when I make time to exercise), the experience of the gadget is a positive one. When I am not well, the experience of number, quantity and tracking is an oppressive one. The question then becomes whether we would like products that monitor negative as well as positive states. This links back to the previous chapter on emotion detection and the question of workplace monitoring discussed above. Spire, for example, provides a clip-on wearable technology that monitors body position, activity and the respiratory behaviour of the body (i.e. breathing patterns). Along with a standalone app that also interacts with Apple's Healthkit, Spire's product is an example of what we accounted for as empathic media. Spire's app tells me whether I am active, tense, focused or calm. The idea is that if I am in negative states of mind, I can recognise this and become more 'mindful' and attentive in moments that may trigger stress. When I used the product this included moments before giving a presentation and, more peculiarly, when writing tricky emails.

The broader question then becomes one of not just tracking when we are well, but when we are not. From the point of view of the data industry, they do not care whether individuals are well or not. Incoming information is simply data and, as we saw in Chapter 9 on big data, the processing takes place in black boxes. Instead it is *we* who are asked to qualitatively live with these devices. Do we want to be tracked so extensively and intensively? Do we want physical and mental well-being to be transparent to the data and insurance industry?

CRITICAL CONCERNS

For people interested in privacy and data protection these developments raise a number of questions and concerns. After all, what is proposed is an unfolding of our very self because the logic of wearable devices is based on rendering intimate data about ourselves for both personal and organisational use. These organisations may be health providers, employers, companies and, potentially, government signals intelligence agencies. The coming sections of this chapter address this by attending to the role of the body in privacy, the nature of objectification, transparency, critical thinking about objectification through wearables, but also questions of infrastructure and whether this data is being stored safely.

THE BODY

Although we typically think of privacy today in terms of surveillance, social media, data and digital matters, privacy is much more basic than this. In addition to who knows what, it is also the degree of control we have over our bodies. This is a large topic, but in relation to privacy scholarship it is best addressed by feminist literature. This looks at privacy in two ways: the first is the extent to which we are in control of our bodies; and the second is that privacy may hide crimes committed against women. The latter complicates over-simplified ideas about privacy as an always positive outcome. Feminists such as Catherine MacKinnon (1989) are concerned with the disturbing side of what privacy affords, particularly in terms of hiding and facilitating domestic abuse, repression, and the exercising of power over women and their bodies. Privacy seen this way is a negative condition that acts as a hermetic seal against public visibility so to facilitate unaccountable behaviour. MacKinnon (1989) has been instrumental in questioning the dominant liberal conception of privacy (that speaks of freedom, autonomy and independence without interference) because, for her, this liberal narrative privileges men over women. Thus, the 'right to be let alone' is, for MacKinnon, the right for men to oppress women in private spaces such as the home, without easy recourse to a public authority.[8] For MacKinnon this is why feminism has to make the personal political and open up what is private for public inspection and social intervention when wrongdoing is taking place. This invites questions beyond the remit of this chapter about unintended consequences and whether private spaces should be regulated by the state and open to inspection.[9]

In regard to the body itself, MacKinnon has been highly vocal on abortion, rights to choice and the ways in which women's bodies are treated like objects for men. Privacy in this context refers to bodily intrusion, objectification and control. By means of feminism's close attention to the materiality of the body, the ways in which it is put to work (be this through images in ads or prostitution), objectification and a less informational view of privacy, we may learn lessons about how to address wearable technologies. Anita Allen (1988), for example, defines privacy in terms of *restricted access*. This involves people being inaccessible in terms of body, mind and information. As more information about our bodies makes its way into the databanks owned by workplaces, corporations and authorities alike, privacy readily connects with notions such as the rights to reserve, intimacy and modesty. Allen's access-based perspective on privacy is worth exploring. It is predicated on: restricting access, limiting access to the individual, protecting from unwanted access to others, denial of access to information about personal intimacies, control of disclosure to selected people/groups, and limiting access to a person's life experiences and engagements. Privacy itself, for Allen, is a condition of inaccessibility, and losses can be said to occur when others assume access to our selves. The lessons we can take away from a feminist account of privacy are a renewed interest in the body, the question of objectification and the role of consent. Although objectification is typically discussed in sexual terms, the principles of ownership, instrumentality and commodification also play a role.

TRANSPARENCY

What wearables represent is a greater push towards personal transparency, or an unfolding of the body, physiological condition, behaviour, emotions, location, communication, preferences, activities and tastes. By means of intimate devices the possibility exists for the data industry to map bodies and physiology as well as communications, personal histories and our friend networks. While seamless and frictionless technology means communication and transactions will certainly be more convenient, it also means we will be less aware of what data we are sharing and with whom. Ease of use also dims awareness. There is then the question of who accesses this data, where it goes, how it is used, lifespan and the security of the cloud centres to which this data is be uploaded. Governments and security services accounted for in the first part of this book are undoubtedly interested in this data (location, activities, behaviour, physiology, emotion and communication).

There are clear benefits to self-tracking and personal sousveillance, not least the capacity to understand our bodies better and take greater control of our own health. However, we should investigate the principle of transparency because although our society has constructed it to be a 'good' thing, there are significant questions to be raised. I will explore these in reference to the work of Clare Birchall, Dave Eggers's novel *The Circle* and my own work on transparency (McStay, 2014). As Birchall (2012) discusses, transparency is less a thing but rather has more in common with cleanliness – a virtue. It sits at the opposite end of the scale to privacy. One can think of this as a visibility slider where on the one side we have utter transparency and the other utter opacity (Bakir and McStay, 2016). The notion of transparency finds roots in the Enlightenment and its concern with clarity and visibility, and ridding society of superstition (Kant, Rousseau and Bentham all figure within this). This is undoubtedly positive but, as Birchall suggests, while transparency has appeal, it too easily slides into totalitarianism, surveillance and singularity of approach. As we saw in Chapter 2 on 'nothing to hide, nothing to fear', resistance to transparency is taken as a sign of guilt.

As Bennington (2011) suggests, transparency acts as a kind of veil. What might this mean? For a tangible example, Facebook preaches transparency of our friendships, networks and interests, so as to be able to 'connect' us with more people and businesses, but the ways by which they process and analyse our data is impenetrable.

Thus, while the Facebook brand impresses us with openness and transparency, its functioning is highly opaque. In less highbrow literature (yet wildly thoughtful), these ideas are taken up by Dave Eggers in his novel *The Circle*. This sees the lead character, Mae, descend into deeper and farther-reaching participation and transparency, as she opens her life for all to see through always-on wearable cameras (perhaps a non-subtle allusion to Google Glass). The book is a satire of modern life, social media, popularity, self-tracking, wearable technologies, Silicon Valley, tech giants and the ubiquity of transparency. This is a modern-day perverse enlightenment where transparency and absolute openness is indexical with virtue. Three of The Circle's catchphrases are 'ALL THAT HAPPENS MUST BE KNOWN', 'SECRETS ARE LIES' and 'PRIVACY IS THEFT', thus meaning secrecy equates to deceit, and to keep an experience private equates to selfishness and denial of access to others. The idea is to remove all filters so to see everything at all times. The overall aim of The Circle is nothing less than the mediation of *all* aspects of human existence.

CONCLUSION

Wearable technology and self-tracking practices have positive and potentially negative characteristics. I have focused here on personal sousveillance, the quantified self, and the ways by which people use self-tracking and automated sensing to understand their bodies and minds. While much of this is useful, enjoyable and health enhancing, there are consequences of this technological development – especially regarding who else may put this data to work. It is early days but marketers, advertisers, social media companies, the financial sector, insurance, human resources departments and even Disney are interested in using data from wearables to track the self-trackers. This information derived from wearables about the body represents a new degree of transparency and data intimacy. As argued in relation to feminist discussion of privacy, access, ownership and objectification, the key is in the extent to which we are in control of this process. We might note that as wearable technology potentially merges into the fabric of clothing and everyday life, this effectively removes data collection and processing from view. I wonder, will privacy terms and conditions be placed on the label along with washing instructions?

Research and challenges

1 To what extent do wearables entail an increase in personal transparency? Also, account for the ways in which this is potentially positive and negative.

2 Should citizens be concerned about the granularity of data about the body being collected about them?

(Continued)

---

3 In what ways may sousveillance turn into surveillance? Provide cases and examples not given in this chapter.

4 In what ways does transparency act as a veil?

NOTES

1 Available from www.entrepreneur.com/video/252940.
2 Notably there was consumer interest as the kGoal crowdfunding campaign attracted 2,200 backers who contributed $266,917. This significantly surpassed the original $90,000 funding goal.
3 In 2015 Google created a parent company called Alphabet. Verily was formerly known as Google Life Sciences, but it is now a separate company in the Alphabet family.
4 They also constructed a computer that fits inside a cigarette packet. The computer allowed a player to time the revolutions of the ball on a roulette wheel and increase chances of predicting where it would end up. Used after the ball was launched (but with the casino still taking bets), the device boosted chances of the ball falling on the gambler's five favoured numbers by 44 per cent (Thorp, 1969).
5 The Quantified Self community can be found at http://quantifiedself.com/.
6 Apple was criticised for not including menstruation in the original Healthkit app launched in 2014, despite covering almost every other human metric. Having received criticism for this, Apple provided menstruation tracking a year later.
7 More detail about Project Jacquard available at www.theverge.com/2015/5/28/8682957/touch-sensitive-fabric-and-tiny-radar-chips-hands-on-with-ataps.
8 In 2015, in the UK, it affects 1 in 4 women and 1 in 6 men in their lifetime. It is also the violent crime least likely to be reported to the police.
9 Anita Allen (1988) critiques MacKinnon directly stating that she is wrong to reject domestic privacy wholesale because of the historic unequal treatment of women. Instead, Allen again points to progress made on being able to enjoy privacy in the home, healthier relationships, birth control, access to education, the workplace, liberal divorce laws and wider opportunities in public life. She comments, 'Instead of rejecting privacy as "male ideology" and subjugation, women can and ought to embrace opportunities for privacy and the exercise of reproductive liberty in their private lives' (1988: 56).

12

BEING YOUNG AND SOCIAL
INTER-PERSONAL PRIVACY
AND DEBUNKING SECLUSION

Key questions

- Is social media a necessity of modern life?
- What are the strengths and weaknesses of a context-based approach to privacy?
- Can you think of your own examples of when contexts collide?
- How useful is a protocol-based approach to privacy?

Key concepts

- Social privacy
- Context management
- Affective protocol
- Networked privacy

Ofcom, the UK's communications regulator, carries out an annual survey of media usage. Made publicly available each year on their website, in 2015 they found that in the UK the age and percentage of people with a social media profile breaks down to:

- 16–24 (93 per cent);
- 25–34 (90 per cent);
- 35–44 (80 per cent);
- 45–54 (68 per cent);
- 55–64 (49 per cent);
- 65+ (28 per cent).

Social media is used across almost all socio-economic groupings. Looking more closely, women are more likely to have a profile than men (74 versus 67 per cent) and Facebook is by far the most popular service as almost 97 per cent of UK adults with a social media profile say they use it. Fifty-two per cent of people with a Facebook account also have another social media profile. These are spread across a range of services, including Twitter (26 per cent), WhatsApp (24 per cent), YouTube (17 per cent), Instagram (16 per cent), LinkedIn (14 per cent), Google+ (12 per cent) and Snapchat (10 per cent). Ofcom's findings for 16–24-year-olds (as young as the survey goes) found that this age group is more likely than older people to have a profile on other social media platforms. Second profiles are: Twitter (40 per cent), WhatsApp (37 per cent), YouTube (32 per cent), Instagram (35 per cent), Snapchat (26 per cent), Tumblr (8 per cent) and Vine (4 per cent) (Ofcom, 2015c: 94–96).

Although people clearly derive gratification from use of social media, the price of not participating in social media is high, particularly for young people. While no one is physically coerced, for many, staying out of the loop is to risk being ostracised. This means not being invited to events; actively choosing not to stay in ambient contact with family members; missing out on interaction with peers; non-participation in 'group' activities (be this family, friends or school class work); not keeping up with events near and far; and missing opportunities for detailing achievements, reputation building, professional networking and there-after employability. Thus, although strictly speaking use of social media is a choice, it is perhaps more realistic to think of it as a *weak necessity* of modern life. Between the personal and professional, few people are unaffected. However, this chapter is less about how social platforms may or may not be taking advantage of the impulse to network and share content, but what happens to our privacy when we engage in these mediated relationships. As all users of social media will be aware, relationship management can be awkward and, sometimes, hurtful.

We have already discussed privacy in terms of organisations and institutions (be this governmental or commercial), surveillance, forced transparency, datafication of behaviour, the pre-eminence of advertising revenue, and commercialisation of the body and emotional life, but this chapter adopts a different approach to privacy. I am much less interested in institutions than what people do online, particularly young people. Here I assess the idea that perhaps one of the most interesting aspects of privacy is not surveillance by companies and computers, but the ways in which social media users watch each other, and how social media users deal with that. Be this unwanted sharing of photos, tagging, mistimed comments from friends, coping with parents who want to be 'friends' or bosses who want to 'follow' us, the media environment is an increasingly complex place and a minefield of potential embarrassment. Indeed, what social media tells us is that privacy is not just about what we choose to share, because the actions of others can implicate and potentially negatively affect us. As we will see, the consequence of this is that privacy is more than being about personal decisions of whether to post information, consent, or some other decision where an individual chooses what to share. Sometimes responsibility for privacy is out of our hands as others post, tag, implicate and mark us online.

Part of the problem is that our social media systems do not care. This accusation is less about the people running the networks than how technologies are indifferent to whether a viewer of an image is a boss, potential employer, ex-lover, grandmother, teacher or trusted friend. Although people are quite masterful in discriminating between how we behave and communicate with different people and groups in our lives, the capacity to control where pictures and posts go is more difficult online. This is a problem of context management. In assessing peer-based privacy, this chapter examines the work of danah boyd,[1] Sherry Turkle, Alice Marwick, Kate Raynes-Goldie, Sonia Livingstone and Helen Nissenbaum, who have each developed and explored the notion of a more flexible account of privacy, whereby we wish to share information with some people at certain times and under specific conditions, so we know what happens with our information. Although discussion of social privacy applies to all users of social media, I take my cue from the empirical work conducted by these scholars and assess it in relation to young people.

PUBLIC CONTEXTS

A famous sociologist named Erving Goffman wrote a book titled *The Presentation of Self in Everyday Life* (1990 [1959]). This depicts everyday life in theatrical terms where people, as actors, alter their performances to suit the setting. Likewise, privacy is employed in a number of ways, contingent on context, situation, place, technologies, people, roles and status, and what people are trying to achieve. There is a great deal of truth to this as we behave differently depending on where we are and whom we are with. From a privacy point of view, the value of this insight is that it tells us that we do not simply have private and public lives, but multiple public lives and modes of interacting with people. This is a rejection of simplistic binary accounts of privacy (private/public, in/out, on/off or yes/no) and recognition that as we move through daily public life situations, our privacy requirements change depending on the nature of the relationships we have with people in that situation. The key fact here is that in everyday life there is not just one 'public' – but many. Also, despite the fact that social media are highly useful for networking, building contacts, messaging, creating personal profiles, letting the world know what we think, and sharing creative and intellectual content, it is not very good at privacy. Although each site contains privacy settings, the default mode is to share with one great big public. This is unlike offline life, where we have different privacy rules for various situations, organisations, groups and people.

An extreme example of context management is sexting (addressed in full in the next chapter) because many people are happy to share intimate photos of themselves with selected individuals, but are appalled if these images are shared with unintended others. Although the nature of the photo plays a role, the privacy harm does not arise from the content of the photo itself, but the sharing of the photo outside of the intended context (that is, beyond the trusted partner to their friends). Irwin Altman was arguably the first to recognise that privacy is a 'dialectical' phenomenon. In our case, this means that values emerge from the relationship between two or more given actors. In the case of sexting, when person B (Bob) shared the image that person A (Sally) sent them, person B violated a dialectical understanding of privacy. Altman's (1975) dialectical conception of privacy is useful and prescient. He recognised that privacy in everyday life is about control and management of privacy norms in changing circumstances, with different actors and environments. This underlines a key argument being made throughout this book. That is, privacy is not just about seclusion because people seek interaction, as well as to restrict it. Thus, privacy should not be seen in negative terms (such as hiding), but as a positive assertion of choice regarding what to share and with whom.

Helen Nissenbaum similarly argues that privacy norms are dictated by social contexts (2004, 2010). This is because contexts have their own internal norms that in turn govern how and what personal information is shared and communicated. For example if I visit my bank manager, discuss the reasons for my financial situation and ask for an overdraft, I can reasonably assume that she will not share this information with friends during after-work drinks. Although the norm is not written or stated (or at least it is not available to me), we both understand this would be a breach of my privacy. This view understands privacy in terms of situation, appropriateness, the type and nature of information, and what and with whom information is being shared. It attempts to dissolve absolute privacy norms through the observation that people do not require complete privacy and different norms apply in different circumstances. It recognises that experiences of privacy are contingent upon who is involved, what the information is, how it is transmitted, who might be affected if a breach occurs and the difficult ways in which social contexts can overlap. Seen this way, privacy is a phenomenon generated from the actors in relationships within a network. This means that according to context-based arguments, which are ultimately pragmatic in nature, privacy norms are not once-and-for-all objective, but neither are they solely subjective. Instead privacy is specified and co-constituted by means of the nature of the relationship we have with people, organisations, institutions, and even technologies.

The nature of the relationship is made up of multiple factors. These involve: roles within a context, such as student, lecturer, medical receptionist, waiter and so on; activities, or what people are seeking to achieve, such as buy a book online, vote, report a lost wallet or share a photo; norms that define the duties, expectations, actions, privileges and what is acceptable for a person or technology fulfilling a role; and values that refer to the goal of a system. The latter recognises that we are always trying to achieve something. This might be obtaining education, staying healthy, being social, staying close to family, promoting one's professional reputation, or simply having fun or procrastinating. For Nissenbaum, the test for any updates to existing privacy arrangements is to measure it against existing practices and check whether it tallies with the objective of the system. This means assessing the extent to which it violates or complies with the existing norm. This is quite pragmatic as new practices are both assessed on their own merits, compared with existing practices, and thereafter judged by a cost–benefit analysis (see 2010: 171–179). The cost part of the analysis is not simply financial, but judged in relation to the ends, goals, purposes and values implicit within the system and its network of users. Her ideas about privacy have proven popular with technologists, policy-makers and the interested public because they are simple, workable and applicable to the development of new media technologies.

Seen this way, privacy takes on the characteristics of *protocol* (McStay, 2014). This refers to the rules, codes and norms that inform how elements of a system should behave. This echoes the work of Irwin Altman (1975) and more recent privacy scholars who recognise that a one-size-fits-all conception of privacy is of little use in everyday life. Instead, privacy has dynamic and emergent characteristics. An emergent and protocol-based view of privacy norms has two characteristics:

1 It is generated by behaviour of people within the network.
2 It also prescribes behaviour of people within that network.

This means that privacy norms are not imposed from without, but generated from within, and they are also tacitly, or explicitly, negotiated. This is a systemic understanding of privacy, whereby privacy regulates social behaviour. It sees privacy as an organisational principle in that it helps order the behaviour of institutions, technologies and, in the case of this chapter, social life. A systemic approach to privacy recognises that, as a protocol, it guides, facilitates, constrains and makes possible appropriate collection and movement of information. Within this is a key lesson: privacy norms are not dictated by external normativity, but by local values and objectives of contexts. Privacy is akin to language in that the content and expression of language changes over time, but language itself is a fact of human life. The same can be said of privacy in that there are different forms and expressions of privacy, but it is apparent in all societies, albeit in very different ways (Ford and Frank, 1951; Hall, 1969; Moore, 1984; Westin, 1984 [1967]).

THE FALLACY THAT 'KIDS' DON'T CARE

Nissenbaum's observation that privacy norms are social and contextually specific is a useful one. Likewise, the notion of protocol helps us understand that privacy is a code of sorts that can either be internalised (such as knocking on doors before entering), or discussed and debated, such as whether it is permissible to tell parents about how a student is performing at university (lecturers in the UK cannot do this due to data protection laws). Contextual and protocol-based understandings of privacy allow us to stop searching for an all-encompassing definition of privacy and instead approach it from an interactionist perspective, or one in which value systems are co-constructed by participants within a situation according to roles, activities, norms, values and goals.

Recognition that privacy is socially dependent is useful, but a contextual approach to privacy is the start rather than the end of the conversation. This is because when applied to the social media environment we have to deal with the fallout of when contexts overlap, when they are not neat and separate, and when we are asked to live out complex social lives in a public space that does not readily acknowledge privacy and separation of life contexts we enjoy offline. In addition to the fact that it is not always easy to separate life contexts online, we should also consider what users do online. At least in part, this is characterised by *social surveillance*, or the ways in which: 1) people scrutinise the content of others; but also 2) people self-monitor and attempt to understand how others perceive the content we post (Marwick, 2012). In other words, social media can be a messy place full of nosey 'friends' from different contexts, with a wide range of motivations and temperaments. This in turn generates a range of user behaviours to negotiate collapsed contexts and unwanted attention, and to ensure that the right people are receiving intended messages. These observations have led specialists in social media and privacy, such as Alice Marwick and danah boyd (2014), to contend that privacy norms are more dynamic and fast moving than Nissenbaum suggests. They argue that:

> Networked privacy goes further [than Nissenbaum's theory of contextual integrity] to suggest that information norms and contexts are co-constructed by participants and frequently shifting. There are differing skill levels to understanding context, and context slips and changes according to fluctuating social norms and technological affordances. (Marwick and boyd, 2014: 1064)

It is a pernicious myth that young people do not care about privacy. They do, but they hold social as well as institutional concerns, particularly when contexts collide. The reason for the continued life of this myth is that 'parents, journalists, and entrepreneurs often use teens' deep engagement with and willingness to share information on social media as "proof" that they eschew privacy' (Marwick and boyd, 2014: 1052). This is echoed by an earlier study by Sonia Livingstone (2008) of 13–16-year-olds. She points to media coverage of the 'MySpace generation' who were said to have no sense of privacy or shame, and to be more narcissistic than those that had gone before. Even worse, she highlights that it was commonly held that social networking is a waste of time, socially isolating, left children prone to being groomed by paedophiles, or teenagers ensnared into suicide pacts. This is classic moral panic grist. While outlying cases exist, the motivation for social media use is that:

> Selves are constituted through interaction with others and, for today's teenagers, self-actualization increasingly includes a careful negotiation between the opportunities (for identity, intimacy, sociability) and risks (regarding privacy, misunderstanding, abuse) afforded by internet-mediated communication. (Ibid., 2008: 407)

What Livingstone identifies is that growing up is not just a personal trajectory, but it is deeply wed to peer groups. Social media are, to an extent, the mediation and committing to digital memory of this experience. Identity is a key factor to social networking, particularly for an age group where members are viscerally undergoing identity development. In Livingstone's study (conducted in the 2000s) she observed how this manifested in choice of network (Bebo and then MySpace for young kids, followed by graduation to Facebook). Identity was also expressed through the design of personal pages, particularly sites that grant personalisation, such as highly decorated pages for younger members, and plainer more 'sophisticated' designs for older kids. Designs were also informed by the general stylistic orientation of a member's peer network.

What is missing is recognition that just because a person participated in online social life, this does not mean that person has jettisoned privacy from their lives. Given that social networking entails presentation of selfhood, identity management, and the creation of a biography of the self, privacy is always going to be an issue because one is (selectively) exposing aspects of one's self. This, for example, can invite nasty and abusive comments from others. As with offline life, we both seek to participate in public life, withdraw when we wish and have control over what we share and with whom. The key is that most people enjoy participating in public life and for many social media users, they are keen to let peers know when they are down as well as when life is going well (as well as the seemingly mundane middling bits of daily experience). This can involve very raw experiences, such as documenting how we feel when parents break up.

Livingstone found in her interviews that to believe that teenagers are not interested in privacy is utterly misguided, not least because it was one of the livelier topics of her conversations. Although users shared insights and information about themselves, they were also careful not to give information away they are not willing to share. Among all her participants she found careful consideration 'about what, how and to whom they reveal personal information' (2008: 404). Many also turned to more private channels of communication for highly intimate conversations (such as MSN and internet relay chat channels). This approach to privacy tallies with the liberal construction of privacy we developed in Chapter 2 that sees privacy in terms of control, management, autonomy and informational self-determination. It also aligns with an overall argument being made in this book that to see privacy in terms of seclusion makes no sense. For the bulk of the population who participate in offline and online public arenas, what matters is control over information so as to modulate and selectively reveal parts of the self. This is done with a view to enjoying more authentic and intimate relationships with others. Although today Facebook allows for different friend groupings, there is still a disparity between how networks and friendships are subtly managed offline, and the properties of social media platforms online that still tend towards context collision.

Similarly, in an ethnographic study Raynes-Goldie (2010) found that her participants care overall about privacy, but are more concerned about controlling access to personal information rather than how Facebook might use that information. This includes factors such as friend selection, inappropriate friend requests, lack of control over which friends see what and the problem of when different parts of our lives collide (such as the weekend party animal, the aspiring professional or the dutiful daughter). This manifests, for example, when another 'friend', such as a sibling, comments upon status updates intended for peers. Marwick and boyd (2014) relay the content of one interview they conducted where a 14-year-old boy says that although he is friends with his sister on Facebook, she should recognise that not all Facebook conversations are intended for her to comment upon. In interview, boyd probed this point and asked how should she know what is OK to comment upon and what is not. The boy responded by saying 'I think it's just the certain way that you talk. I will talk to my sister a different way than I'll talk to my friends at school' (2014: 1057). This is complex privacy protocol and an attempt to claim a modicum of control over interaction through linguistic and social cues. They also give another example of when a teenage girl underwent a break-up with her boyfriend. While her first inclination was to post song lyrics that reflected how she was feeling, she knew her mother would be reading so she posted 'Always look on the bright side of life' from the Monty Python film *Life of Brian*. This staved off unwanted attention from her mother (who thought it was a positive status update), but her friends spotted the intention of the post and texted her to see how she is doing. From the point of view of privacy this is interesting because the communication is taking place in a highly public space with little opportunity for privacy (unlike offline life where we have walls and geographic distance), so the teenage girl was forced to hide in plain sight. Marwick and boyd explain this in terms of stenography, or a form of encoding, where meaning is only accessible to those who know the codes. They also highlight the role of *sub-tweeting*, or the act of indirectly posting something about a person without mentioning their name. The key to this is that even though the person's name is not mentioned, it is clear whom the person being indirectly talked about is. On Twitter for example, it can involve either communication without the @ sign so the person in question will not be notified, or it can be more oblique and not contain any name at all. Thus, for example, if students wanted to chat about a particularly bad lecture I gave, they might refer to 'the lecturer' (or something worse!) without mentioning me by name. This gives plausible deniability, if I were to somehow stumble across the posts. This is another example of encoding and hiding in plain sight.

Part of the problem is that 'friend' is a deeply laden term. As boyd (2010) highlights, friends lists are not a cascade of people we trust and are affectionate with, and who we turn to in difficult times, but they are often political and social. Identifying a sentiment that most will have experience of, she remarks: 'In choosing who to include as Friends, participants more frequently consider the implications of excluding or explicitly rejecting a person as opposed to the benefits of including them' (2010: 5). Many of us simply accept all requests from people who we consider to be relevant. These people may well be individuals we have never met, or worse, people such as bosses and teachers.[2] This returns us to the problem of context and while some people find mixing different social contexts acceptable, for others it is an unwanted overlapping of parts of our lives. There is a key theoretical lesson here for privacy and media studies in that privacy is not simply about withholding information, but complex and dynamic management of information, how this is presented, contexts and their overlaps. In the case of social media context management, we are happy to share certain insights with some people, but not with others. The question of how to manage contexts entails recognition of the problem that 'being public' to all friends means our usual techniques of sorting life contexts does not work online. Again, privacy is less a binary question of privacy/public, in/out, see/don't see or share/withhold, but on social media entails difficulties in controlling the flow and interpretation of information in networked life.

In most cases, the outcome of context collision is simply awkwardness and possibly a little embarrassment ('did my Muslim auntie see that photo of me scuba-diving in a bikini?'), but it is an important feature of privacy in networked life. This is a broadly interactionist conception of privacy in that problems arise because we struggle to manage how we present ourselves. This is less about holding everything back or revealing all information about the self, but the lack of ability to manage how the self is presented to different people in our contextually complex lives. A photo of a drunken night is not innately problematic, particularly in regard to the friends whom we were out with, but embarrassment occurs when evidence of this transcends that peer group (and witnessed by family members, bosses or teachers). The problem of context need not be just about embarrassing photos, but even how we speak online. This is because in offline life we manage multiple public lives with moderately different forms of 'us'. On social media, to our friends, there is only one form of public life that is open for all our 'friends' to see.

LACK OF INDIVIDUAL CONTROL

Sherry Turkle's (2011) interview-based research with teenagers also brings to light a number of inter-personal privacy issues, particularly in terms of surveillance and stalking. She observed that on Facebook stalking and following without the subject knowing is quite normal, although it remains somewhat creepy. One of Turkle's interviewees remarks that while it is not against Facebook rules to look at other people's wall-to-wall conversations, most Facebook users do it, and 'it's like listening to a conversation that you are not in, and after stalking I feel like I need to take a shower' (2011: 252). Stalking, or less sensationally the act of watching and listening in to interactions that one has not been invited to, has become a voyeuristic norm. Turkle also goes on to highlight another interviewee who would not sign online political petitions, or even attend live demonstrations, for fear of being photographed and not being able to control where those photos might end up. Other examples of inter-personal surveillance include employers who follow employees, who might be reprimanded for an ill-judged comment after a bad day at work. While only anecdotal evidence, conversations in seminars with my own students revealed that even those in non-professional part-time jobs (working for hotels, furniture retailers and restaurants) were being questioned about content appearing on their Twitter and Facebook accounts.

Management problems extend beyond 'friends' to ways in which the construction of social media sites can be circumvented to access people's images without their permission. Raynes-Goldie (2010), for example, speaks of users she interviewed who found ways to access the accounts of ex-partners (by means of using other people's accounts). Images were also shared by right-clicking, saving and distributing. Photo albums were also ingeniously accessed by person A friending person B who is a friend of person C. When person B comments on person C's album, this allows person A to click the comment and access the album (this is to 'creep' a profile).

We can see that a notable feature of privacy matters on social networks is that it is difficult for individuals to have control over their own privacy. This has led scholars who specialise in social media and privacy to suggest that sites such as Facebook have forced teens to change their understanding of privacy to account for the networked nature of social media (Marwick and boyd, 2014). Part of this is due to the fact that privacy in the social media environment is dictated by: a) the actions of others; and b) the affordances of the platform, or what opportunities and constraints the technology places on online networking. Livingstone (2008), for example, highlights that some of her interviewees were hesitant to show her how privacy settings can be changed. We should note that although these interviews were done some years ago and Facebook's privacy settings have been through a number of iterations, literacy and confidence using privacy settings remains a concern. Further, although Facebook's privacy settings allow a degree of control over contexts and who sees what posts, this becomes more difficult if members of two of a user's social contexts are already friends (such as family, workplace, at university or friends from a user's hometown). It is also difficult (if not impossible) to control what friends post and although we might try to keep our social media profiles respectable, friends may view social media differently. Again, Marwick and boyd (2014) depict another interview in which a young man trying to maintain a professional profile to help win a college scholarship is unwittingly let down by a friend with a juvenile sense of humour who posts unwanted comments on the young man's photos. The problem is one of context in that person A has professional motives for using social media, while the latter sees it as a domain of banter and fun.

Social media sites, not least Facebook, contain privacy settings that can be difficult to understand and, even if understood and considered adequate, one's reputation is still prone to the behaviour of others. If someone posts an embarrassing photo and tags that person, or posts a rant about why Steve was such a bad boyfriend, there is not a great deal that he or she can do. Marwick and boyd report that in an environment where information can be rapidly disseminated, shared, replicated and altered, they find that teenagers' understanding of privacy entails 'an ability to control their situation, including their environment, how they are perceived, and the information that they share' (2014: 1056). This leads them to introduce the principle of *networked privacy*. This is 'the ongoing negotiation of contexts in a networked ecosystem in which contexts regularly blur and collapse' (2014: 1063). Seen this way, privacy is not a thing, or a state of being, but an active process of management and negotiation with people and technical systems. It also implies that it is not just a personal act, but also a collective responsibility. This is because social environments are just that, spaces which are made up of people. As such, *privacy is a common good*, to be achieved by co-constructed means. This is a key argument that is slightly different to the personal and control-based account that dominates understanding of privacy. We will return to this discussion in Chapter 13 on sexting.

PRIVACY: A FACT OF LIFE

We are routinely told that privacy is dead and people do not care anyhow. Both are inaccurate, for two different reasons. What industry, governmental and academic surveys repeatedly show is that most internet users are not at all happy about exchanging privacy (control over what happens with their information) for discounts and services, but feel powerless to stop their data being collected and used by marketers. The truth is that people do not do a cost–benefit analysis, but instead they feel resigned to the situation. Indeed, there is an implicit assumption in much of the social privacy literature that young people only care about online inter-personal privacy, rather than what businesses and governments do with their information. The evidence suggests that this is simply not true. A report published by DATA-PSST and DCSS (Bakir et al., 2015) – of which I am one of the contributors – found that younger people are very keen to have control over their privacy online (this figure is consistently over 80 per cent). However, institutions are not the focus of this chapter, but rather inter-personal privacy. It is here where we see how ridiculous the suggestion that privacy might somehow disappear is, but also that it *is* prone to redefinition. A 'norm' is just that; it is a standard practice and as such is open to being modified. As it is not an immutable law, privacy understood as a protocol is receptive to change. However, to say that privacy is somehow altogether defunct is to misunderstand the very nature of privacy as a core factor in how we relate to each other, and how we manage and enjoy relationships with other people (with some people we are deeply intimate, but we are not quite so intimate with everybody!). Likewise, the reader only has to look up from the book or screen to see doors, locks, curtains and blinds, to recognise that privacy matters pervade, construct and mediate everyday life.

CONCLUSION

Young people care about privacy and to argue that they only care about inter-personal rather than institutional privacy is to swallow a fallacy happily promoted by industries that mine data. However, much interest in privacy has focused on the role of government and the data industry, and for young people in particular, the micro-politics of privacy on social media are deeply significant and important. What teenagers implicitly understand is that privacy is not just about seclusion and avoidance of situations whereby they are required to share information. Instead they recognise that intimacy, sharing of experience and connections with their peer groups requires a degree of exposure. In many ways this is healthy because intimate conversation about personal topics is healthy. However, when mediated online, these privacy decisions come with a degree of risk, not least of context collision, and the posting of unwanted content about them. A key reason why this is so is because social media are highly public. Whereas in offline life there are multiple publics (such as home, workplace, university, pubs, bars and so on), in an online setting contexts tend to collide. Young people are acutely aware of this and attempt to manage these contexts in novel ways. This chapter has drawn on the research of danah boyd, Alice Marwick, Sherry Turkle, Kate Raynes-Goldie and Sonia Livingstone to articulate some of the techniques employed. This involves language play, cultural references, sub-tweeting and use of the technical properties of social media platforms. The intention of this is to exercise control over the social media environment, different contexts within this environment, reputation and the flow of information. What each of these interview-based studies shows is that privacy within social media environments is far more nuanced than laws, regulations, philosophical writings and theory typically depicts. Thus, whereas in earlier chapters we have discussed institutions, what teenagers' use of social media shows is a deeply tactical approach to this social communicative space. Critically too, whereas privacy is usually conceived in terms of personal control and ownership, on social media users may not be able to control what someone says or posts about them. Legal, regulatory, institutional and technical approaches to privacy tend not to reflect these cultural and micro-political aspects of lived privacy.

Research and challenges

1   This chapter uses insights and data about young people, but myself and other researchers cited in this chapter are beyond our early 20s. How do the views contained compare with your experience and that of your peer group? Also see a blog post titled 'A Teenager's View on Social Media: Written by an Actual Teen'.[3]

2   What privacy and identity management techniques do young people employ on social media other than Facebook?

3   If privacy is at least in part subject to redefinition, what factors lead to this development?

NOTES

1   See her autobiographical webpage for reasons for lack of capitalisation at www.danah.org/aboutme.html.

2   This applies to lecturers too: many of us have balanced the offence caused by snubbing a friend request from a student with the wish to protect one's private life.

3   Available from https://backchannel.com/a-teenagers-view-on-social-media-1df 945c09ac6#.vx8ozi72y.

13
SEXTING
EXPOSURE, PROTOCOL
AND COLLECTIVE PRIVACY

Key questions

- How does affect contribute to understanding of privacy?
- To what extent is privacy a collective responsibility?
- Given the risks, why do people send sexts?
- To what extent is sexting a form of cyber-bullying?

Key concepts

- Unwanted exposure
- Affect
- Affective protocol
- Collective privacy

Sexting refers to the practice of people sending nude or explicit images of themselves, usually through social media. It is also referred to as cybersex, sending nudes, sexts, dodgy pix, fanpics or just selfies. People typically do this to create erotica, enliven their sex lives and generate greater closeness. Married couples and people in long-term relationships do it but, as this chapter will explore, so do younger people. This brings with it questions about pressure, motivation and laws about the dissemination of explicit images of children. There are a variety of tools used for sexting, such as email and images sent via text and messaging services, but also mobile apps such as Snapchat, Kik, Whatsapp, HouseTab, Frankly and Tinder. Some of these, such as Snapchat and Frankly, promise disappearing messages, videos and images, although screenshots of images can be saved and third-party applications exist that get around Snapchat's privacy features. This chapter discusses sexting with smartphones in mind, although images snapped on mobiles may be viewed and shared on tablets and computers. Conversely, sexting may be captured via webcam, but seen and shared on phones.

As this chapter will detail, sexting invokes every understanding of privacy employed so far in this book. When sexting goes wrong and images end up where they should not be, this is clearly a traumatic event. From the point of view of privacy, it illustrates principles of informational control and management, which in turn draws upon liberal notions of autonomy, and respect for selfhood and the sovereignty of others. This chapter adds to this by introducing the affective dimension of privacy that refers to corporeal experiences of privacy. Too often privacy is thought of in abstract terms of data and information flow, whereas experience of privacy matters can quite literally be gut wrenching. Another key fact that sexting teaches us about privacy is the role of protocol and behavioural norms that guide what people do in groups. I introduced this social conception of privacy in Chapter 12, but its role is even more important here. This is because sexting, a practice engaged in by around 20 per cent of all smartphone users, entails not just personal, but collective privacy responsibility.

WHO DOES IT?

Although initially more popular with people in their 20s and 30s, recent years have seen an increase of interest from teenagers. As presented in Table 13.1, US research by the Pew Research Center (2014a) depicts the percentage of smartphone users who use their phones to receive, send and forward sexts.

Table 13.1 Breakdown of smartphone users who use their phones to receive, send and forward sexts

Age	Receiving sexts (%)	Sending sexts (%)	Forwarding sexts (%)
18–24	44	15	6
25–34	34	22	5
35–44	22	11	2
45–54	15	5	2
55+	4	Less than 1	Less than 1

Until 2013, sexting was more popular with 25–34-year-olds, but the survey shows an increase so that 18–24-year-olds are now receiving more than 25–34-year-olds, although notably the older group continue to send more. The survey also shows that:

- 9 per cent of adult cell owners have sent a sext of themselves to someone else, up from 6 per cent of cell owners who said this in 2012.
- 20 per cent of cell owners have received a sext of someone else they know on their phone, up from 15 per cent who said this in 2012.
- 3 per cent of cell owners have forwarded a sext to someone else – unchanged since 2012.
- Married and partnered adults are just as likely as those not in a relationship to say they have sent sexts; single adults are more likely to report receiving and forwarding such images or videos.

Notably, it is not just single people on the dating scene taking part in sexting, because people in relationships send sexts at almost the same rate compared to those who are single. This invites speculation on the medium (smartphones) and their role in relationships. Rather than just being means of buying, searching and organising, media technologies also enhance emotional intimacy in relationships. The survey supports this observation by pointing out that 21 per cent of internet users or smartphone owners who are in committed relationships 'have felt closer to their partner because of exchanges or conversations they had online or by text message'. Another 9 per cent have 'resolved an argument with their partner online or by texting that they had difficulty resolving in person' (Pew Research Center, 2014a).

For people who do not sext, this might lend a degree of understanding to why people do it. It is less about communication but enhancing intimacy, reducing distance, nurturing closeness, and sharing emotional and erotic feelings from afar. Such behaviour must be seen in the context of trust and desire for open and authentic relationships with others. Sexting is thus an extension of pre-existing intimate behaviour. However, things go wrong, particularly when relationships breakdown. For example, a US-based study by McAfee (2014) found that 36 per cent of people have sent or intend to send intimate content to their partners, but also that one in ten ex-partners threatened to expose risqué photos online – a threat carried out 60 per cent of the time.[1] The reasons for partner actions that lead to the exposure of personal data are as follows: lied (45 per cent); cheated (41 per cent); broke up with me (27 per cent); called off wedding (14 per cent); posted picture with someone else (13 per cent); and other (13 per cent). The gender breakdown is also interesting because McAfee's study finds that in 2013, despite the risks, 36 per cent of Americans still planned to send private sexual images to their partners via email, text and social media on Valentine's Day. Notably more men plan to do so, compared with women (43 vs. 29 per cent), even though men get threatened to have their photos exposed online more than women (12 vs. 8 per cent) and often have the threats carried out more than women (63 vs. 50 per cent). What is clear from the study is that private sharing of intimate imagery is an entrenched part of sex and relationships in digital life, but it comes with risks.

WHAT ABOUT YOUNGER PEOPLE?

As a number of studies show, the negative outcomes of sexting are not just restricted to adults. It is very popular among younger people who are still considered children. In 2015 the UK's National Crime Agency (NCA) and CEOP (Child Exploitation and Online Protection Centre) reported that child protection officers were investigating an average of one case involving sexting every day. There are five areas of concern:

1 Young people are targeted by strangers who attempt to blackmail them over images and videos they have been tricked into taking and sharing.
2 Private messages between friends can be forwarded to others without the sender's consent.
3 Users post pictures of themselves on websites or social media with low privacy settings, so more people than anticipated see them.
4 In the UK it is illegal for anyone under 18 to take, possess or share 'indecent images' even if they are the person in the picture.[2]
5 If in trouble, children are reticent to tell their parents for fear of being judged or having their phones taken away.

As the National Society for the Prevention of Cruelty to Children (NSPCC) highlight in their description of sexting, many young people see it as flirtation and part of normal life (NSPCC, 2015). To appreciate the nature of sexting for young people, we should recognise that sexting does not happen in isolation from offline life. As Ringrose et al. (2012) highlight, this takes place in a broader domain in which media culture has become increasingly sexualised. The reasons for this are multiple, but clearly associated with media saturation of sexualised bodies (advertising and music videos for example), normalisation of pornography, and mainstreaming of lap-dancing and pole-dancing (such as becoming a fitness activity and not just a feature of the sex industry). The situation is a complex one, but what is clear is the connection with pornography as girls' bodies are being expressed, collected and mediated through the language of online pornography. Although girls are quite clearly the victims here, a point made by Salter (2015) illustrates the somewhat poignant nature of collecting 'nudes' and sexting. He highlights that a number of females he spoke to expressed sadness about the loss of platonic opposite-sex friendships with males who could no longer be trusted.

To explore sexting and children, I draw heavily on a report produced for the NSPCC by Jessica Ringrose, Rosalind Gill, Sonia Livingstone and Laura Harvey titled *A Qualitative Study of Children, Young People and 'Sexting'*.[3] This contains findings and insights from qualitative research by the authors with schoolchildren from London. What is immediately notable is that the fun dimension of sexting seems notably absent for girls and that they are under enormous pressure to conform to the wishes of boys. Indeed, many of the examples the authors give are nothing less than alarming. For example, they report that one common practice of sexting is when schoolboys request, and schoolgirls send, an image of either the whole body, or a part, where a boy's name has been written in black marker pen. This is to indicate male ownership of the girl's body. This would then be uploaded to a social networking service such as Facebook or Bebo. Connected, in-school harassment is also common as many boys assume that the bodies of girls are *for them*. Examples include boys being controlling over what clothes their girlfriends wear. This is less about defending the interests of the girl, but the reputation of boys (who do not want a 'slag' for a girlfriend). Also, because of unwanted touching and groping, girls have had to resort to wearing shorts under skirts to avoid 'touching up' by boys. Verbal objectification includes requests to ejaculate upon a girl's face and demands for oral sex. Even more alarming, interviewees also described 'daggering', which 'involves being "rushed" or pushed down by a group of boys and enduring them "daggering" (that is thrusting one's penis, "dry humping" or masturbating against you from behind), usually in the school corridor' (Ringrose et al., 2012: 33).

SEXTING: A FORM OF CYBER-BULLYING?

Cyber-bullying by definition takes place through electronic communication, such as through social networks, phone calls, text messages or email. It entails threats, harassment or public humiliation. Much of this applies to child sexting too, despite beginning as a way of enhancing pre-existing relationships. Ringrose et al. (2012: 24) depict a range of sexting formats and situations:

1 Asking for 'bare' photos (mostly boys asking girls for photos in bra, bikini or topless);
2 Posting sexually explicit BlackBerry pin broadcasts and messages;[4]
3 Collecting bare photos (such as girls in bra or cleavage);
4 'Exposing', or sharing, posting or distributing without the sender's permission, sexually revealing or compromising photos;
5 Screen munching: when 'sex talk', for instance promising a 'blow job', can be made public through munch screens on digital teen social networks and phones;
6 Posting a sexually explicit photo (peer produced or professionally produced pornography including animated images) on Facebook, BlackBerry (or other peer digital networks);
7 Harassing others with sexually explicit images, for instance pornography on phones or by tagging other young people in the images.

Online, girls on social media and BBM peer networks are repeatedly asked to perform sexual acts and for photos by boys. One boy says he asked for a photo of a girl's cleavage to have as his profile picture, with another boy saying that he enjoyed the satisfaction that he could ruin a girl's reputation. The authors also highlight that requests for sex acts are not just sporadic, but for many girls daily (the researchers witnessed pings and phone activity even as the interviews were being conducted). The boys get angry on being turned down, not least because they seek to improve their own 'ratings'. This is established by how many girls they can get to send them sexts (extra kudos is awarded for getting pictures of girls who would not be expected to send them) (also see Ringrose et al., 2013). This is known as 'snaking', where a boy befriends a girl, asks for sexts and then shares them among peers. Arguably, the sharing of nudes and dodgy pix is an extension of pre-existing shared pornography within male peer groups. This comes under the category of what Flood (2008) refers to as a 'homosocial bonding practice' that includes factors such as telling stories about sexual exploits. Deeply heterosexual, these typically reinforce hegemonic masculinities, homophobia, negative gender relationships, humiliation of women for male amusement and approval from other males.

CONTROL AND CONSENT

Much has been made in this book of understanding privacy through the principles of control and consent. Posting naked or sexual selfies is a strong example of this because when 'Send' is pressed, the content is out of control of the sender and the image is effectively public. While one might reasonably ask why anyone would send such images, the answer is that they are not aimed at the public. Intended for a trusted other, the sharing of such images is meant to be playful, flirtatious, caring and to enhance a relationship. Further, young people, particularly girls, can feel pressured into posting content they might not otherwise have done. A number of scholars have found that girls have been compelled by their boyfriends to deliver images, for example by them saying they only want it because they appreciate them and they want a memento of them (Ringrose et al., 2012; Salter, 2015). There is also the possibility of being under the influence of alcohol or other substances.

Although coercion and high levels of pressure are very real factors, what is perhaps most interesting is low-pressure conditions. From a privacy and media studies point of view (that is, typically interested in technology, autonomy, control, capacity to manage information flows and rights over one's body), this is important because it points to environmental factors impacting on privacy behaviour. As we have discussed earlier in relation to behavioural advertising, consent is a key feature of privacy because it involves rational exercising of control over information. In the case of advertising, in theory, we only give consent when we have weighed up the pros and cons of granting advertising networks access to information about us. In the case of sexting, we see that consensual sexting (and sharing of intimate images of the body) is potentially affected by need to participate in youth culture, dating, to have a boyfriend, gossip, flirtation and not to be ostracised. This leads to situations that elide the distinctions of rational consent theory as young people voluntarily and consensually engage in such practices, but do so in an environment that can feel pressured. Although girls are mindful of what happens when sexts go public and result in them being called 'skets' and 'sluts', this can be contrasted with a wish not to be seen as prudish or stuck-up (Lippman and Campbell, 2014). However, we should also note that girls who sext and send nudes may be chastised by other girls for being an attention seeker, as slutty and as deserving retribution (Tolman, 2002). Another notable social dynamic is when the female victim is a popular girl who enjoys high social rank. For example, an interviewee of Salter (2015) said that if a boy of a low social rank circulated an image of the high-ranking girl, this would have challenged the stratification of hierarchy, and potentially caused physical retaliation by the 'popular' boys.

EXPOSURE AND AFFECT

When theorising privacy we often examine laws, regulations and how technologies work, and we think of privacy in terms of information, where it goes, whom it is shared with and the degree of control we have over this information. These characteristics are all true, but we would have a very blank account of privacy if we ignored the role of feeling. In the case of sexting gone wrong, this is deeply visceral and occurs when images are 'exposed', typically by circulation through networks, posting on dedicated sites and creation of social media profiles (normally on Facebook) to display the images. A video produced in 2011 by CEOP (Figure 13.1) graphically illustrates the fallout of when sexting goes wrong and the girl (Dee) is 'exposed' to her peers.[5] It depicts how girl meets boy, they enjoy a relationship, girl sends non-explicit selfie, boy responds saying how 'fit' he finds her and how she arouses him, and girl decides she wants to demonstrate love for him by going further and sending naked selfies. Inevitably this goes wrong and the boyfriend who 'wasn't thinking' shares the images with his friend who then shares it with others. The video goes on to offer practical advice on what young people who find themselves in this position can do.

Exposure is something that young girls are regularly threatened with, even if they have not actually posted anything. This takes the form of a boy making up a sexual event and then others affirming the lie so for it to become truth. In the aforementioned investigation *A Qualitative Study of Children, Young People and 'Sexting'*, the exposure theme was a recurrent one and the study talked about it in terms of mental impact, depression, rumours, people saying negative things and 'haters' (Ringrose et al., 2012). The fear of exposure is not just about the revealing of body parts to a public audience. Sexting-gone-wrong draws on a longer social history of the good, pure and chaste woman that exists in the 'private' sphere; who contrasts with the whore and supposedly amoral and promiscuous 'public' woman[6] (Landes, 1998; Salter, 2015). Indeed, the construction of the public woman is an 'epithet for one who was seen as the dregs of society, vile, unclean'

Figure 13.1 Screen-grab of *Exposed*

(Matthews, 1992: 4). Modern-day language in schools of skets, sluts and slags is not too far away. What this tells us is that privacy harms done by sexting are not fixed and innate, but derive from the fact that self-published images of boys and girls are subject to very different standards of reception. Salter's (2015) study, for example, discussed one image a boy took of his own genitals that was considered funny and representative of 'gross-out' humour, thus positively raising his profile among peers. At worst, unwanted circulation of male sexts are temporarily privately embarrassing, and publicly shrugged off by a 'whatever', although Salter tells of one scenario where a boy with a small penis sent a 'dick pic'[7] and subsequently suffered social ignominy. However, in general, girls experience something more adverse, injurious and negative.

Indeed, one literal approach to privacy is to see it as *unwanted exposure*. The legal privacy scholar Julie Cohen, for example, accounts for informational privacy by means of phrasing it in terms of 'interest against exposure' (2012: 12). This leads her to define privacy as that which 'operates at the interface between evolving subjectivity and surveillance' (ibid.: 17), and that in thinking about how we should manage privacy at a societal level, we might conceive of it as a way of creating a border, boundary or buffer zone. She continues by asserting that 'Privacy law does not exist to protect fixed, exogenously constituted selves from the effects of technological and social dynamism; it exists to shelter dynamic, emergent subjectivity from informational and spatial constraint' (ibid.).

The point about emergent subjectivity is both important and less obvious than privacy as unwanted exposure. The idea of this is liberal in origin as it connects with principles of autonomy, the importance of selfhood and the belief that people should be able to develop in all sorts of ways, assuming no harm to others. It recognises that although the self is inimically bound to environment and society (the life context we grow out of), a liberal approach provides space for autonomy in which one can explore and develop self and identity away from unwanted attention from other people. Unwanted exposure in the case of sexting has multiple possibilities in that it may involve exposure of: a) what one party in the relationship believed to be authentic, personal, erotic and intimate moments; but also b) where images may be taken under a degree of coercion, which the sender may have preferred not to send in the first place. Whereas the first involves unwanted exposure of authentic sexuality and what was believed to be sexual fun/co-development with a partner, the latter entails exposure of a version of the self that the sender was pressured into being.

The reality and principle of unwanted exposure highlights the affective dimension of privacy (McStay, 2014). This tends to get lost in the assessment of legal, political and theoretical modelling of privacy. Indeed, privacy is by definition affective. This understanding separates it from rights, such as those based on property violations. For example, if someone steals my cash I will certainly be annoyed, but this is qualitatively different from a privacy violation. Notably too, if one has one's home broken into, the concern is less about the material objects taken than the sense of violation of personal space through trespass. An affective approach to privacy also applies to camera-enabled surveillance, tracking of emotions (even if not personally identifiable), or simply being irked by unwanted sharing of personal information with marketers. An affective understanding of privacy requires that privacy scholars recognise that privacy is not just about information, data, flow and systems, but embodied lived experience. In academic terms, we refer to this in terms of 'affect', or the role that emotion, feelings and sensations play in life (cf. Clough, 2007; Gregg and Seigworth, 2010). Although the point may be extremely obvious in that privacy events are very acute and often painful, we should ensure that we do lose sight of this when we progress to theorise privacy. Affective understanding is useful because it involves a refusal of abstraction and will not allow us to depart, deny, lose sight of or reject the lucid sense of a privacy event (McStay, 2014).

TOWARDS NON-MALE GRATIFICATION

Ringrose et al. (2012) point out that sexting pressure placed upon girls by boys allows little opportunity for them to articulate their own sexual desires, not least because they are cast into the subject position of 'slut'. This depressing account is deeply sexist, geared towards serving men and shows total absence of interest in female pleasure. Hasinoff (2012) also highlights that sexting is a distinctly gendered debate, although for slightly different reasons. This splits into: boys and their consumption of pornography (and what is done *to* them); and negative implications of girls' sexting activities (what is done *by* them). An undesirable outcome of this is that girls are held as responsible for their own online abuse. Academics who study sexting closely also point out the latter incites warnings to girls to focus on not being immodest online in order to reduce the risk of sexual harm or reputational damage (Albury and Crawford, 2012). If the situation for young girls is not already disturbing, Hasinoff points to a tendency within the US media to link acts of sexting with licentiousness and lack of moral compass. She cites as an example a CBS News *Sunday Morning* online article. This discussed a teenage girl who posted a photo of her in a bra taken by a friend at a sleepover when she was 12 years old. This was later distributed without her consent. The story goes on to detail that the teenager in the photo became pregnant at 15. For Hasinoff this implies a strong link between pregnancy and sexting, and thereafter that sexting somehow involves moral failings, being out of control, and a negative view of teenagers, girls and their behaviour.

Mobile phones play a pivotal role in modern social life. Both the handset itself, along with communication carried out on them, act as tools for building self-image, reputation, popularity, winning acceptance, and participation and performance in friendship networks. Central to this chapter, they also play a key role in forming, maintaining and manipulating intimate relationships (Bond, 2011). Although sexting has recently had a boost in press exposure, it has been taking place for some time. Mobile phones have been used for sexual purposes and to enhance relationships since at least the mid-2000s. Indeed, in relation to children, Bond suggests that 'the mobile phone is central to understanding children's sexuality and reflexivity in their construction of self-identity' (2011: 588). For her, this takes place against a social context where children's sexuality is effectively silenced in favour of a more innocent construction of childhood. Somewhat paradoxically, this lack of discussion takes place in a situation where sexual texts (not least online pornography) are abundant. Bond found in her series of focus groups of 11–17-year-olds that they thought mobile phones to be core to their experience of growing up and both 'supportive but also potentially damaging' (2011: 592). This led her to frame this insight in the social theory of Anthony Giddens (1990) who discusses the double-edged nature of modernity. This phrasing refers to the fact that modern technologies offer comforts and boons, but also the production of social, physiological and environmental risks. In the case of children's relationships with phones, positive characteristics included reassurance, security, enhanced friendships, with negative dimensions including uncertainty, isolation and loneliness (if there are no calls or messages). The 'temporal' dimension (which means sense of time) of mobile phones is also an important one that tends towards the need for perpetual contact, ambient sociality (such as constant messaging) and ongoing streams of communication throughout the day.

Bond says that in discussion of downloaded and user-generated sexual content on mobile phones, 'What was very apparent from the data was the blurring of the boundaries between the public and the private. What could be perceived as being private – the naked body or the sexual act – is transformed into being public by the technology' (2011: 595). This occurs by content first being shared between partners and then, potentially, more publicly. She argues that the intimacy shared between people who are communicating sexual content generates a private space. Likening it to the 'bike shed' of previous generations where much teenage fumbling took place, the creation of these virtual spaces possesses different rules than other spaces. These are fuelled by what is perceived to be a trusting relationship, although in reality this carries with it a significant degree of risk. What is notable in Bond's paper is that for some teenagers, there is also a degree of exhibitionism. Focus group members, for example, recounted one boy they knew who masturbated via a webcam and who 'flashed' his own genitalia with a view to getting a similar response from girls. Notably too, on occasion content was sent to the wrong person. Participants also highlighted that often they could not see what the images are before they opened it which led to difficulties in managing reception of unwanted pictures and risk. Despite this, Bond says that her participants believed themselves to be responsible for keeping themselves safe. Rather than abandoning responsibility (which may be an initial reaction to the suggestion of sexting), they saw themselves as weighing up risks and making reasonable choices given the social circumstances they are faced with.

Hasinoff (2012) attempts to build a more positive and liberational account of girls and sexting. While aware of the literature surrounding dangers and harm of sexting (Powell, 2010; Ringrose et al., 2012), Hasinoff (2012) also asks that we pay academic attention to the possible pleasures and benefits of sexting as well. For her, the positive dimension of sexting seems to be that it enables sexual confidence and that sexting should be investigated to 'help girls find new ways to express their sexual needs and desires and even perhaps re-write some of the gender norms that ask girls to be passive and acquiescent in intimate heterosexual relationships' (2012: 455–456). This entails greater sexual confidence to initiate sexual encounters and be more demanding of partners. Her argument is inspired by the work of the media scholar Henry Jenkins, who since the 1990s has explored at length participatory cultures, self-publishing, blogging and the shifting of emphasis from media elites to one in which media content production is something we all engage in. It is predicated on the suggestion that self-generated content leads to more authentic points of view. Hasinoff (2012) highlights techniques that use media technologies to help girls counter dominant objectifying narratives ubiquitous in mass-media content. However, sense of sexual emancipation through sexting should be counterbalanced with observations that girls seem to replicate the practices of commercial pornography (Grisso and Weiss, 2005; Thiel-Stern, 2007). Hasinoff (2012) responds to this by highlighting that sexting along with other behaviour takes place in a complex world of sexual representations that young girls do not control, further arguing that although they may draw upon the visual language of pornography, this does not mean that their behaviour is non-consensual. She progresses to argue that by taking control of the means of media production, engaging with the languages and politics of pornography, challenging conventional representation, and by embracing sexting as a means of critique (along with expression and pleasure), there is scope to challenge the norms of pornography (for example, in relation to female passivity).

NETWORKED NORMS

Although responsibility of sending sexts lies with the person who sent the message, there is also the question of the responsibility of the receiver. All life situations have codes and protocols that guide behaviour and, in the case of sexting, the responder is expected to delete the message (and clearly not share it with friends or others). In the previous chapter we considered the work of danah boyd and Alice Marwick who suggest privacy is best understood in terms of the norms of a given peer group. Helen Nissenbaum (2010) has developed the related idea of contextual integrity and elsewhere I have argued that privacy is best seen in terms of protocol (McStay, 2014). This entails the norms that guide the behaviour of both people and technical systems.

The observation that privacy is not just about the self but the networks and contexts we participate in (offline and online) applies to sexting. Given its popularity what matters is not just the personal decision about risk, trust and unanticipated outcomes, but also reception of the messages and what we do with them. This, for example, entails not just abstaining from sharing with friends, but also deleting them in case of loss of phone. For sexters, this is good practice, but from the point of view of privacy theory it highlights that privacy has a collective character based on trust and mutuality. This is a very different sentiment from how we usually think about privacy (that entails control over *my* body, *my* personal details and *my* information). Let us state this clearly: what we shall term *collective privacy* is an ethic, a responsibility, good practice and a decent way of behaving that is mutually advantageous for all who participate in flirtatious and erotic online culture. Thus, those who breach protocol and share images without the consent of the sender do not just offend the sender, but the community of sexters. As discussed earlier, this is not a niche community as one reliable survey says that 20 per cent of adult smartphone owners have received a sext of someone else they know on their phone (and 9 per cent of adult smartphone owners have sent a sext of themselves to someone else) (Pew Internet Center, 2014a).

CONCLUSION

The chapter has explored the relationship between sexting and privacy. Although routinely defined in terms of people sending explicit images of themselves, we might also recognise sexting as a technical extension of pre-existing domains of intimacy. Use of mobile phones in this way can enhance relationships. However, as with all performances of intimacy, there is a possibility of exposure and privacy harms. Unwanted exposure in the case of sexting can include making public what were believed to be authentic, personal, erotic and intimate moments. However, worse is when images are produced under coercion, where the sender may have preferred not to produce the image. Although it is difficult to argue against the fact that individuals remain the ultimate gatekeeper for what is produced and exposed, we must balance this with understanding of the growing ubiquity of sexting, smartphones and pressure on girls in particular to participate. We should also recognise that the internet was not built for children and contains few safeguards against types of content and misadventure. Sexting is only likely to continue as we further embrace media technologies and use them to enhance intimate dimensions of personal and inter-personal life. What sexting also highlights is the affective dimension of privacy, or the visceral and emotional experiences we undergo when we are publicly exposed without consent. Too often the affective dimension is omitted from definitions of privacy.

However, sexting also allows us to think beyond individuals to recognise that privacy is a collective responsibility and a public good. This has led me to suggest the term *collective privacy* whereby a break in privacy protocol does not just harm the person who has been exposed, but the community at large that use media technologies to enhance intimacy. Seen in this way, privacy is less about borders, barriers, seclusion and hermitage, but responsibility regarding the privacy of others so as to maintain a common good (capacity for mediated intimacy). This is quite a leap from how we usually think about privacy because we tend to think of it in highly liberal and individualistic terms. I pointed to this in the previous chapter but the idea that privacy is a protocol that guides the informational behaviour of a social context becomes highly apparent with sexting. As in the last chapter, we can also push the principle of protocol beyond the privacy of people to the behaviour of the technology too, such as apps that delete images immediately and promote responsible sexting (see also Chapter 5 which discusses privacy-by-design).

Some readers will understandably continue to argue that if a person does not want images unwantedly shared, they should not post them to anyone under any circumstances, but this is to ignore the gratification that people gain from sexting and how it enhances pre-existing domains of intimacy. Given its growing popularity it is of little use to chastise people for sexting, but rather for them to be both aware of the personal risks and, critically, to take collective responsibility for maintaining good privacy protocol. In the case of sexting this entails not sharing without consent and regularly deleting content. However, sexting among school children presents difficult additional challenges, not least that it is illegal (in the UK). The report produced for the NSPCC by Ringrose et al. (2012) contains six pages of detailed recommendations, but what is clearly required is greater understanding among academics and policy-makers of what is taking place in schools. This is a tall order, but includes: the extent of coercive sexting; gender relationships in schools; the emerging nature of the relationship between children and technology; what parents can do; the effectiveness of existing sex-education teaching; and how teachers can discuss sexually explicitly content and support students. What is not viable is to ban child sexting and although we may prefer it disappears from the social radar, this is highly improbable.

Research and challenges

1 In what ways do smartphones mediate modern relationships?

2 In groups, make use of reports cited in this chapter and provide workable recommendations to education policy-makers about what can be done to reduce negative aspects of sexting.

3 In what ways might teachers and other responsible adults support young people who have undergone negative sexting experiences?

NOTES

1 Study available from www.mcafee.com/uk/about/news/2013/q1/20130204-01.aspx.

2 In the UK, if another child has indecent images or videos of somebody who is under 18, they would technically be in possession of an indecent image of a child – even if they were the same age. This is an offence under the Protection of Children Act 1978 and the Criminal Justice Act 1988.

3 Report available from www.nspcc.org.uk/globalassets/documents/research-reports/qualitative-study-children-young-people-sexting-report.pdf.

4 The authors found a preference for BlackBerry because of its free messaging service, such as BlackBerry Messenger (BBM) or Ping, and that communication was less likely to be monitored by parents, teachers or uninvited family members.

5 Available from www.youtube.com/watch?v=4ovR3FF_6us.

6 For origins of this gendered split of private and public domains also revisit Chapter 2 and discussion of Aristotle and the masculine city-state.

7 Where males send females unsolicited images of their genitals.

14

CONCLUSION
WHAT DO MEDIA
DEVELOPMENTS TELL US
ABOUT PRIVACY?

What should be clear by now is that privacy is a far-reaching topic that reaches into multiple domains of media. I will even go as far to suggest that privacy is the number one issue for critical accounts of media today. The reason for this is because wittingly and unwittingly we are communicating (or mediating) more information about ourselves than ever. In this book we have touched upon, but not exhausted, a wide range of subjects. Specialists on any of the matters broached in this chapter may point to a lack of nuance and analytical sophistication, but this book was not written with specialists in mind. It is aimed at people who want an overview of the relationship between privacy and media. Hopefully, by working through multiple privacy perspectives to address diverse media, we have developed an overall appreciation of the centrality of privacy to media today. I began by exploring the background to privacy in Chapter 2. Although the word is one we used a great deal, it is one lacking in agreed meaning. However, rather than searching for a definitive, sentence-long definition, it seemed to me more productive to understand the context of the word as we use it in the West. This is primarily based in liberal politics and philosophical writing from around the seventeenth and eighteenth centuries. These are positive approaches to privacy based on freedom, consent, autonomy, self-determination, dignity and non-interference from unwanted others, although also recognition that security and liberty can be a difficult balance to achieve. More negative accounts also have roots in philosophy, not least Plato's shifty citizen from ancient Greece who does not want to participate in public life.

Our first foray into media culture in Chapter 3 was journalism. This has multiple relationships with privacy because, as a practice, it is about making facts public, while trying to protect the privacy of its sources. This raises ethical questions about public interest. After all, 'what is in the public interest' and 'what is of interest to the public' are quite different things. At the noble end of the scale, journalism reveals governmental and corporate misdeeds, but at the other end it is hurtful, damaging, salacious and more interested in readership, clicks and audience numbers for advertisers. Samuel Warren and Louis Brandeis's (1984 [1890]) essay 'The Right to Privacy', written almost 130 years ago, is arguably more relevant today than ever because it is based on the fact that new media technologies deeply affect the nature of journalism. Be these new modes of visuality (drone journalism) or the flow of information across the internet (that makes injunctions untenable), emergent media continue to challenge and contribute to redefinitions of rights to privacy.

Chapter 4 discussed surveillance, the chilling effect and the impact of the Edward Snowden leaks of June 2013. What he did was of deep historic significance because he revealed the extent of secret surveillance, bulk data collection, and storage and analysis of citizens' digital communications by 'Five Eyes' nations (Australia, Canada, New Zealand, United Kingdom and the United States). A central argument of this chapter is that being pro-privacy does not mean being anti-surveillance. Phrased another way, the supposed balance between liberty and security turns out to be suspect under closer scrutiny. Although one might assume that having more information is a good thing, this only makes sense if it can be analysed. An increase in noise to signal ratio, or the proportion of useful information to useless information in any given batch of data, makes the work of surveillance harder. This leads William Binney, a whistle-blower and ex-NSA employee of 36 years, to argue that mass surveillance simply does not work. Further, while there is no published evidence that predictive surveillance works, what is clear is that security forces are typically already aware of perpetrators of terrorism. What this tells privacy and media scholars is that the Hobbesian binary argument of security versus privacy is problematic because there is no public evidence that mass surveillance stops terrorism. Perhaps what is needed is smarter rather than ubiquitous surveillance?

Chapter 5 continued the discussion of surveillance but focused on encryption. Although at heart privacy is a basic fact of living in groups, technologies play a key role today in mediating communication. A key technique employed to help do this in a privacy-friendly manner is encryption. Used by many of our favourite devices and apps, encryption means to encode information so only authorised parties can read it. This is an example of privacy-by-design and, when implemented properly, means that meaningful content of communication is hidden not just from prying eyes, but the company that owns the communications platform. Apple in particular has made a lot of PR noise about privacy in recent years and while it is unclear whether this reflects libertarian politics popular among technologists, a wish to do the right thing, or understanding of a strategic opportunity to sell goods, the net result is a stand-off between leaders of the technology industry and national governments.

Chapter 6 departed from questions of governmental surveillance to consider the prominence of platforms of media culture, and beyond. In sum, platforms are organisations of the internet age because they do not make things, but mediate connections between people and organisations, and facilitate services. Before the web, we had not really seen anything like these before (although the internet itself is arguably the mother of all platforms). The logic behind the platform business model is to gain the maximum amount of users because more people using a service typically equates to higher revenue and a better end-user experience. Another notable factor is that platforms are based on software upon which much of everyday life is carried out. They tend to be systems that organise human activity, yet also disrupt existing ways things are done. This applies to buying and selling second-hand goods (eBay), shopping (on Amazon), taxi rides and personal mobility (Uber), searching for information (Google), buying craft items (Etsy), paying for goods (PayPal), leaving holiday reviews (TripAdvisor) and Alibaba (which is a platform for platforms). Each of these leverages the principle of connectivity. As platforms are able to supply smaller businesses with a larger customer base, this drives existing companies to work with the platforms and become part of it. Taxi drivers and second-hand booksellers may not like Uber and Amazon, but they cannot ignore them. Although revenue may be gained through sales, commissions, subscriptions and donations, they typically use data to create value. The problem is that each platform is very oblique in what it does with people's data. The lesson for privacy is that although we typically see it in personal control-based terms, individuals should not be left to take responsibility for processes that are difficult and potentially impossible to manage. Privacy is not just personal, but requires trusted stronger actors working on our behalf to create meaningful regulations about what is acceptable.

The role of advertising in funding media and driving platform development is a very under-appreciated fact. In Chapter 7 we investigated the state of advertising today and plotted its trajectory. The role of advertising becomes clearer if we consider a company such as Google. Although they create services and platforms that many people rely upon, over 90 per cent of Google's total revenue comes from advertising. Likewise, advertising funds an overwhelming number of social networking services, news sites, video players, forums and other sources of information and entertainment. Much of this is based on understanding our online behaviour. Behavioural advertising is typically done by third parties so, for example, when we log on to our favourite news sites, our devices do not just share information with these sites, but other actors too who serve ads on their news sites and collect data about our online behaviour. These third parties place tracking cookies on our computers that allow them to effectively follow us and track our online behaviour. Today this process is intensifying so all our devices are tracked so third-party data and location data can be merged with other data about 'people like us'. This is programmatic advertising whose objective is to reach the right people with the right messages at the right time. A problem with this is that, at least in Europe, this is supposed to be based on consent whereby we clearly indicate our preference about whether we prefer to be tracked and receive tailored advertising, or not. The extent to which this is meaningful consent is highly questionable. This should be placed in context of research that finds that people care deeply about online privacy. Note too, this is not just academic work, but this is echoed in studies carried out for the advertising industry that finds that 89 per cent of people 'want to be in control of their online privacy'. In practical, legal and philosophical terms, consent is the fundamental lynchpin. The chapter progressed to consider critical scholarship on the commodification of mediated life. Although typically dressed by Marx-inspired commentators in terms of labour (generation of value for others), Marx's notion of alienation is a better fit. This means to be estranged from something that belongs to us, but has come to be separate from us. In its original usage it referred to material products of work and labour, but in a digital context alienation reflects a lack of control over how information about ourselves ends up being presented back to us in the form of ads and marketing that seeks to extract further value from us. This chapter also addressed the relationship between media scholarship on privacy and Marx, highlighting problems with property and an uncomfortable lack of interest from Marxist writing in human rights.

Chapter 8 explored what happens when the right to privacy collides with the right to freedom of expression. This is what transpired with the 'right to be forgotten' case in Europe that began in 2009. More formally known as *Google Spain SL, Google Inc. v Agencia Española de Protección de Datos, Mario Costeja González*, this eventually led the Court of Justice of the European Union to rule that internet search engines must remove information deemed inaccurate, inadequate, irrelevant or excessive for the purposes of data processing. This was not just a legal ruling, but also an ethical right to have unwanted information fade from public view and be forgotten. This runs counter to the search industry, not least Google, and its narrative that it can organise the world's information to provide a one-stop window into a global memory. In practice, if a person wants to have linked stories removed from Google, they apply to Google who assesses each individual request to decide whether there is public interest in keeping the information on its search results. What the 'right to be forgotten' case brings to light is the nature of modern media and memory, and changes in news rhythm and temporality. From the point of understanding the relationship between privacy and the media, it tells us that the ethics of privacy are not always easy and one-sided. In the case study, the 'right to be forgotten' sees rights to speech, expression and knowledge clash with privacy. The court ruling itself was a good example of both practical and philosophical pragmatism.

Chapter 9 considered big data, machine learning and critical approaches to algorithms. Although the big data moniker is often maligned and overused, when one considers that it does not just refer to lots of data, but also different forms of data being processed in real time, the term has analytical value. Along with platforms discussed earlier, big data processing reflects key changes in domains that rely on information. These include surveillance, health, policy making, insurance, marketing, manufacturing, pharmaceuticals/life sciences, retail, technology, education and media. Recent scholarship in media studies has paid attention to these developments and questioned the terms by which 'correlations' are discerned.[1] In particular, it has noted that machines are prone to discrimination and longstanding cultural biases. Ultimately this is not the fault of machines but the people that supervise them in direct and indirect ways. Trust and faith placed in machines also leads to lack of critical questioning about how machines arrived at their insights, decisions and suggestions. This is important because judgements made by machines are gradually shaping important parts of our lives, such as decisions about health, insurance, employability, surveillance, creditworthiness and likelihood of criminality. A key problem is that the algorithms and the 'black boxes' that contain them are only accessible to very few people. The chapter ended by calling for effective oversights and greater transparency over automated decision-making.

Chapter 10 focused on how emotions are being quantified. Here I suggested that analytical technologies employed to understand emotions and intentions are showing characteristics of empathy. This is based on technologies developed in the field of affective computing. To understand emotions, sensors in our devices and environments assess and interpret speech, gestures, gaze direction, facial cues and other bodily signals. This might be through wearables, webcams, digital assistants, input devices for games, microphones/cameras in smartphones and tablets, or sensors embedded in public spaces. To explore the latter I examined out-of-home advertising that employs facial coding of emotions so as to evolve and improve advertising in real time. Notably, the Bahio case examined does not make use of personally identifiable data. This is very important because this case study raises questions not just about data protection, but the very usefulness of the concept of privacy itself. The problem is that certainly in a legal setting, if not elsewhere, privacy is wedded to identification. What is required is critical attention not just to privacy, but intimacy and the affective properties of information.

Chapter 11 addressed wearables. These take multiple forms from the well-known Apple Watch to the weird and bizarre that track the most personal of activities, such as the male 'thrust' tracker called Sexfit from Bondara (which also allows wearers to share and compare data with other users). The impulse for personal sousveillance and quantification of the self is not especially recent. Even those who care little for technology often possess bathroom scales, but today the industrial interest in data about our bodies is palpable. This includes aforementioned platforms such as Google, Apple and a long list of start-up firms, but notably also employers and insurance companies. Employers are keen on data from wearable technology to reduce insurance costs and better understand the workforce, their behaviour, location and psychological states (such as stress). Insurance companies themselves are interested in wearable data to better manage risk by means of understanding more about customers' health. From a privacy point of view, there is a coercive element to this in that it is quite conceivable that those who do not wear wearables may be required to pay more (or wearers will receive lower premiums), and those who can afford the best health tracking devices (such as the Apple Watch) will obtain lowest rates. To understand this situation I examined these concerns in relation to the larger picture of generalised commercial interest in the body and its unfolding for commercial purposes. Feminist literature has the most experience of privacy and the body, arguing for rights in relation to access, objectification, intrusion, reserve, modesty and dignity. In general, losses to privacy occur when others assume and/or force access to our selves.

Much of this book has focused on institutions, but Chapter 12 examined inter-personal privacy and the subtle defences (and attacks) of privacy achieved by young people's use of social media. Some of these are technical, but they also employ tactical language play, cultural references and sub-tweeting. We can learn a great deal from social media because what adult and youthful use shows is that people are very willing to share insights and information about themselves, yet still require privacy. Is this a paradox? No. We can see this in our offline lives in that we are constantly exposing and being intimate with others to varying degrees. What social media also tells us about privacy is that it not just an individual act, but a collective responsibility because the behaviour of others can impact and affect us. Although experiences of privacy are certainly personal, privacy is to be defended as a common good.

Chapter 13 continued an interest in networked privacy and the idea that privacy is collective and structural. This means it is guided by privacy protocol that emerges from affordances of the platform itself (what it allows/denies) and cultures of use (that both guides users and is created by users). We focused on sexting (or sending nudes). This allowed us to consider motivations and pressures to send deeply personal images, how smartphones are embedded in relationships, the affective nature of privacy when sexting goes wrong, connections with cyberbullying, the influence of ratings from other parts of the social web and the deep gender divide that sexting highlights. This is especially evident in personal and group reactions when personal images are exposed and go public. Boys are able to fall back on 'gross out' humour, while girls suffer accusations of being a whore, promiscuous, dirty, and today's vernacular of skets, sluts and slags. The growing use of sexting among young people and adults shows us that, again, privacy is not just a personal experience of borders, breaches and seclusion; but a collective responsibility, a code of conduct and a fundamental ethic in modern mediated life. All intimacy involves risk and while sexting can go badly wrong, when seen in the context of need for intimacy, close, deep and authentic relationships with others, it becomes more understandable. All meaningful relationships entail trust, unanticipated outcomes and potential pain.

THE BIG PICTURE

What media developments tell us about privacy is that privacy is not about seclusion because people are willing to share and communicate the most intimate of details about themselves under the right conditions. Despite the fact that this entails selected openness and transparency, this is still privacy behaviour. Also, despite its liberal origins in respect of selfhood, autonomy and control, it is clear that privacy includes these principles, but is not synonymous with them. Instead, it is increasingly understood in terms of group behaviour, the values embedded in our media technologies, and finally the protocols that affect how people and machines behave. These protocols are both written and unwritten scripts of what is right, wrong, allowed, disallowed and acceptable in a given situation. Critically, this applies to the behaviour of technologies as well as people.

To end the conclusion and this book, there are a few final points I'd like to highlight. These are musings rather than arguments. The first is that where possible we should avoid dystopian narratives of privacy and media matters. To make sense of anything we do not properly understand, people (not least academics in the media and cultural studies field) take recourse to metaphor to understand, explain, relate and theorise. Although articulating complex information in simpler form is useful, it runs the risk of distortion. For privacy and surveillance matters, Orwell's 'Big Brother' from the novel *1984* is the most obvious crutch, but my more general suggestion is the avoidance of invocation of vague unseen conspiratorial powers.[2] This is not always easy because much of what the data industry and surveillance agencies do is oblique, but that only means we should look harder, or look at what is around it, so as to better understand its shape and composition. This involves study of industry reports; participating in public industry webinars; going to free industry/policy conferences (and blagging into ones with fees); following thought leaders and relevant figures on social media; assessing financial records and laws; asking what citizens think (surveys/interviews/focus groups); learning what policy-makers think and do; meeting people in the media and technology industry (who are of course regular people!); reading patents of technologies (a brilliant source of what companies want to do); analysing public speeches (that are deeply crafted and considered), and of course interrogating the technologies themselves. This does not require us to be computer scientists, but instead comprehend how technologies achieve the purpose they were constructed for, whom they serve, what they deny, what their properties are and how they promote or weaken privacy.

Although I suggest avoidance of dystopian accounts, this does not mean we should be a-political. My argument is quite the opposite. As we have seen in this book, power is exercised in both overt and subtle ways. These include: attempts to force journalists to reveal sources (or for the state to hack their devices); by surveilling entire populations with no democratic conversation about whether this is the right thing to do; platforms that are playing increasingly key roles in social life to collect data; advertising and its meaningless consent mechanisms; use of emotions to help marketers shape how we think (and, on the horizon, to help governments regulate cities by mapping emotions to geographic regions); information about our bodies to further interests of employers and the insurance industry; and social media and the ways in which schoolchildren may leverage a very visceral form of power over fellow schoolchildren. In spite of this, there is little point in lamenting and decrying the current state of affairs. Rather, we should get on with the business of understanding the situation in detail and, if the case is important enough to us, we should try to do something about it. The opportunities here are diverse and include changing our own behaviour, recommending neighbours do the same, and joining a privacy group (such as Electronic Frontier Foundation, Privacy International, Open Rights Group or any other easily found on a search engine). The reader might also ensure they write to their local politicians when current affairs involving privacy flare up. All of this is helped when we remember the key argument of this book: *privacy is positive*; it is not about seclusion or hiding, but it is an expression of the right to selfhood. Sometimes we will share a great deal, but our willingness to do this should never be assumed.

As we look to the future for privacy and media studies, inexorably those interested in data will want to know more about intimate life. As we saw in the book's later chapters, there is a considerable increase in: the amount of data being collected; the corporeal (bodily) nature of data being collected; automated data collection about emotions; and more broadly the fact that oblique machinic decision-making shapes important factors of human life (such as our behaviour, financial decisions, the workplace, policing, social policy, health and more). These require that we not only attend to the ethical dimension of privacy, but also remain attentive to new technologies, industrial trends, governmental behaviour, laws and social practices.

NOTES

1 See, for example, the journal *Big Data & Society*.
2 My dislike for 'hidden forces' and 'vague threats' is better expressed by the pragmatist philosopher Richard Rorty (1998), who goes as far to argue that supposed hidden forces are simply knowledge claims that keep intellectuals in business. Bruno Latour (2005) similarly says that we should avoid intellectual investigation that begins with the assumption that mysterious forces of 'power' are in play, but get on with the business of tracing and understanding the mechanics of asymmetries regarding data and information.

REFERENCES

Acquisti, A. and Grossklags, J. (2006) *What Can Behavioral Economics Teach Us About Privacy?* http://www.heinz.cmu.edu/~acquisti/papers/Acquisti-Grossklags-Chapter-Etrics.pdf, accessed 20 January 2016.

Adobe (2015) *Adobe Privacy Center/Analytics and on-site personalization services*, www.adobe.com/privacy/analytics.html?f=2o7, accessed 16 May 2015.

Albury, K. and Crawford, K. (2012) Sexting, consent and young people's ethics: beyond Megan's story, *Continuum: Journal of Media & Cultural Studies*, 26(3): 463–473.

Allen, A.L. (1988) *Uneasy Access: Privacy for Women in Free Society*. Totowa, NJ: Rowman & Littlefield.

Allen, A.L. (2003) *Why Privacy Isn't Everything: Feminist Reflections on Personal Accountability*. Lanham, MD: Rowman & Littlefield.

Altman, I. (1975) *The Environment and Social Behaviour: Privacy, Personal Space, Territory, Crowding*. Monterey, CA: Brooks/Cole.

Anderson, C. (2008) The end of theory: the data deluge makes the scientific method obsolete, *Wired*, http://archive.wired.com/science/discoveries/magazine/16-07/pb_theory, accessed 22 September 2014.

Anderson, D. (2015) *A Question of Trust: Report of the Investigatory Powers Review*, https://terrorismlegislationreviewer.independent.gov.uk/wp-content/uploads/2015/06/IPR-Report-Web-Accessible1.pdf, accessed 13 October 2015.

Andrejevic, M. (2013) *Infoglut: How Too Much Information is Changing the Way We Think and Know*. New York: Routledge.

Android Official Blog (2014) A sweet lollipop, with a Kevlar wrapping: new security features in Android 5.0, http://officialandroid.blogspot.co.uk/2014/10/a-sweet-lollipop-with-kevlar-wrapping.html, accessed 3 March 2015.

Apple (2016) A message to our customers, www.apple.com/customer-letter/, accessed 3 June 2016.

Aristotle (1995 [350 BC]) *Politics*. Oxford: Oxford University Press.

Article 29 Working Party (2010) *Opinion 2/2010 on online behavioural advertising*, http://ec.europa.eu/justice/policies/privacy/docs/wpdocs/2010/wp171_en.pdf, accessed 3 March 2015.

Article 29 Working Party (2014a) *Opinion 06/2014 on the notion of legitimate interests of the data controller under Article 7 of Directive 95/46/EC*, www.cnpd.public.lu/fr/publications/groupe-art29/wp217_en.pdf, accessed 3 March 2015.

Article 29 Working Party (2014b) *Opinion 05/2014 on Anonymisation Techniques*, http://ec.europa.eu/justice/data-protection/article-29/documentation/opinion-recommendation/files/2014/wp216_en.pdf, accessed 12 November 2014.

Bakir, V. (2010) *Sousveillance, Media and Strategic Political Communication: Iraq, USA, UK*. Continuum: New York.

Bakir, V. (2015) 'Veillant panoptic assemblage': mutual watching and resistance to mass surveillance after Snowden, *Media and Communication*, 3(3): 12–25.

Bakir, V. (forthcoming) Sousveillance, in B. Arrigo (ed.) *The Sage Encyclopedia of Surveillance, Security and Privacy*. Thousand Oaks, CA: Sage.

Bakir, V., Cable, V., Dencik, L., Hintz, A. and McStay, A. (2015) *Public Feeling on Privacy, Security and Surveillance: A Report by DATA-PSST and DCSS*, http://data-psst.bangor.ac.uk/policy.php.en, accessed 20 January 2016.

Bakir, V. and McStay, A. (2016) Theorising transparency arrangements: assessing interdisciplinary academic and multi-stakeholder positions on transparency in the post-Snowden leak era, *Ethical Space: Journal of Communication*, 3(1): 24–31.

Ball, J. (2015) GCHQ captured emails of journalists from top international media, *Guardian*, www.theguardian.com/uk-news/2015/jan/19/gchq-intercepted-emails-journalists-ny-times-bbc-guardian-le-monde-reuters-nbc-washington-post, accessed 20 January 2015.

Barocas, S. and Nissenbaum, H. (2014) Big data's end run around anonymity and consent, in J. Lane, V. Stodden, S. Bender and H. Nissenbaum (eds) *Privacy, Big Data, and the Public Good Frameworks for Engagement*. Cambridge: Cambridge University Press.

Beniger, J.R. (1986) *The Control Revolution: Technological and Economic Origins of the Information Society*. Cambridge, MA: Harvard University Press.

Bennington, G. (2011) Kant's open secret, *Theory, Culture & Society*, 28(7–8).

Birchall, C. (2012) Introduction to 'secrecy and transparency': the politics of opacity and openness', *Theory, Culture & Society*, 28(7–8): 7–25.

Blair, T. (2010) *A Journey*. London: Random House.

Bloustein, E.J. (1984 [1964]) Privacy as an aspect of human dignity: an answer to Dean Prosser, in F.D. Schoeman (ed.) *Philosophical Dimensions of Privacy: An Anthology*. Cambridge: Cambridge University Press. pp. 156–202.

Bond, E. (2011) The mobile phone = bike shed? Children, sex and mobile phones, *New Media & Society*, 13(4): 587–604.

Boyce, G. (1978) The Fourth Estate: the reappraisal of a concept, in G. Boyce, J. Curran and P. Wingate (eds) *Newspaper History from the Seventeenth Century to the Present Day*. London: Constable. pp. 19–40.

boyd, d. (2008) *Taken Out of Context: American Teen Sociality in Networked Publics*. PhD Dissertation, School of Information, University of California-Berkeley, Berkeley, CA.

boyd, d. (2010) Social network sites as networked publics: affordances, dynamics, and implications, in Z. Papacharissi (ed.) *Networked Self: Identity, Community, and Culture on Social Network Sites*. London: Routledge. pp. 39–58.

boyd, d. and Crawford, K. (2012) Critical questions for big data, *Information, Communication & Society*, 15(5): 662–679.

Bruns, A. (2006) 'Towards produsage: futures for user-led content production', in F. Sudweeks, H. Hrachovec and C. Ess (eds) *Proceedings*: *Cultural Attitudes towards Communication and Technology 2006*, Perth: Murdoch University, http://produsage. org/files/12132812018_towards_produsage_0.pdf, accessed 9 September 2015.

Callon, M. (2012 [1987]) Society in the making: the study of technology as a tool for socio-logical analysis, in W.E. Bijker; T.P. Hughes and T. Pinch (eds) *The Social Construction of Technological Systems: New Directions in the Sociology and History of Technology.* Cambridge, MA: MIT. pp. 77–104.

Carlyle, T. (2007 [1840]) *Sartor Resartus, and On Heroes, Hero-Worship, & the Heroic in History.* London: J.M. Dent & Sons.

Chadwick, P. and Mullaly, J. (1997) *Privacy and the Media.* Melbourne: Communications Law Centre.

Clifford, D. (2014) EU data protection law and targeted advertising: consent and the Cookie Monster – tracking the crumbs of online user behaviour, *JIPITEC*, 5, www.jipitec.eu/ issues/jipitec-5-3-2014/4095, accessed 12 September 2016.

Clough, P. (2007) *The Affective Turn: Theorizing the Social.* Durham, NC: Duke University Press.

Cohen, J.E. (2012) Configuring the networked self: law, code, and the play of everyday practice, www.juliecohen.com/page5.php, accessed 10 February 2016.

Cohen, J.L. and Arato, A. (1992) *Civil Society and Political Theory.* Cambridge, MA: MIT.

Council of Europe (2010 [1950]) *European Convention on Human Rights*, www.echr.coe. int/Documents/Convention_ENG.pdf, accessed 5 October 2015.

Cranor, L.F., Hoke, C., Leon, P.G. and Au, A. (2014) *Are They Worth Reading? An In-Depth Analysis of Online Advertising Companies' Privacy Policies*, http://ssrn.com/ abstract=2418590, accessed 10 June 2016.

Darwin, C. (2009 [1872]) *The Expression of the Emotions in Man and Animals.* London: Harper.

DeCew, J.W. (1997) *In Pursuit of Privacy: Law, Ethics, and the Rise of Technology.* New York: Cornell University Press.

Dworkin, R. (2011 [1977]) *Taking Rights Seriously.* London: Bloomsbury.

Economist, The (2014) Every step you take, www.economist.com/news/leaders/ 21589862-cameras-become-ubiquitous-and-able-identify-people-more-safe guards-privacy-will-be, accessed 30 December 2014.

Economist, The (2016) Frankenstein's paperclips, www.economist.com/news/special-report/21700762-techies-do-not-believe-artificial-intelligence-will-run-out-control-there-are, accessed 29 June 2016.

Ekman, P. and Friesen, W.V. (1971) Constants across cultures in the face and emotion, *Journal of Personality and Social Psychology*, 17(2): 124–129.

Ekman, P. and Friesen, W.V. (1978) *Facial Action Coding System: A Technique for the Measurement of Facial Movement.* Palo Alto, CA: Consulting Psychologists Press.

Engelhardt, H.T. Jr. (2000) Privacy and limited democracy: the moral centrality of persons, *Social Philosophy & Policy*, 17(2): 120–140.

Flood, M. (2008) Men, sex and homosociality: how bonds between men shape their sexual relations with women, *Men and Masculinities*, 10(3): 339–359.

Ford, C.S. and Frank, F.A. (1951) *Patterns of Sexual Behaviour.* New York: Harper & Brothers.

Fridlund, A.J. (1991) The sociality of solitary smiles: effects of an implicit audience, *Journal of Personality and Social Psychology*, 60: 229–240.

197

Fridlund, A.J. (1995) *Human Facial Expression: An Evolutionary View*. San Diego, CA: Academic Press Inc.

Fried, C. (1984 [1968]) Privacy [a moral analysis], in F.D. Schoeman (ed.) *Philosophical Dimensions of Privacy: An Anthology*. Cambridge: Cambridge University Press. pp. 203–222.

Fuchs, C. (2012) The political economy of privacy on Facebook, http://fuchs.uti.at/wp-content/uploads/polec_FB.pdf, accessed 5 October 2015.

Fuchs, C. (2016) *Reading Marx in the Information Age: A Media and Communication Studies Perspective on Capital Volume 1*. New York: Routledge.

Gandy, O.H. (2009) *Coming to Terms with Chance: Engaging Rational Discrimination and Cumulative Disadvantage*. Burlington, VT: Ashgate.

Gellman, B. and Poitras, L. (2013) U.S., British intelligence mining data from nine U.S. Internet companies in broad secret program, *Washington Post*, www.washingtonpost.com/investigations/us-intelligence-mining-data-from-nine-us-internet-companies-in-broad-secret-program/2013/06/06/3a0c0da8-cebf-11e2-8845-d970ccb04497_story.html, accessed 20 October 2015.

Giddens, A. (1990) *The Consequences of Modernity*. Cambridge: Polity Press.

Gillespie, T. (2010) The politics of 'platforms', *New Media & Society*, 12(3): 347–367.

Goffman, E. (1990 [1959]) *The Presentation of Self in Everyday Life*. London: Penguin.

Goodman, B. and Flaxman, S. (2016) EU regulations on algorithmic decision-making and a 'right to explanation', http://arxiv.org/pdf/1606.08813v1.pdf, accessed 11 July 2016.

Gregg, M. and Seigworth, G.J. (eds) (2010) *The Affect Theory Reader*. Durham, NC and London: Duke University Press.

Greenwald, G. (2014) *No Place to Hide: Edward Snowden, the NSA and the U.S. Surveillance State*. New York: Metropolitan Books.

Grisso, A.D. and Weiss, D. (2005) What are gURLs talking about? Adolescent girls' construction of sexual identity on gURL.com, in S. Mazzarella (ed.) *Girl Wide Web: Girls, the Internet, and the Negotiation of Identity*. New York: Peter Lang. pp. 31–49.

Grotius, H. (2001 [1625]) *On the Law of War and Peace*. Kitchener, ON: Batoche Books.

Guardian (2014) GCHQ views data with no warrant, government admits, www.theguardian.com/uk-news/2014/oct/29/gchq-nsa-data-surveillance?CMP=EMCNEWEML6619I2, accessed 29 October 2014.

Hall, E.T. (1969) *The Hidden Dimension*. New York: Anchor.

Harding, P. (2012) Journalism in the public interest, in R.L. Keeble and J. Mai (eds) *The Phone Hacking Scandal: Journalism on Trial*. Bury St Edmunds: Abramis. pp. 309–320.

Hardy, J. (2014) *Critical Political Economy of the Media*. London: Routledge.

Hasinoff, A.A. (2012) Sexting as media production: rethinking social media and sexuality, *New Media & Society*, 15(4): 449–465.

Hayashi, K. (2006) 'The Public' in Japan, *Theory, Culture & Society*, 23: 615.

Hinton, G. (2016) Deep Learning, http://deeplearning.net/tag/geoffrey-hinton/, accessed 20 June 2016.

Hobbes, T. (1985 [1651]) *Leviathan*. London: Penguin.

Hobbes, T. (1998 [1668/1642]) *Man and Citizen (De Homine and De Cive)*. Indianapolis: Hackett.

Hoofnagle, C. (2013) How the fair credit reporting act regulates big data, http://papers.ssrn.com/sol3/papers.cfm?abstract_id=2432955, accessed 20 September 2015.

Hosein, G. (2004) Privacy and or as Freedom, http://personal.lse.ac.uk/hosein/pubs/mit_chapter_gus.pdf, accessed 15 October 2016.

House of Commons Science and Technology Committee (2016) *The big data dilemma*, www.publications.parliament.uk/pa/cm201516/cmselect/cmsctech/468/468.pdf, accessed 20 June 2016.

IAB (2012) *Consumers and Online Privacy 2012 – Bitesize Guide*. Retrieved from www.iabuk.net/sites/default/files/Consumers%20and%20Online%20Privacy%202012%20-%20Bitesize%20Guide.pdf, accessed 20 September 2015.

IAB (2015a) 15% of Britons online are blocking ads, www.iabuk.net/about/press/archive/15-of-britons-online-are-blocking-ads, accessed 20 September 2015.

IAB (2015b) IAB believes in PRIVACY, www.iabuk.net/blog/the-iab-believes-in-privacy, accessed 20 September 2015.

IAB (2016) Ad blocking software – consumer usage and attitudes Feb 16, www.iabuk.net/research/library/ad-blocking-software-consumer-usage-and-attitudes-feb-16, accessed 20 June 2016.

Ilardi, V. (2007) *Renaissance Vision from Spectacles to Telescopes*. Philadelphia, PA: American Philosophical Society.

Information Commissioner's Office (2014) *Anonymisation: Managing Data Protection Risk Code of Practice*, http://ico.org.uk/~/media/documents/library/Data_Protection/Practical_application/anonymisation-codev2.pdf, accessed 23 October 2014.

Inside BlackBerry (2015) *The Encryption Debate: a Way Forward*, http://blogs.blackberry.com/2015/12/the-encryption-debate-a-way-forward/, accessed 20 June 2016.

International Institute of Communications (2012) Personal data management: the user's perspective, www.iicom.org/open-access-resources/doc_details/226-personal-datamanagement-the-users-perspective, accessed 1 February 2016.

ISC (2015) Privacy and security: a modern and transparent legal framework, House of Commons, http://isc.independent.gov.uk/, accessed 15 February 2016.

Jenkins, H. (2006) *Convergence Culture*. New York: New York University.

Kant, I. (1983 [1784]) 'An Answer to the Question: What is Enlightenment?' in *Perpetual Peace and Other Essays*. Indianapolis: Hackett. pp. 33–48.

Kant, I. (2004 [1764]) *Observations on the Feeling of the Beautiful and Sublime*. Berkeley, CA: University of California Press.

Kaye, S. (2015) *Report of the Special Rapporteur on the promotion and protection of the right to freedom of opinion and expression*, www.ohchr.org/EN/HRBodies/HRC/RegularSessions/Session29/Documents/A.HRC.29.32_AEV.doc, accessed 13 January 2016.

Kegan, S. (1992) The structure of normative ethics, *Philosophical Perspectives, Ethics*, 6: 223–242.

Kitchin, R. (2014) Big Data, new epistemologies and paradigm shifts, *Big Data & Society*, 1–12.

Koehler, J.O. (1999) *Stasi: The Untold Story of the East German Secret Police*. Boulder, CO: Westview.

Kosta, E. (2013) *Consent in European Data Protection Law*. Leiden: Martinus Nijhoff Publishers.

Kronos (2016) *Productivity Resource Centre*, www.kronos.co.uk/productivity-resource-centre.aspx, accessed 22 May 2016.

Kücklich (2005) Precarious playbour: modders and the digital games industry, *Fibreculture*, 5(25), http://five.fibreculturejournal.org/fcj-025-precarious-playbour-modders-and-the-digital-games-industry/, accessed 15 October 2015.

Lafkey, D. (2009) The safe harbor method of de-identification: an empirical test, *ONC Presentation*, 8 October, www.ehcca.com/presentations/HIPAAWest4/lafky_2.pdf, accessed 18 April 2014.

Landes, J. (ed.) (1998) *Feminism, the Public and the Private*. New York: Oxford University Press.

Laney, D. (2001) *3D Data Management: Controlling Data Volume, Velocity and Variety*, http://blogs.gartner.com/doug-laney/files/2012/01/ad949-3D-Data-Management-Controlling-Data-Volume-Velocity-and-Variety.pdf, accessed 15 April 2015.

Latour, B. (1987) *Science in Action*. Cambridge, MA: Harvard University Press.

Latour, B. (2005) *Reassembling the Social: An Introduction to Actor-Network-Theory*. Oxford: Oxford University Press.

Lieshout, M.v., Kool, L., Schoonhoven, B.v. and Jonge, M. de (2011) Privacy by design: alternative for existing practices in safeguarding privacy? Paper prepared for EuroCPR. pp. 1–29.

Lippman J.R. and Campbell S.W. (2014) Damned if you do, damned if you don't ... if you're a girl: relational and normative contexts of adolescent sexting in the United States, *Journal of Children and Media*, 8(4): 371–386.

Livingstone, S. (2008) Taking risky opportunities in youthful content creation: teenagers' use of social networking sites for intimacy, privacy and self-expression, *New Media & Society*, 10(3): 393–411.

Lloyd, J. (2012) Exposed: the 'swaggering arrogance' of the popular press, in R.L. Keeble and J. Mair (eds) *The Phone Hacking Scandal: Journalism on Trial*. Bury St Edmunds: Abramis. pp. 1–3.

Locke, J. (2005 [1689]) *Two Treatises of Government and A Letter Concerning Toleration*. Stilwell, KS: Digireads.com.

Lupton, D. (2016) *The Quantified Self*. Cambridge: Polity.

Lyon, D. (2001) *Surveillance Society: Monitoring Everyday Life*. Buckingham: Open University Press.

Lyon, D. (2015) *Surveillance After Snowden*. Cambridge: Polity.

MacKinnon, C. (1989) *Toward a Feminist Theory of the State*. Cambridge, MA: Harvard University Press.

Madden, M. (2014) Public perceptions of privacy and security in the post-Snowden era, *Pew Research Internet Project*, www.pewinternet.org/files/2014/11/PI_PublicPerceptions ofPrivacy_111214.pdf, accessed 14 November 2014.

Mann, S. (2004) Sousveillance: inverse surveillance in multimedia imaging. In International Multimedia Conference: Proceedings of the 12th Annual ACM International Conference on Multimedia, *ACM Press*, http://idtrail.org/content/view/135/42/, accessed 20 January 2016.

Mann, S., Nolan, J. and Wellman, B. (2003) Sousveillance: inventing and using wearable computing devices for data collection in surveillance environments, *Surveillance & Society*, 1(3): 331–355.

Marcuse, H. (1955 [1941]) *Reason and Revolution: Hegel and the Rise of Social Theory*. London: Routledge.

Marthews, A. and Tucker, C. (2014) Government surveillance and internet search behavior, *SSRN*, http://dx.doi.org/10.2139/ssrn.2412564, accessed 8 November 2014.

Marwick, A.E. 2010. Status update: celebrity, publicity and self-branding in web 2.0, www.tiara.org/blog/wp-content/uploads/2010/09/marwick_dissertation_statusupdate.pdf, accessed 22 May 2016.

Marwick, A.E. (2012) The public domain: social surveillance in everyday life, *Surveillance & Society*, 9(4): 378–393.

Marwick, A.E. and boyd, d. (2014) Networked privacy: how teenagers negotiate context in social media, *New Media & Society*, 16(7): 1051–1067.

Marx, G.T. (2002) What's new about the 'new surveillance'? Classifying for change and continuity, *Surveillance & Society*, 1(1): 9–29.

Marx, K. and Engels, F. (2011 [1844]) *Economic and Philosophic Manuscripts of 1844*. Blacksburg, VA: Wilder.

Matthews, G. (1992) *The Rise of Public Woman: Women's Power and Woman's Place in the United States 1630–1970*. New York: Oxford University Press.

McAfee (2014) Study reveals majority of adults share intimate details via unsecured digital devices, www.mcafee.com/uk/about/news/2014/q1/20140204-01.aspx, accessed 4 February 2016.

McStay, A. (2011) *The Mood of Information: a Critique of Online Behavioural Advertising*. New York: Continuum.

McStay, A. (2012) I consent: an analysis of the cookie directive and its implications for UK behavioural advertising, *New Media and Society*, 15(4): 596–611.

McStay, A. (2013) *Creativity and Advertising: Affect, Events and Process*. London: Routledge.

McStay, A. (2014) *Privacy and Philosophy: New Media and Affective Protocol*. New York: Peter Lang.

McStay, A. (2016) *Digital Advertising* (second edition). London: Palgrave Macmillan.

McStay, A. (2017) *Empathic Media: The Surveillance of Emotional Life*. London: Sage.

Mill, J.S. (1962 [1859]) *Utilitarianism, On Liberty, Essay on Bentham*. London: Fontana Press.

Mislove, A. Viswanath, B. Gummadi, K.P. and Druschel, P. (2010) *You Are Who You Know: Inferring User Profiles in Online Social Networks*, www.ccs.neu.edu/home/amislove/publications/Inferring-WSDM.pdf, accessed 26 January 2016.

Moore, B. Jr. (1984) *Privacy: Studies in Social and Cultural History*. New York: M.E. Sharpe.

National Crime Agency (2015) Sexting becoming the norm for teens, www.nationalcrimeagency.gov.uk/news/632-sexting-becoming-the-norm-for-teens, accessed 26 January 2016.

Nissenbaum, H. (2004) Privacy as contextual integrity, *Washington Law Review*, 79(1): 119–158.

Nissenbaum, H. (2010) *Privacy in Context: Technology, Policy, and the Integrity of Social Life*. Stanford, CA: Stanford University Press.

NSPCC (2015) Sexting: advice for parents, www.nspcc.org.uk/preventing-abuse/keeping-children-safe/sexting/, accessed 12 June 2015.

Ofcom (2015a) *Promoting Investment and Innovation in the Internet of Things: Summary of Responses and Next Steps*, http://stakeholders.ofcom.org.uk/binaries/consultations/iot/statement/IoTStatement.pdf, accessed 2 February 2015.

Ofcom (2015b) *The Communications Market Report: International*, http://stakeholders. ofcom.org.uk/market-data-research/market-data/communications-market-reports/ cmr15/international/, accessed 2 February 2015.

Ofcom (2015c) *Adults' Media Use and Attitudes*, http://stakeholders.ofcom.org.uk/binaries/ research/media-literacy/media-lit-10years/2015_Adults_media_use_and_attitudes_ report.pdf, accessed 20 February 2016.

Ohm, P. (2009) Broken promises of privacy: responding to the surprising failure of anonymization, *UCLA Law Review*, 57: 1701–1777, http://uclalawreview.org/pdf/57-6-3.pdf, accessed 13 October 2014.

Omand, D. (2010) *Securing the State*. London: Hurst & Company.

Pasquale, F. (2015) *The Black Box Society: The Secret Algorithms that Control Money and Information*. Cambridge, MA: Harvard University Press.

PEN America (2013) *Chilling Effects: NSA Surveillance Drives U.S. Writers to Self-Censor*, www.pen.org/sites/default/files/Chilling%20Effects_PEN%20American.pdf, accessed 12 November 2014.

Pew Internet Center (2014a) *Couples, the Internet, and Social Media*, www.pewinternet. org/2014/02/11/couples-the-internet-and-social-media/, accessed 10 January 2016.

Pew Internet Center (2014b) *Public Perceptions of Privacy and Security in the Post-Snowden Era*, www.pewinternet.org/2014/11/12/public-privacy-perceptions/, accessed 10 May 2015.

Pew Internet Center (2015) *Americans' Privacy Strategies Post-Snowden*, www.pewinter net.org/files/2015/03/PI_AmericansPrivacyStrategies_0316151.pdf, accessed 10 May 2015.

Pew Research Center (2016) *Privacy and Information Sharing*, www.pewinternet. org/2016/01/14/privacy-and-information-sharing/, accessed 20 January 2015.

Picard, R.W. (1995) *Affective Computing*. MIT Media Laboratory Perceptual Computing Section Technical Report No. 321, www.pervasive.jku.at/Teaching/_2009SS/Seminaraus PervasiveComputing/Begleitmaterial/Related%20Work%20(Readings)/1995_ Affective%20computing_Picard.pdf, accessed 15 January 2014.

Picard, R.W. (1997) *Affective Computing*. Cambridge, MA: MIT.

Plato (2004 [306 BC]) *The Laws*. London: Penguin.

Podesta, J., Pritzker, P., Moniz, E.J., Holden, J. and Zients, J. (2014) Big data: seizing opportunities, preserving values, The White House, www.whitehouse.gov/ sites/default/files/docs/big_data_privacy_report_5.1.14_final_print.pdf, accessed 13 November 2014.

Posner, R.A. (1983) *The Economics of Justice*. Cambridge, MA: Harvard University Press.

Powell, A. (2010) Configuring consent: emerging technologies, unauthorised sexual images and sexual assault, *Australian and New Zealand Journal of Criminology*, 43: 76–90.

PricewaterhouseCoopers (2014) *PwC's Global Data & Analytics Survey 2014: Big Decisions*, www.pwc.com/gx/en/issues/data-and-analytics/big.../2014-survey.html, accessed 1 January 2015.

Prosser, W.L. (1984 [1960]) 'Privacy [A legal analysis]', in F.D. Schoeman (ed.) *Philosophical Dimensions of Privacy: An Anthology*. Cambridge: Cambridge University Press. pp. 104–155.

Rawls, J. (1999 [1971]) *A Theory of Justice*. Cambridge, MA: Belknap Press of Harvard University Press.

Raynes-Goldie, K. (2010) Aliases, creeping, and wall cleaning: understanding privacy in the age of Facebook, *First Monday*, 15(1), http://firstmonday.org/article/view/2775/2432, accessed 5 January 2016.

Regulation of Investigatory Powers Bill standing committee: Clause 5, 2000-03-21, www. publications.parliament.uk/pa/cm199900/cmstand/f/st000321/am/00321s02.htm, accessed 29 October 2014.

Richards, N. (2015) *Intellectual Privacy: Rethinking Civil Liberties in the Digital Age*. New York: Oxford University Press.

Ringrose, J., Gill, R., Livingstone S. and Harvey, L. (2012) *A Qualitative Study of Children, Young People and 'Sexting': A Report Prepared for the NSPCC*. London: National Society for the Prevention of Cruelty to Children.

Ringrose, J., Harvey, L., Gill, R. and Livingstone, S. (2013) Teen girls, sexual double standards and 'sexting': gendered value in digital image exchange, *Feminist Theory*, 14(3): 305–323.

Rorty, R. (1998) *Truth and Progress: Philosophical Papers 3*. Cambridge: Cambridge University Press.

Rozenburg, J. (2004) *Privacy and the Press*. Oxford: Oxford University Press.

Rusbridger, A. (2012) Hackgate reveals failure of normal checks and balances to hold power to account, in R.L. Keeble and J. Mair (eds) *The Phone Hacking Scandal: Journalism on Trial*. Bury St Edmunds: Abramis. pp. 129–144.

Rushe, D. (2015) SIM card database hack gave US and UK spies access to billions of cellphones, *Guardian*, www.theguardian.com/us-news/2015/feb/19/nsa-gchq-sim-card-billions-cellphones-hacking, accessed 20 February 2015.

RUSI (2015) *A Democratic Licence to Operate: Report of the Independent Surveillance Review*, London: Royal United Services Institute for Defence and Security Studies, https://rusi.org/publication/whitehall-reports/democratic-licence-operate-report-independent-surveillance-review, accessed 15 February 2016.

Salter, M. (2015) Privates in the online public: sex(ting) and reputation on social media, *New Media & Society*, 1–17.

Scahill, J. and Begley, J. (2015) The great SIM heist: how spies stole the keys to the encryption castle, *The Intercept*, https://firstlook.org/theintercept/2015/02/19/great-sim-heist/, accessed 20 February 2015.

Schauer, F. (1978) Fear, risk and the first amendment: unraveling the chilling effect, *Boston University Law Review*, 58/5: 685–732.

Schmidt, E. and Cohen, J. (2013) *The New Digital Age: Reshaping the Future of People, Nations and Business*. London: John Murray.

Shirky, C. (2008) *Here Comes Everybody: How Change Happens when People Come Together*. New York: Penguin.

Simcox, R. (2015) *Surveillance after Snowden: Effective Espionage in an Age of Transparency*. London: The Henry Jackson Society.

Sledge, M. (2013) CIA's Gus Hunt on big data: we 'try to collect everything and hang on to it forever', *The Huffington Post*, www.huffingtonpost.com/2013/03/20/cia-gus-hunt-big-data_n_2917842.html, accessed 7 July 2014.

Smythe, D.W. (1977) 'Communications: blindspot of Western Marxism', *Canadian Journal of Political and Social Theory*, 1(3): 1–27.

Stoycheff, E. (2016) Under surveillance: examining Facebook's spiral of silence effects in the wake of NSA internet monitoring, *Journalism & Mass Communication Quarterly*, 1–16.

Sweeney, L. (2002) *Achieving k-Anonymity Privacy Protection Using Generalization and Suppression*, dataprivacylab.org/dataprivacy/projects/kanonymity/kanonymity2.pdf, accessed 7 July 2014.

Thiel-Stern, S. (2009) Femininity out of control on the internet: a critical analysis of media representations of gender, youth, and MySpace.com in international news discourses, *Girlhood Studies: An Interdisciplinary Journal*, 2: 20–39.

Thorp, E.O. (1969) Optimal gambling systems for favorable game. *Review of the International Statistical Institute*, 37(3): 273–293.

Timberg, C. (2014) Newest Androids will join iPhones in offering default encryption, blocking police, *The Washington Post*, www.washingtonpost.com/blogs/the-switch/wp/2014/09/18/newest-androids-will-join-iphones-in-offering-default-encryption-blocking-police/, accessed 3 March 2015.

Tolman, D.L. (2002) *Dilemmas of Desire: Teenage Girls Talk about Sexuality*. Cambridge, MA; London: Harvard University Press.

TRUSTe 2014 (2013) UK Consumer Data Privacy Study: Advertising Edition. Retrieved from www.truste.com/resources/privacy-research/uk-consumer-confidence-index-2014/

Turkle, S. (2011) *Alone Together: Why We Expect More from Technology and Less from Each Other*. New York: Basic Books.

Turner, J. (1997) *The Institutional Order*. New York: Longman.

US Chamber of Commerce (2014) *Re: Big Data and Consumer Privacy in the Internet Economy* [Docket No. 140514424– 4424–01], www.ntia.doc.gov/files/ntia/us_chamber.pdf, accessed 17 August 2014.

Venkataramanan, M. (2014) Madhumita Venkataramanan: my identity for sale, *Wired*, www.wired.co.uk/magazine/archive/2014/11/features/my-identity-for-sale, accessed 25 December 2014.

Wack, R. (2010) *Privacy: A Short Introduction*. Oxford: Oxford University Press.

Warnick, J. (2012) James Whittaker: how to change the way people think in four easy steps, http://news.microsoft.com/stories/people/james-whittaker.html, accessed 20 January 2015.

Warren, S. and Brandeis, L. (1984 [1890]) The right to privacy [the implicit made explicit], in F.D. Schoeman (ed.) *Philosophical Dimensions of Privacy: An Anthology*. Cambridge: Cambridge University Press. pp. 75–103.

Warwick, K. (2012) *Artificial Intelligence: The Basics*. Abingdon: Routledge.

Westin, A. (1984 [1967]) The origins of modern claims to privacy, in F.D. Schoeman (ed.) *Philosophical Dimensions of Privacy: An Anthology*. Cambridge: Cambridge University Press. pp. 56–74.

Young, A.L. and Quan-Haase, A. (2013) Privacy protection strategies on Facebook: the internet privacy paradox revisited, *Information, Communication & Society*, 16(4): 479–500.

Zimmer, M. (2014) Mark Zuckerberg's theory of privacy, www.washingtonpost.com/lifestyle/style/mark-zuckerbergs-theory-of-privacy/2014/02/03/2c1d780a-8cea-11e3-95dd-36ff657a-4dae_story.html, accessed 20 June 2016.

INDEX

9/11 attacks, 44, 50
1984, 193

abortion, 155
Acer, 147, 148
adblockers, 93
Adebolajo, Michael, 51
Adebowale, Michael, 51
Adobe, 87–8
advertising, 6, 64, 75, 83–4, 86, 141–2, 178,
        189–90, 194
    see also behavioural advertising;
        programmatic advertising
advertising networks, 86–7
Adwords, 76
Affdex, 136
affect, 179–81, 185
Affectiva, 7, 136, 138, 140, 141, 142, 143
affective computing, 136–8, 191
affective privacy, 8, 192
affective protocol, 150 *see also* protocols
a-historical, 112, 121
Airbnb, 72
algorithms, 7, 58–9, 64, 116, 120, 126, 127–8,
        129, 130, 190, 191
Alibaba, 72, 189
alienation, 97, 190
Allen, Anita, 155–6, 158
Alphabet (Google), 158
al-Qaeda, 44
Altman, Irwin, 162, 163
Amazon, 6, 64, 72–3, 189
American Civil Liberties Union, 51
Amnesty International, 46

analytics, 39, 117
Ancient Greek philosophy, 14–15, 16–17,
        18–19, 127, 187
Anderson, Chris, 126
Anderson, David, 46
Andrejevic, Mark, 7, 48, 126, 127
Android, 71, 74, 76
anonymisation, 122–5
anonymity, 67, 121
AOL, 42, 45
Apple, 6, 42, 45, 57–8, 61–2, 63–5, 66, 67, 71,
        72, 73, 145, 151, 154, 188, 191, 192
Arato, A., 34
Aristotle, 15, 16
arousal, 139
Article 8 (European Convention on Human
        Rights), 28, 30–2, 38–9, 46, 104
    see also right to privacy
Article 10 (European Convention on Human
        Rights), 28, 31–2, 38–9, 46, 107, 113
    see also freedom of expression
Article 17 (General Data Protection
        Regulations), 104
Article 29 Working Party, 122
Article 80 (General Data Protection
        Regulations), 104
artificial emotional intelligence *see* empathic
        media
audience-as-commodity, 85, 96–7, 98
Audit Bureau of Circulation (ABC), 116–17
auto-completion, 127
autonomy, 18, 20, 174, 181, 187
Avaaz, 72
Aviva, 154

backdoors, 61
Bahio, 141–2, 191
Bakir, V., 150
Barocas, S., 123–4
Bebo, 165, 177
behavioural advertising
  audience-as-commodity, 96–7
  big data, 116
  consent, 7, 91–6
  how it works, 86–8
  nature of, 6, 84–5, 189
  personal data, 91–6
  see also programmatic advertising
Beniger, James, 117
Bennington, G., 156
Bentham, Jeremy, 6
Big Brother, 193
Big Brother Watch, 49
big data
  anonymisation, 122–5
  behavioural advertising, 116
  black boxing, 129–30, 154
  discrimination, 127–9
  early feedback practices, 116–17
  early market research, 116–17
  mythologies, 125, 128
  nature of, 7, 117–20, 190–1
  and policy, 122
Binney, William, 49–50, 53, 55, 188
biometrics, 120–1, 138
Birchall, Clare, 6, 156
Bitcoin, 71
black boxing, 129–30, 154, 191
BlackBerry, 64–5, 177, 186
Blair, Tony, 32–3
Bloustein, E.J., 34
bodies, 155–6, 192
Bond, E., 182–3
Bondara, 148, 191
Bourne, Iain, 22–3, 24, 25
Boyce, G., 29
boyd, d., 126, 161, 164, 166–7, 169,
  170, 184
Brandeis, L., 25, 28, 36–7, 38, 39,
  112, 188
BSkyB, 30

Callon, Michel, 66
Cameron, David, 61
Carlyle, Thomas, 28–9
CBS, 182
CCTV, 22, 23, 24

celebrities, 30, 31
Change.org, 72
Charlie Hebdo, 51, 61
Child Exploitation and Online Protection
  Centre (CEOP), 176, 179, 180fig
child protection, 176
children, 176–7
chilling effect, 33, 42, 51–3, 54
Chrome, 74, 84
ciphers, 58
The Circle, 156, 157
CitizenFour, 42
city-state, 15
Clarkson, Jeremy, 37
Click, 143
code of practice (PCC), 33–4
Cohen, J.E., 65, 180–1
Cohen, J.L., 34
collective privacy, 184, 185
commodification, 96–7, 121, 156, 190
common ownership, 98
*Communications: Blindspot of Western
  Marxism*, 96
communications data, 45
congealing, 97
consent, 6–7, 18, 84, 85, 91–6, 122, 178–9,
  187, 189–90
context collision, 2, 8, 164, 167
context dependent privacy, 161–4
context management, 161, 162–4, 167
contextual integrity, 184
contract, 21, 23, 24
control, 3–4, 19–20, 28, 78, 79, 84, 178–9
Cook, Tim, 57, 63, 64
cookies, 86–8, 89, 92, 94–5, 189
corporate wellbeing, 152
corporation tax, 76
correlationism, 126, 128, 191
Court of Justice of the European Union,
  105–6, 113, 190
covert surveillance, 35
Crawford, K., 126
credit reports, 130
creeping, 168
crime maps, 129
crimes, 108–9, 128–9, 155
critical political economy, 85
culture, 76–7
cyber-bullying, 177–8, 192
cyber-crime, 68
cybersex, 8, 173
CyborgLogs, 150

daggering, 177
Darwin, Charles, 139
data
  alienation, 97
  analytics, 39, 117
  controllers, 106, 108
  deletion, 104 *see also* right to be forgotten
  importance of, 75
  protection, 25, 38, 40, 84, 94, 95, 104, 105,
    114, 123, 125, 143
  retention, 122
  visualisation, 129
data management platforms (DMPs), 89
Data Protection Act (1988), 38, 40, 125
Data Protection Directive (EU), 94, 95, 104, 105
DATA-PSST, 170
DCSS, 170
DeCew, Judith, 98
Deep Face, 120
deletion *see* de-listing; right to be forgotten
de-listing, 106–9, 111, 112, 113, 190
democracies, 15, 18, 20, 27, 28–9, 44
derogable, 32
dialectical, privacy as, 162
digital footprint, 115
digital labour, 97
dignity tort, 34
Directive 95/46/EC, 94, 95, 104
Directive 2002/58/EC, 94
Disconnect, 86
discrimination, 127–9, 191
Disney Park, 148
domestic abuse, 155
Doubleclick, 86, 87, 88
Dowler, Milly, 30
drones, 28, 38, 39
Dworkin, Ronald, 34
dystopias, 193

eBay, 72, 189
*Economic and Philosophic Manuscripts of
  1844*, 97
The Economist, 44
Eggers, Dave, 156, 157
Ekman, Paul, 139–40
Electronic Frontier Foundation, 194
Electronic Privacy Information Center (EPIC),
  63, 64
emancipation, 98
Emotient, 139, 140, 141, 142, 143
emotion-detection technologies *see* emotion-
  sensitive technologies

emotions, 7, 139, 181, 185, 191, 194
emotion-sensitive technologies, 136, 138,
  140, 143
empathic media, 135–44, 191
empathy, 7, 135, 136, 137
employers, 191
encryption
  arguments against, 60–1
  Google, 58, 63, 66
  and libertarianism, 64–5
  nature of, 6, 58–9, 188
  privacy-by-design, 65, 66, 67
  privacy-enhancing technologies, 65, 66, 67
  social construction of technology, 65–6
  tech industry, 61–4
  United Kingdom, 61–2
  United States of America, 61–2
  value of, 59–60
Engels, F., 97
e-Privacy Directive, 94
Equifax, 90
erasure, right to, 104
Etsy, 72, 189
European Convention on Human Rights, 28,
  30–2, 38–9, 46, 104, 107, 113
  see also freedom of expression; right to
    privacy
European Union Select Committee, 38, 40
eXelate, 89
expert systems, 129
explicit consent, 95, 96
exposure, 179–81, 185
*The Expression of the Emotions in Man and
  Animals*, 139
Exterion Media, 142
eyeglasses, 149

face recognition, 120–1
Facebook, 42, 43, 45, 53, 58, 64, 72, 73, 76, 78,
  120, 156–7, 160, 165, 166, 168, 177
Facebook Connect, 88
FaceNet, 120
Facial Action Coding System (FACS), 139
facial coding, 136, 138–41, 142, 191
facial expressions, 7
Federal Trade Commission, 78
feedback practices, 116–17
feminist perspectives, 8, 155–6, 192
FindFace, 121
First Amendment, 52, 63
first-party data, 89
Five Eyes, 42, 63, 188

Flood, M., 178
forced openness, 109–11, 113, 121
forced transparency, 17
Fourth Estate, 28, 29
Frankly, 173–4
free press, 28–30, 37
freedom, 14
freedom of expression, 7, 31–2, 34, 38, 52, 61,
    104, 106, 107–8, 111, 113, 190
    see also Article 10 (European Convention on
        Human Rights)
Freedom of Information Act (2000), 32–3
Fridlund, A.J., 139–40
Fried, C., 20
Friends (Facebook), 166–7, 168–9
Friesen, Wallace, 139
Fuchs, Christian, 97, 99

gagging, 28, 37
Gamestation, 92
gamification, 154
Gandy, O.H., 128
gay, 60, 68
GCHQ (Government Communications
    Headquarters), 23, 35, 46, 47, 48, 50, 63
gender, 128, 181–4
General Data Protection Regulations (GDPR),
    104, 108, 122, 130, 142
General Motors, 147
Ghostery, 85, 88
Giddens, Anthony, 129, 182
Giggs, Ryan, 37
Gill, Rosalind, 176–7
Gillespie, Tarleton, 74–5, 127
Glass (Google), 150, 157
Gmail, 3
Goffman, Erving, 161
González, Mario Costeja, 105, 113
    see also Google, Google Spain v AEPD and
        Mario Costeja González
Goodwin, Fred, 37
Google
    advertising, 6, 64, 75, 86, 189
    Alphabet, 158
    Android, 71, 74, 76
    auto-completion, 127
    corporate philosophy, 106
    corporation tax, 76
    de-listing content, 106–9, 111, 112, 113
    Docs, 43
    Doubleclick, 87
    encryption, 58, 63, 66
    Glass, 150, 157

Google cont.
    Gmail, 3
    Google Spain v AEPD and Mario Costeja
        González, 7, 103, 104, 105–6, 111,
        113, 190
    Google Transparency Report, 107
    Google Trends study, 52
    Google+, 86, 160
    Images, 127
    Maps, 84
    platforms, 72, 73–4
    Project Jacquard, 151–2
    right to be forgotten, 103, 104, 105–6, 111,
        113, 190
    self-driving car, 120
    surveillance, 45, 62
    Trends study, 52
Government Communication Headquarters
    (GCHQ), 23, 35, 46, 47, 48, 50, 63
Greenwald, Glenn, 45, 46, 47
Grotius, Hugo, 19
Group Insurance Commission (GIC), 124
Guardian, 33, 35, 39, 42, 45, 46, 88

Hannigan, Robert, 50, 63
hard biometrics, 138
Harvey, Laura, 176–7
hashing, 58
Hasinoff, A.A., 182, 183–4
Hayashi, K., 15–16
health
    data, 124, 125
    information, 4–5
    research, 116
Healthkit (Apple), 73, 151, 154
heat lists, 128–9
Hemming, John, 37
hierarchical sousveillance, 150
Hobbes, Thomas, 5, 18, 21, 22, 23, 188
homosocial bonding practice, 178
Hosein, G., 32
Huffington Post, 48
Huhne, Chris, 35
human rights, 17–18, 19, 20, 21, 25, 99, 190
Human Rights Act (1998), 40
Hunt, Gus, 48

i2MediaResearch, 142
iCloud, 64
ICO, 122, 125, 132
incentivisation, 66
Information Commissioner's Office, 9, 22, 25
information society, 116, 117

injunctions, 28, 37, 39
insights, 119
Instagram, 160
institutional privacy, 78
insurance, 153–4, 191–2
The Intercept, 42, 52
interest against exposure, 180
Internet Advertising Bureau, 93
Internet of Things (IoT), 119, 146
Internet Protocol version 6 (IPv6), 118–19
inter-personal privacy, 168, 169, 170, 192
inter-personal surveillance, 168
intimacy, 142, 143, 175, 185, 191, 192
intrusion, 32, 33, 34
invasion, 28, 33, 34
invasive-by-design (IBD), 65
Investigatory Powers Bill, 50
Investigatory Powers Tribunal, 47
iPhone, 138, 147, 151
IPv6 (Internet Protocol version 6), 118–19
ISIS, 53, 74
IXI Services, 89–90

Japan, 15–16, 147
Jenkins, Henry, 183
jihadi, 51
journalism, 5, 27–40, 187–8
A Journey, 32

Kant, Immanuel, 20, 132, 156
Kaye, David, 60
Kegan, S., 111
KGoal Smart Kegel Trainer, 148
King, Rodney, 150
Kitchin, R., 127
Kronos, 152

La Vanguardia, 105
Lafkey, D., 125
Latour, B., 129, 194
The Laws, 16–17
Le Monde, 35, 45
legislation, 19, 66
legitimate interests, 96
Leveson inquiry, 30
Levi Strauss, 151
Leviathan, 21, 23
libel, 36
liberalism, 5, 7, 14, 18–19, 29, 181, 187
libertarianism, 62, 63, 64–5, 78, 79, 188
liberty, 21–4
Liberty (organisation), 46
Lightbeam, 85

likelihood test, 125
LinkedIn, 72, 160
Linux, 71
Livingstone, Sonia, 164–6, 168, 170, 176–7
Locke, John, 18, 20
Looncup, 148
Lyon, David, 43

M&C Saatchi, 141–2
machine learning, 7, 48, 120–2, 140, 190, 194
MacKinnon, Catherine, 155, 158
MagicBands, 148
Mail on Sunday, 35
Mann, Steve, 8, 149–50, 151
market research, 116–17
Marr, Andrew, 37
Marwick, A.E., 151, 164, 166–7, 169, 170, 184
Marx, Gary, 43
Marxist perspectives, 96, 97, 98–9, 190
Mastercard, 147
McAfee, 175
McDaniel, Robert, 128–9
McLuhan, Marshall, 36
McStay, A., 89
media studies, 1–2
medical research, 116
menstruation, 148, 158
metadata, 45
Microsoft, 42, 45, 62–3, 84, 142, 147–8
Mill, John Stuart, 29, 156
Millward Brown, 141
Mislove, A., 123–4
Mitchell, Andrew, 40
mobile data, 3
mobile phones, 182–3, 184
    see also smartphones
mosaic effect, 124–5
motivated intruder test, 125
MySpace, 165
mythologies, 125, 128

Narrative Clip, 150
National Crime Agency (NCA), 176
National Institute of Justice (NIJ), 129
National Security Agency (NSA), 41, 42, 44,
    46, 47, 49, 50, 53, 58
National Society for the Prevention of Cruelty
    to Children (NSPCC), 176–7, 186
Naughton, Eileen, 76
Netflix, 116, 120
network effects, 71
networked norms, 184
networked privacy, 169, 192

neural networking, 120, 121, 130
neuromarketing, 141
New York Times, 35, 45, 86
News Corporation, 30
news cycles, 112
News of the World, 30
Newton-Dunn, Tom, 35
Nissenbaum, H., 20, 123–4, 161, 162, 163,
    164, 184
No Place to Hide, 47
non-derogable, 32
non-interference, 18
nothing to hide, nothing to fear, 16–18, 22, 43,
    50, 156
NSA (National Security Agency), 41, 42, 44,
    46, 47, 49, 50, 53, 58
NSPCC (National Society for the Prevention of
    Cruelty to Children), 176–7, 186

Obama, Barack, 62
objectification, 146, 155, 156, 192
Ofcom, 159–60
Ohm, P., 124, 125
oikos, 15
online advertising, 6–7
online profiling, 84
Open Rights Group, 50, 194
openness, 109–11, 113, 121
Ophan, 39
opt-in consent, 122
opt-out consent, 95, 96
Orwell, George, 193

Paltalk, 42, 45
paparazzi, 30, 31, 36, 38
participatory cultures, 74, 183
Pasquale, F., 130
patents, 77
Patriot Act, 44
PayPal, 6, 72, 189
peer-based privacy, 8, 161
PEN America, 52, 55
personal data, 89–96, 104, 113, 170
personal freedom, 18
personal sousveillance, 150, 152, 153, 156,
    157, 191
Pew Internet Survey, 3–4, 25, 184
Pew Research Center, 174–5
photojournalism, 5, 28
Picard, Rosalind, 136–7, 143
Ping, 186
platforms, 6, 71–9, 188–9, 193–4
Plato, 16–17, 18–19, 187

Plebgate, 35, 40
Poitras, Laura, 42, 44–5
policing, 128
polis, 15
Pomader Watch, 149
pornography, 176, 177, 178, 182, 184
Posner, Richard, 109–10
post-privacy, 143
predictive policing, 128
The Presentation of Self in Everyday Life, 161
Press Complaints Commission (PCC), 32, 33
Pretty Good Privacy (PGP), 59
PRISM, 45, 62
Prism Skylabs, 140–1
Privacy International, 46, 194
privacy-by-design (PbD), 6, 58, 65, 66, 67, 188
privacy-enhancing technologies (PETs), 65,
    66, 67
privacy-invading technologies (PITs), 65
privare, 15
privatum, 15
privo, 15
programmatic advertising, 84, 88–9, 92, 96–7,
    116, 120, 147, 189–90
Project Jacquard, 151–2
property-based perspectives, 98, 99
Prosser, W.L., 34
protocols, 163–4, 166, 174, 184, 185, 192, 193
pseudoanonymisation, 58–9
public anonymity, 121
public interest, 28, 32–4, 187
public leaks, 139
public women, 179–80
Pulse, 152
purpose limitation, 122

Quantified Self community, 150
*A Qualitative Study of Children, Young People
    and 'Sexting,'* 176–7, 179

racism, 127–8
Raynes-Goldie, Kate, 161, 166, 168, 170
reactivity, 117
Reddit, 64
Regulation of Investigatory Powers Act (RIPA),
    35, 46, 47
Rehabilitation of Offenders Act, 109, 111
re-identification, 124–5
respect for others, 20–1
restricted access, 155
retail, 140–3
retail engagement, 142
re-targeting, 97

retention, data, 122
Richards, N., 37
right of access, 32
right to be forgotten, 7, 18, 103–14, 190
  see also Google, *Google Spain v AEPD and Mario Costeja González*
right to be let alone, 18, 25, 37, 39, 110
right to erasure, 104
right to know, 32
right to privacy, 28, 30, 31–2, 36, 38, 39, 40
The Rights to Privacy, 28, 36, 39, 188
Ringrose, J., 176–7, 181, 186
RIPA (Regulation of Investigatory Powers Act), 35, 46, 47
risk, 153
Rorty, Richard, 194
Rousseau, John-Jacques, 18, 156
Rowling, J.K., 31
Rozenburg, J., 31–2
Rusbridger, Alan, 33

Salter, M., 176, 178, 180
Schmidt, E., 65
Science, Technology and Society (STS), 68
screen munching, 177
search engines, 7, 103, 104, 105, 106, 107, 112, 113, 190
  see also Google
Seaver, Nick, 127
seclusion, 8, 21, 39, 67, 162, 166, 170, 185, 192, 193, 194
second-party data, 89
security, 3, 5, 21–4
self-censorship, 52
self-determination, 18, 19, 20, 28, 187
self-driving car, 120
self-knowledge through numbers, 151
self-tracking, 8, 150–4, 156, 157
self-work, 151
September (2001), 44, 50
servers, 86
Sexfit, 148, 191
sexting
  children, 176–7
  context management, 162
  control and consent, 178–9
  cyber-bullying, 177–8, 192
  exposure and affect, 179–81, 185
  gender differences, 181–4
  illegality, 186
  nature of, 8–9, 173–4, 177, 192
  networked norms, 184
  who does it, 174–5

sexualisation, 176
Shannon, Claude, 149
Signal, 66
Signals Intelligence (SIGINT), 49
singling out, 123–4, 142
skets, 179, 180
Skype, 42, 45, 58
slander, 36
sluts, 179, 180, 181
smartphones, 8, 79, 88–9, 148, 150, 174–5, 184, 185, 192
  see also mobile phones
SmartWig, 147
Smith, David, 38
Smythe, Dallas, 96
snaking, 178
Snapchat, 66, 150, 160, 173–4
Snow, Charles, 127
Snowden, Edward, 5, 22, 23, 24, 35, 41–5, 52, 53, 57, 62, 93, 188
Snowden Archives, 42
social contract, 23, 24
social graph, 46
social institutions, 72, 73, 75–6
social media
  advertising, 84
  collective responsibility, 192
  context dependent privacy, 161–4
  digital labour, 97
  gagging orders, 37
  impact of non-use, 160
  peer-based privacy, 8
  platforms, 71–2
  usage, 159–60
  user privacy concerns, 4
social privacy, 78, 161, 169, 174
social surveillance, 164
socialisation, 151
soft biometrics, 138
Sony, 147
Sony Walkman, 149
Sorrell, Sir Martin, 142–3
sources, journalistic, 28, 35, 38, 187, 193
sousveillance, 8, 149–50, 152, 153, 156, 157, 191
  see also surveillance
spam email, 120
Spectacles, 150
Spire, 154
Stacey, Chris, 110–11
stalking, 168–9
state of nature, 23
subjectivity, 180–1
sublime, 126, 127, 132

sub-tweeting, 166–7, 170
Sun, 35
Sunday Express, 31
Sunday Herald, 37
Sunday Morning, 182
super-injunctions, 28, 37
supervised learning, 120, 121, 127
surveillance, 18, 22–4, 35, 41–54, 62, 152,
    153–4, 181, 188, 193
    see also sousveillance
Surveillance & Society, 42
surveys, 3–4
Sweeney, L., 124
sympathy, 136

tabloid journalism, 28
tax, 76
Telegram, 66
Telegraph, 37
television, 3, 9
TEMPORA, 46
Terms and Conditions May Apply, 92
terrorism, 51, 188
Terry, John, 37
third parties, 86
third-party data, 89, 189
Thomas, Imogen, 37
Thorp, Edward, 149, 158
Time, 78
timepieces, 149
Tinder, 121, 173
transparency, 5–6, 17, 18, 38, 44, 121, 130,
    156–7, 193
TripAdvisor, 72, 189
TrustE, 93
Turkle, Sherry, 168, 170
Twitter, 37, 43, 74, 160, 166–7, 168
Two Cultures, 126, 127

Uber, 72, 74, 189
unambiguous consent, 95

Universal Declaration of Human Rights, 21,
    25, 60–1
Unlock, 109, 110, 113
unsupervised learning, 120, 121–2, 127
unwanted exposure, 180, 181, 185
UPSTREAM, 46
US Federal Trade Commission, 78
USA Patriot Act, 44

Vaz, Keith, 35
Venkataramanan, Madhumita, 90
The Verge, 128
Verily, 148, 158
Virgin, 152

Warren, S., 25, 28, 36–7, 38, 39, 112, 188
Washington Post, 35, 45, 78
Watch (Apple), 145, 154, 191, 192
watches, 149
wearable media, 7–8, 138, 145–58, 191, 192
wearables *see* wearable media
Westin, Alan, 19–20
WhatsApp, 66, 160, 173
whistle-blowers, 35, 42
Whittaker, James, 84
Wikileaks, 24
Wikipedia, 72
Winner, Langdon, 68
Wired, 90, 126, 132
women, 15
    see also gender
World Wide Web, 3
WPP, 143

XKEYSCORE, 46

Yahoo! 42, 45
YouTube, 42, 45, 74, 76, 160

Zimmer, Micheal, 78
Zuckerberg, Mark, 13, 62, 78